By Carlos Castaneda

THE EAGLE'S GIFT

THE SECOND RING OF POWER

TALES OF POWER

JOURNEY TO IXTLAN: *The Lessons of don Juan*

A SEPARATE REALITY: *Further Conversations
with don Juan*

THE TEACHINGS OF DON JUAN: *A Yaqui Way of Knowledge*

The Eagle's Gift

BY

CARLOS CASTANEDA

SIMON AND SCHUSTER
New York

PUBLISHED BY SIMON AND SCHUSTER
A DIVISION OF GULF & WESTERN CORPORATION
SIMON & SCHUSTER BUILDING
ROCKEFELLER CENTER
1230 AVENUE OF THE AMERICAS
NEW YORK, NEW YORK 10020
SIMON AND SCHUSTER AND COLOPHON ARE TRADEMARKS OF
SIMON & SCHUSTER
DESIGNED BY EVE METZ
MANUFACTURED IN THE UNITED STATES OF AMERICA

3 5 7 9 10 8 6 4 2

LIBRARY OF CONGRESS CATALOGING IN PUBLICATION DATA

CASTANEDA, CARLOS.
THE EAGLE'S GIFT.

1. CASTANEDA, CARLOS.   2. HALLUCINOGENIC DRUGS AND
RELIGIOUS EXPERIENCE.   3. ANTHROPOLOGISTS—MEXICO—
BIOGRAPHY.   4. YAQUI INDIANS—RELIGION AND MYTHOLOGY.
5. INDIANS OF MEXICO—RELIGION AND MYTHOLOGY.
I. TITLE.
F1221.Y3C373   299'.792   80-27841
ISBN 0-671-23087-5

Contents

PROLOGUE   7

Part One
THE OTHER SELF

1. The Fixation of the Second Attention 15
2. Seeing Together 34
3. Quasi Memories of the Other Self 54
4. Crossing the Boundaries of Affection 71
5. A Horde of Angry Sorcerers 91

Part Two
THE ART OF DREAMING

6. Losing the Human Form 115
7. Dreaming Together 131
8. The Right and the Left Side Awareness 154

Part Three
THE EAGLE'S GIFT

9. The Rule of the Nagual 175
10. The Nagual's Party of Warriors 191
11. The Nagual Woman 215

CONTENTS

12. The Not-Doings of Silvio Manuel   *232*

13. The Intricacies of Dreaming   *249*

14. Florinda   *268*

15. The Plumed Serpent   *299*

Prologue

Although I am an anthropologist, this is not strictly an anthropological work; yet it has its roots in cultural anthropology, for it began years ago as field research in that discipline. I was interested at that time in studying the uses of medicinal plants among the Indians of the Southwest and northern Mexico.

My research evolved into something else over the years as a consequence of its own momentum and of my own growth. The study of medicinal plants was superseded by the study of a belief system which seemed to cut across the boundaries of at least two different cultures.

The person responsible for this shift of emphasis in my work was a Yaqui Indian from northern Mexico, don Juan Matus, who later introduced me to don Genaro Flores, a Mazatec Indian from central Mexico. Both of them were practitioners of an ancient knowledge, which in our time is commonly known as sorcery, and which is thought to be a primitive form of medical or psychological science, but which in fact is a tradition of extremely self-disciplined practitioners and extremely sophisticated praxes.

The two men became my teachers rather than my informants, but I still persisted, in a haphazard way, in regarding my task as a work in anthropology; I spent years trying to figure out the cultural matrix of that system, perfecting a taxonomy, a classificatory scheme, a hypothesis of its origin and dissemination. All were futile efforts in view of the fact that in the end, the compelling inner forces of that system derailed my intellectual pursuit and turned me into a participant.

Under the influence of these two powerful men my work has been transformed into an autobiography, in the sense that I have been forced from the moment I became a participant to report what happens to me. It is a peculiar autobiography because I am not reporting about what happens to me in my everyday life as an average man, nor am I reporting about my subjective states generated by daily living. I am reporting, rather, on the events that unfold in my life as a direct result of having adopted an alien set of interrelated ideas and procedures. In other words, the belief system I wanted to study swallowed me, and in order for me to proceed with my scrutiny I have to make an extraordinary daily payment, my life as a man in this world.

Due to these circumstances I am now faced with the special problem of having to explain what it is that I am doing. I am very far away from my point of origin as an average Western man or as an anthropologist, and I must first of all reiterate that this is not a work of fiction. What I am describing is alien to us; therefore, it seems unreal.

As I enter deeper into the intricacies of sorcery, what at first appeared to be a system of primitive beliefs and practices has now turned out to be an enormous and intricate world. In order to become familiar with that world and to report about it, I have to use myself in increasingly complex and more refined ways. Whatever happens to me is no longer something I can predict, nor anything congruous with what other anthropologists know about the belief systems of the Indians of Mexico. I find myself, consequently, in a difficult position; all I can do under the circumstances is present what happened to me *as it happened.* I cannot give any other assurance of my good faith, except to reassert that I do not live a dual life, and that I have committed myself to following the principles of don Juan's system in my everyday existence.

After don Juan Matus and don Genaro Flores, the two Mexican Indian sorcerers who tutored me, had explained their knowledge to me to their own satisfaction, they said goodbye and left. I understood that from then on my task was to assemble by myself what I had learned from them.

In the course of fulfilling this task I went back to Mexico and found out that don Juan and don Genaro had nine other apprentices of sorcery; five women and four men. The oldest woman was named Soledad; the next was Maria Elena, nicknamed "la Gorda," the other three women, Lydia, Rosa, and Josefina, were younger, and were called "the little sisters." The four men, in order of age, were Eligio, Benigno, Nestor, and Pablito; the latter three men were called "the Genaros" because they were very close to don Genaro.

I had already known that Nestor, Pablito, and Eligio, who was no longer around, were apprentices, but I had been led to believe that the four girls were Pablito's sisters, and that Soledad was their mother. I knew Soledad slightly over the years and had always called her *doña* Soledad, as a sign of respect, since she was closer to don Juan in age. Lydia and Rosa had also been introduced to me, but our relationship had been too brief and casual to afford me an understanding of who they really were. I knew la Gorda and Josefina only by name. I had met Benigno but had no idea that he was connected to don Juan and don Genaro.

For reasons that were incomprehensible to me, all of them seemed to have been waiting, in one way or another, for my return to Mexico. They informed me that I was supposed to take the place of don Juan as their leader, their Nagual. They told me that don Juan and don Genaro had disappeared from the face of the earth, and so had Eligio. The women and the men believed that the three of them had not died—they had entered another world, different from the world of our every-day life, yet equally real.

The women—especially doña Soledad—clashed violently with me from our first meeting. They were, nevertheless, instrumental in producing a catharsis in me. My contact with them resulted in a mysterious effervescence in my life. From the moment I met them drastic changes took place in my thinking and my understanding. All this did not happen, however, on a conscious level—if anything, after my first visit to them I found myself more confused than ever, yet in the midst of the chaos I encountered a surprisingly solid base. In the impact of our clash I found in myself resources I had not imagined I possessed.

La Gorda and the three little sisters were consummate *dreamers;* they voluntarily gave me pointers and showed me their own accomplishments. Don Juan had described the art of *dreaming* as the capacity to utilize one's ordinary dreams and transform them into *controlled awareness* by virtue of a specialized form of attention, which he and don Genaro called the *second attention.*

I expected that the three Genaros were going to teach me their accomplishments in another aspect of don Juan's and don Genaro's teachings, "the art of *stalking.*" The art of *stalking* was introduced to me as a set of procedures and atti-tudes that enabled one to get the best out of any conceivable situation. But whatever the three Genaros told me about *stalking* did not have the cohesion or the force I had antici-pated. I concluded that either the men were not really prac-titioners of that art, or they simply did not want to show it to me.

I stopped my inquiries in order to give everyone a chance to feel relaxed with me, but all of the men and women sat back and trusted that since I was no longer asking questions I was finally behaving like a Nagual. Each of them demanded my guidance and counsel.

In order to comply I was obliged to undertake a total review of everything don Juan and don Genaro had taught me, to go deeper still into the art of sorcery.

Part One

THE OTHER SELF

1

The Fixation
of the Second Attention

It was midafternoon when I got to where la Gorda and the little sisters lived. La Gorda was alone, sitting outside by the door, gazing into the distant mountains. She was shocked to see me. She explained that she had been completely absorbed in a memory and for a moment she had been on the verge of remembering something very vague that had to do with me.

Later that night, after dinner, la Gorda, the three little sisters, the three Genaros, and I sat on the floor of la Gorda's room. The women sat together.

For some reason, although I had been with each one of them an equal length of time, I had isolated la Gorda as the recipient of all my concern. It was as if the others did not exist for me. I speculated that perhaps it was because la Gorda reminded me of don Juan, while the others did not. There was something very easy about her, yet that easiness was not so much in her actions as it was in my feelings for her.

They wanted to know what I had been doing. I told them that I had just been in the city of Tula, Hidalgo, where I had visited some archaeological ruins. I had been most impressed with a row of four colossal, columnlike figures of stone, called "the Atlanteans," which stand on the flat top of a pyramid.

Each one of the almost cylindrical figures, measuring fifteen feet in height and three feet across, is made of four separate pieces of basalt carved to represent what archaeologists think are Toltec warriors carrying their war paraphernalia. Twenty feet behind each of the front figures on the top of the pyramid, there is another row of four rectangular columns of the same height and width as the first, also made of four separate pieces of stone.

The awe-inspiring setting of the Atlanteans was enhanced by what a friend, who had guided me through the site, had told me about them. He said that a custodian of the ruins had revealed to him that he had heard the Atlanteans walking at night, making the ground underneath them shake.

I asked the Genaros for comments on what my friend had said. They acted shy and giggled. I turned to la Gorda, who was sitting beside me, and asked her directly for her opinions.

"I've never seen those figures," she said. "I've never been in Tula. Just the idea of going to that town scares me."

"Why does it scare you, Gorda?" I asked.

"Something happened to me in the ruins of Monte Alban in Oaxaca," she said. "I used to go to roam around those ruins even after the Nagual Juan Matus told me not to set foot in them. I don't know why but I loved that place. Every time I was in Oaxaca I would go there. Because women alone are always harassed, I would usually go with Pablito, who is very daring. But once I went there with Nestor. He *saw* a glitter on the ground. We dug a little and found a strange rock that fit in the palm of my hand; a hole had been neatly drilled into the rock. I wanted to put my finger through it, but Nestor stopped me. The rock was smooth and made my hand very hot. We didn't know what to do with it. Nestor put it inside his hat and we carried it as if it were a live animal."

All of them started to laugh. There seemed to be a concealed joke in what la Gorda was telling me.

"Where did you take it?" I asked her.

"We brought it here to this house," she replied, and that

statement elicited uncontainable laughter from the others. They coughed and choked laughing.

"The joke is on la Gorda," Nestor said. "You've got to understand that she's muleheaded like no one else. The Nagual had already told her not to fool around with rocks, or bones, or any other thing she might find buried in the ground. But she used to sneak behind his back and get all kinds of crap.

"That day in Oaxaca she insisted on carrying that godawful thing. We got on the bus with it and brought it all the way to this town and then right into this room."

"The Nagual and Genaro had gone on a trip," la Gorda said. "I got daring and put my finger through the hole and realized that the rock had been cut to be held in the hand. Right away I could feel the feeling of whoever had held that rock. It was a power rock. My mood changed. I became frightened. Something awesome began to lurk in the dark, something that had no shape or color. I couldn't be alone. I would wake up screaming and after a couple of days I couldn't sleep any more. Everybody took turns keeping me company, day and night."

"When the Nagual and Genaro came back," Nestor said, "the Nagual sent me with Genaro to put the rock back in the exact place where it had been buried. Genaro worked for three days to pinpoint the spot. And he did it."

"What happened to you, Gorda, after that?" I asked her.

"The Nagual buried me," she said. "For nine days I was naked inside a dirt coffin."

There was another explosion of laughter among them.

"The Nagual told her that she couldn't get out of it," Nestor explained. "Poor Gorda had to piss and shit inside her coffin. The Nagual pushed her inside a box that he made with branches and mud. There was a little door on the side for her food and water. The rest of it was sealed."

"Why did he bury her?" I asked.

"That's the only way to protect anyone," Nestor said. "She had to be placed under the ground so the earth would heal her. There is no better healer than the earth; besides, the Nagual had to fend off the feeling of that rock, which was focused on la Gorda. The dirt is a screen, it doesn't allow anything to go through, either way. The Nagual knew that she couldn't get worse by being buried for nine days; she could only get better. Which she did."

"How did it feel to be buried like that, Gorda?" I asked.

"I nearly went crazy," she said. "But that was just my indulging. If the Nagual hadn't put me in there, I would have died. The power of that rock was too great for me; its owner had been a very large man. I could tell that his hand was twice the size of mine. He held on to that rock for dear life, and in the end someone killed him. His fear terrified me. I could feel something coming at me to eat my flesh. That was what the man felt. He was a man of power, but someone even more powerful got him.

"The Nagual said that once you have an object of that kind, it brings disaster because its power enters into challenges with other objects of its kind, and the owner becomes either a pursuer or a victim. The Nagual said that it is the nature of such objects to be at war, because the part of our attention which focuses on them to give them power is a very dangerous, belligerent part."

"La Gorda is very greedy," Pablito said. "She figured that if she could find something which already had a great deal of power in it, she'd be a winner because nowadays no one is interested in challenging power."

La Gorda assented with a movement of her head.

"I didn't know that one could pick up other things besides the power that the objects have," she said. "When I first put my finger through the hole and held the rock my hand got hot and my arm began to vibrate. I felt truly strong and big. I'm sneaky so no one knew that I was holding the rock in my hand. After a few days of holding it the real horror began. I could feel that somebody had gone after the owner of the rock. I could feel his fright. He was doubtlessly a very powerful sorcerer and whoever was after him wanted not only to kill him but to eat his flesh. That really scared me. I should've dropped the rock then, but the feeling I was having was so new that I kept the rock clutched in my hand like a damn fool. When I finally dropped it, it was too late. Something in me was hooked. I had visions of men coming at me, men dressed in strange clothes. I felt they were biting me, tearing the flesh of my legs with sharp little knives and with their teeth. I went berserk!"

"How did don Juan explain those visions?" I asked her.

"He said that she no longer had defenses," Nestor said. "And because of that she could pick up that man's fixation, his second attention, which had been poured into that rock. When he was being killed he held on to the rock in order to gather all his concentration. The Nagual said that the man's power went out of his body into his rock; he knew what he was doing, he didn't want his enemies to benefit by devouring his flesh. The Nagual also said that the ones who killed him knew this, that's why they were eating him alive, to get whatever power was left. They must have buried the rock to avoid trouble. And la Gorda and I, like two idiots, found it and dug it up."

La Gorda shook her head affirmatively three or four times. She had a very serious expression.

"The Nagual told me that the second attention is the most fierce thing there is," she said. "If it is focused on objects, there is nothing more horrendous."

"What's horrible is that we cling," Nestor said. "The man who owned the rock was clinging to his life and to his power; that's why he was horrified at feeling his flesh eaten away. The Nagual said that if the man would've let go of his possessiveness and abandoned himself to his death, whatever it may have been, there wouldn't have been any fear in him."

The conversation faded. I asked the others if they had anything to say. The little sisters glared at me. Benigno giggled and hid his face with his hat.

"Pablito and I have been in the pyramids of Tula," he finally said. "We've been in all the pyramids there are in Mexico. We like them."

"Why did you go to all the pyramids?" I asked him.

"I really don't know why we went to them," he said. "Perhaps it was because the Nagual Juan Matus told us not to."

"How about you, Pablito?" I asked.

"I went there to learn," he replied huffily, and laughed. "I used to live in the city of Tula. I know those pyramids like the back of my hand. The Nagual told me that he also used to live there. He knew everything about the pyramids. He was a Toltec himself."

I realized then that it had been more than curiosity that made me go to the archaeological site in Tula. The main reason I had accepted my friend's invitation was because at the time of my first visit to la Gorda and the others, they had told me something which don Juan had never even mentioned to me, that he considered himself a cultural descendant of the Toltecs. Tula had been the ancient epicenter of the Toltec empire.

"What do you think about the Atlanteans walking around at night?" I asked Pablito.

"Sure, they walk at night," he said. "Those things have been there for ages. No one knows who built the pyramids, the Nagual Juan Matus himself told me that the Spaniards were not the first to discover them. The Nagual said there were others before them. God knows how many."

"What do you think those four figures of stone represent?" I asked.

"They are not men, but women," he said. "That pyramid is the center of order and stability. Those figures are its four corners; they are the four winds, the four directions. They are the foundation, the basis of the pyramid. They have to be women, mannish women, if you want to call them that. As you yourself know, we men are not that hot. We are a good binding, a glue to hold things together, but that's all. The Nagual Juan Matus said that the mystery of the pyramid is its structure. The four corners have been elevated to the top. The pyramid itself is the man, supported by his female warriors; a male who has elevated his supporters to the highest place. See what I mean?"

I must have had a look of perplexity on my face. Pablito laughed. It was a polite laughter.

"No. I don't see what you mean, Pablito," I said. "But that's because don Juan never told me anything about it. The topic is completely new to me. Please tell me everything you know."

"The Atlanteans are the *nagual;* they are *dreamers.* They represent the order of the second attention brought forward, that's why they're so fearsome and mysterious. They are creatures of war but not of destruction.

"The other row of columns, the rectangular ones, represent the order of the first attention, the *tonal.* They are *stalkers,* that's why they are covered with inscriptions. They are very peaceful and wise, the opposite of the front row."

Pablito stopped talking and looked at me almost defiantly, then he broke into a smile.

I thought he was going to go on to explain what he had said, but he remained silent as if waiting for my comments.

I told him how mystified I was and urged him to continue talking. He seemed undecided, stared at me for a moment, and took a deep breath. He had hardly begun to speak when the voices of the rest of them were raised in a clamor of protest.

"The Nagual already explained that to all of us," la Gorda said impatiently. "What's the point of making him repeat it?"

I tried to make them understand that I really had no conception of what Pablito was talking about. I prevailed on him to go on with his explanation. There was another wave of voices speaking at the same time. Judging by the way the little sisters glared at me, they were getting very angry, especially Lydia.

"We don't like to talk about those women," la Gorda said to me in a conciliatory tone. "Just the thought of the women of the pyramid makes us very nervous."

"What's the matter with you people?" I asked. "Why are you acting like this?"

"We don't know," la Gorda replied. "It's just a feeling that all of us have, a very disturbing feeling. We were fine until a moment ago when you started to ask questions about those women."

La Gorda's statements were like an alarm signal. All of them stood up and advanced menacingly toward me, talking in loud voices.

It took me a long time to calm them and make them sit down. The little sisters were very upset and their mood seemed to influence la Gorda's. The three men showed more restraint. I faced Nestor and asked him bluntly to explain to me why the women were so agitated. Obviously I was unwittingly doing something to aggravate them.

"I really don't know what it is," he said. "I'm sure none of us here knows what is the matter with us, except that we all feel very sad and nervous."

"Is it because we're talking about the pyramids?" I asked him.

"It must be," he replied somberly. "I myself didn't know that those figures were women."

"Of course you did, you idiot," Lydia snapped.

Nestor seemed to be intimidated by her outburst. He recoiled and smiled sheepishly at me.

"Maybe I did," he conceded. "We're going through a very strange period in our lives. None of us knows anything for sure any more. Since you came into our lives we are unknown to ourselves."

A very oppressive mood set in. I insisted that the only way

to dispel it was to talk about those mysterious columns on the pyramids.

The women protested heatedly. The men remained silent. I had the feeling that they were affiliated in principle with the women but secretly wanted to discuss the topic, just as I did.

"Did don Juan tell you anything else about the pyramids, Pablito?" I asked.

My intention was to steer the conversation away from the specific topic of the Atlanteans, and yet stay near it.

"He said one specific pyramid there in Tula was a guide," Pablito replied eagerly.

From the tone of his voice I deduced that he really wanted to talk. And the attentiveness of the other apprentices convinced me that covertly all of them wanted to exchange opinions.

"The Nagual said that it was a guide to the second attention," Pablito went on, "but that it was ransacked and everything destroyed. He told me that some of the pyramids were gigantic *not-doings*. They were not lodgings but places for warriors to do their *dreaming* and exercise their second attention. Whatever they did was recorded in drawings and figures that were put on the walls.

"Then another kind of warrior must've come along, a kind who didn't approve of what the sorcerers of the pyramid had done with their second attention, and destroyed the pyramid and all that was in it.

"The Nagual believed that the new warriors must've been warriors of the third attention, just as he himself was; warriors who were appalled by the evilness of the fixation of the second attention. The sorcerers of the pyramids were too busy with their fixation to realize what was going on. When they did, it was too late."

Pablito had an audience. Everyone in the room, myself included, was fascinated with what he was saying. I understood the ideas he was presenting because don Juan had explained them to me.

Don Juan had said that our total being consists of two perceivable segments. The first is the familiar physical body, which all of us can perceive; the second is the luminous body, which is a cocoon that only seers can perceive, a cocoon that gives us the appearance of giant luminous eggs. He had also said that one of the most important goals of sorcery is to reach the luminous cocoon; a goal which is fulfilled through the sophisticated use of *dreaming* and through a rigorous, systematic exertion he called *not-doing*. He defined *not-doing* as an unfamiliar act which engages our total being by forcing it to become conscious of its luminous segment.

In order to explain these concepts, don Juan made a three-part, uneven division of our consciousness. He called the smallest the first attention, and said that it is the consciousness that every normal person has developed in order to deal with the daily world; it encompasses the awareness of the physical body. Another larger portion he called the second attention, and described it as the awareness we need in order to perceive our luminous cocoon and to act as luminous beings. He said that the second attention remains in the background for the duration of our lives, unless it is brought forth through deliberate training or by an accidental trauma, and that it encompasses the awareness of the luminous body. He called the last portion, which was the largest, the third attention—an immeasurable consciousness which engages undefinable aspects of the awareness of the physical and the luminous bodies.

I asked him if he himself had experienced the third attention. He said that he was on the periphery of it, and that if he ever entered it completely I would know it instantly, because all of him would become what he really was, an outburst of energy. He added that the battlefield of warriors was the second attention, which was something like a training ground for reaching the third attention. It was a state rather difficult to arrive at, but very fruitful once it was attained.

"The pyramids are harmful," Pablito went on. "Especially to unprotected sorcerers like ourselves. They are worse yet to formless warriors like la Gorda. The Nagual said that there is nothing more dangerous than the evil fixation of the second attention. When warriors learn to focus on the weak side of the second attention nothing can stand in their way. They become hunters of men, ghouls. Even if they are no longer alive, they can reach for their prey through time as if they were present here and now; because prey is what we become if we walk into one of those pyramids. The Nagual called them traps of the second attention."

"What exactly did he say would happen?" la Gorda asked.

"The Nagual said that we could stand perhaps one visit to the pyramids," Pablito explained. "On the second visit we would feel a strange sadness. It would be like a cold breeze that would make us listless and fatigued; a fatigue that soon turns into bad luck. In no time at all we'll be jinxed; everything will happen to us. In fact, the Nagual said that our own streaks of bad luck were due to our willfulness in visiting those ruins against his recommendations.

"Eligio, for instance, never disobeyed the Nagual. You wouldn't catch him dead in there; neither did this Nagual here, and they were always lucky, while the rest of us were jinxed, especially la Gorda and myself. Weren't we even bitten by the same dog? And didn't the same beams of the kitchen roof get rotten twice and fall on us?"

"The Nagual never explained this to me," la Gorda said.

"Of course he did," Pablito insisted.

"If I had known how bad it was, I wouldn't have set foot in those damned places," la Gorda protested.

"The Nagual told every one of us the same things," Nestor said. "The problem is that every one of us was not listening attentively, or rather every one of us listened to him in his own way, and heard what he wanted to hear.

"The Nagual said that the fixation of the second attention has two faces. The first and easiest face is the evil one. It happens when *dreamers* use their *dreaming* to focus their second attention on the items of the world, like money and power over people. The other face is the most difficult to reach and it happens when *dreamers* focus their second attention on items that are not in or from this world, such as the journey into the unknown. Warriors need endless impeccability in order to reach this face."

I said to them that I was sure that don Juan had selectively revealed certain things to some of us and other things to others. I could not, for instance, recall don Juan ever discussing the evil face of the second attention with me. I told them then what don Juan said to me in reference to the fixation of attention in general.

He stressed to me that all archaeological ruins in Mexico, especially the pyramids, were harmful to modern man. He depicted the pyramids as foreign expressions of thought and action. He said that every item, every design in them, was a calculated effort to record aspects of attention which were thoroughly alien to us. For don Juan it was not only ruins of past cultures that held a dangerous element in them; anything which was the object of an obsessive concern had a harmful potential.

We had discussed this in detail once. It was a reaction he had to some comments I had made about my being at a loss as to where to store my field notes safely. I regarded them in a most possessive manner and was obsessed with their security.

"What should I do?" I asked him.

"Genaro once gave you the solution," he replied. "You thought, as you always do, that he was joking. He never jokes. He told you that you should write with the tip of your finger instead of a pencil. You didn't take him up on that, because you can't imagine that this is the *not-doing* of taking notes."

I argued that what he was proposing had to be a joke. My self-image was that of a social scientist who needed to record everything that was said and done in order to draw verifiable conclusions. For don Juan one thing had nothing to do with the other. To be a serious student had nothing to do with

taking notes. I personally could not see a solution; don Genaro's suggestion seemed to me humorous, not a real possibility.

Don Juan argued his point further. He said that taking
notes was a way of engaging the first attention in the task of
remembering, that I took notes in order to remember what
was said and done. Don Genaro's recommendation was not a
joke because writing with the tip of my finger on a piece of
paper, as the *not-doing* of taking notes, would force my second
attention to focus on remembering, and I would not accumulate sheets of paper. Don Juan thought that the end result
would be more accurate and more powerful than taking notes.
It had never been done as far as he knew, but the principle
was sound.

He pressed me to do it for a while. I became disturbed.
Taking notes acted not only as a mnemonic device, but
soothed me as well. It was my most serviceable crutch. To
accumulate sheets of paper gave me a sense of purpose and
balance.

"When you worry about what to do with your sheets," don
Juan explained, "you are focusing a very dangerous part of
yourself on them. All of us have that dangerous side, that
fixation. The stronger we become, the more deadly that side
is. The recommendation for warriors is not to have any material things on which to focus their power, but to focus it on
the spirit, on the true flight into the unknown, not on trivial
shields. In your case, your notes are your shield. They won't
let you live in peace."

I seriously felt that I had no way on earth to disassociate
myself from my notes. Don Juan then conceived of a task for
me in lieu of a *not-doing* proper. He said that for someone who
was as possessive as I was, the most appropriate way of freeing
myself from my notebooks would be to disclose them, to
throw them in the open, to write a book. I thought at the time
that that was a bigger joke than taking notes with the tip of
my finger.

"Your compulsion to possess and hold on to things is not unique," he said. "Everyone who wants to follow the warrior's path, the sorcerer's way, has to rid himself of this fixation.

"My benefactor told me that there was a time when warriors did have material objects on which they placed their obsession. And that gave rise to the question of whose object would be more powerful, or the most powerful of them all. Remnants of those objects still remain in the world, the leftovers of that race for power. No one can tell what kind of fixation those objects must have received. Men infinitely more powerful than you poured all the facets of their attention on them. You have merely begun to pour your puny worry on your notes. You haven't gotten yet to other levels of attention. Think how horrible it would be if you would find yourself at the end of your trail as a warrior, still carrying your bundles of notes on your back. By that time the notes will be alive, especially if you learn to write with your fingertip and still have to pile up sheets. Under those conditions it wouldn't surprise me in the least if someone found your bundles walking around."

"It is easy for me to understand why the Nagual Juan Matus didn't want us to have possessions," Nestor said after I had finished talking. "We are all *dreamers*. He didn't want us to focus our *dreaming body* on the weak face of the second attention.

"I didn't understand his maneuvers at the time. I resented the fact that he made me get rid of everything I had. I thought he was being unfair. My belief was that he was trying to keep Pablito and Benigno from envying me, because they had nothing themselves. I was well-off in comparison. At the time, I had no idea that he was protecting my *dreaming body*."

Don Juan had described *dreaming* to me in various ways. The most obscure of them all now appears to me as being the one that defines it best. He said that *dreaming* is intrinsically the *not-doing* of sleep. And as such, *dreaming* affords practitioners the use of that portion of their lives spent in slumber. It is as if the *dreamers* no longer sleep. Yet no illness results from it. The *dreamers* do not lack sleep, but the effect of *dreaming* seems to be an increase of waking time, owing to the use of an alleged extra body, the *dreaming body*.

Don Juan had explained to me that the *dreaming body* is sometimes called the "double" or the "other," because it is a perfect replica of the *dreamer*'s body. It is inherently the energy of a luminous being, a whitish, phantomlike emanation, which is projected by the fixation of the second attention into a three-dimensional image of the body. Don Juan explained that the *dreaming body* is not a ghost, but as real as anything we deal with in the world. He said that the second attention is unavoidably drawn to focus on our total being as a field of energy, and transforms that energy into anything suitable. The easiest thing is of course the image of the physical body, with which we are already thoroughly familiar from our daily lives and the use of our first attention. What channels the energy of our total being to produce anything that might be within the boundaries of possibility is known as *will*. Don Juan could not say what those boundaries were, except that at the level of luminous beings the range is so broad that it is futile to try to establish limits—thus, the energy of a luminous being can be transformed through *will* into anything.

"The Nagual said that the *dreaming body* gets involved and attaches itself to anything," Benigno said. "It doesn't have sense. He told me that men are weaker than women because a man's *dreaming body* is more possessive."

The little sisters agreed in unison with a movement of their heads. La Gorda looked at me and smiled.

"The Nagual told me that you're the king of possessiveness," she said to me. "Genaro said that you even say goodbye to your turds before you flush them down."

The little sisters rolled down on their sides laughing. The Genaros made obvious efforts to contain themselves. Nestor, who was sitting by my side, patted my knee.

"The Nagual and Genaro used to tell great stories about

you," he said. "They entertained us for years with tales about a weird guy they knew. We know now that it was you."

I felt a wave of embarrassment. It was as if don Juan and don Genaro had betrayed me, laughing at me in front of the apprentices. Self-pity took over. I began to complain. I said out loud that they had been predisposed to be against me, to think that I was a fool.

"That's not true," Benigno said. "We are delighted that you are with us."

"Are we?" Lydia snapped.

All of them became involved in a heated argument. The men and the women were divided. La Gorda did not join either group. She stayed sitting by my side, while the others had stood up and were shouting.

"We're going through a difficult time," la Gorda said to me in a low voice. "We've done a lot of *dreaming* and yet it isn't enough for what we need."

"What do you need, Gorda?" I asked.

"We don't know," she said. "We were hoping that you would tell us that."

The little sisters and the Genaros sat down again in order to listen to what la Gorda was saying to me.

"We need a leader," she went on. "You are the Nagual, but you're not a leader."

"It takes time to make a perfect Nagual," Pablito said. "The Nagual Juan Matus told me that he himself was crappy in his youth, until something shook him out of his complacency."

"I don't believe it," Lydia shouted. "He never told me that."

"He said that he was very crummy," la Gorda added in a low voice.

"The Nagual told me that in his youth he was a jinx, just like me," Pablito said. "He was also told by his benefactor not to set foot in those pyramids and because of that he practically lived there, until he was driven away by a horde of phantoms."

Apparently no one else knew the story. They perked up.

"I had completely forgotten about that," Pablito explained. "I've only just remembered it now. It was just like what happened to la Gorda. One day after the Nagual had finally become a formless warrior, the evil fixations of those warriors who had done their *dreaming* and other *not-doings* in the pyramids came after him. They found him while he was working in the field. He told me that he saw a hand coming out of the loose dirt in a fresh furrow to grab the leg of his pants. He thought that it was a fellow worker who had been accidentally buried. He tried to dig him out. Then he realized that he was digging into a dirt coffin: a man was buried there. The Nagual said that the man was very thin and dark and had no hair. The Nagual tried frantically to patch up the dirt coffin. He didn't want his fellow workers to see it and he didn't want to injure the man by digging him out against his will. He was working so hard that he didn't even notice that the other workers had gathered around him. By then the Nagual said that the dirt coffin had collapsed and the dark man was sprawled on the ground, naked. The Nagual tried to help him up and asked the men to give him a hand. They laughed at him. They thought he was drunk, having the d.t.'s, because there was no man, or dirt coffin or anything like that in the field.

"The Nagual said that he was shaken, but he didn't dare tell his benefactor about it. It didn't matter because at night a whole flock of phantoms came after him. He went to open the front door after someone knocked and a horde of naked men with glaring yellow eyes burst in. They threw him to the floor and piled on top of him. They would have crushed every bone in his body had it not been for the swift actions of his benefactor. He *saw* the phantoms and pulled the Nagual to safety, to a hole in the ground, which he always kept conveniently at the back of his house. He buried the Nagual there while the ghosts squatted around waiting for their chance.

"The Nagual told me that he had become so frightened that

he would voluntarily go back into his dirt coffin every night to sleep, long after the phantoms had vanished."

Pablito stopped talking. Everyone seemed to be getting ready to leave. They fretted and changed position as if to show that they were tired of sitting.

I then told them that I had had a very disturbing reaction upon hearing my friend's statements about the Atlanteans walking at night in the pyramids of Tula. I had not recognized the depth at which I had accepted what don Juan and don Genaro had taught me until that day. I realized that I had completely suspended judgment, even though it was clear in my mind that the possibility these colossal figures of stone could walk did not enter into the realm of serious speculation. My reaction was a total surprise to me.

I explained to them at great length that the idea of the Atlanteans walking at night was a clear example of the fixation of the second attention. I had arrived at that conclusion using the following set of premises: First, that we are not merely whatever our common sense requires us to believe we are. We are in actuality luminous beings, capable of becoming aware of our luminosity. Second, that as luminous beings aware of our luminosity, we are capable of unraveling different facets of our awareness, or our attention, as don Juan called it. Third, that the unraveling could be brought about by a deliberate effort, as we were trying to do ourselves, or accidentally, through a bodily trauma. Fourth, that there had been a time when sorcerers deliberately placed different facets of their attention on material objects. Fifth, that the Atlanteans, judging by their awe-inspiring setting, must have been objects of fixation for sorcerers of another time.

I said that the custodian who had given my friend the information had undoubtedly unraveled another facet of his attention; he might have unwittingly become, if only for a moment, a receptor for the projections of ancient sorcerers' second attention. It was not so farfetched to me then that the man may have visualized the fixation of those sorcerers.

If those sorcerers were members of don Juan's and don Genaro's tradition, they must have been impeccable practitioners, in which case there would have been no limit to what they could accomplish with the fixation of their second attention. If they intended that the Atlanteans should walk at night, then the Atlanteans would walk at night.

As I talked, the three little sisters became very angry and agitated with me. When I finished, Lydia accused me of doing nothing else but talking. Then they got up and left without even saying goodbye. The men followed them, but stopped at the door and shook hands with me. La Gorda and I remained in the room.

"There is something very wrong with those women," I said.

"No. They're just tired of talking," la Gorda said. "They expect some action from you."

"How come the Genaros are not tired of talking?" I asked.

"They are more stupid than the women," she replied dryly.

"How about you, Gorda?" I asked. "Are you also tired of talking?"

"I don't know what I am," she said solemnly. "When I am with you I'm not tired, but when I am with the little sisters I'm dead tired, just like them."

During the following uneventful days I stayed with them, it was obvious that the little sisters were thoroughly hostile to me. The Genaros tolerated me in an offhand way. Only la Gorda seemed to be aligned with me. I began to wonder why. I asked her about it before I left for Los Angeles.

"I don't know how it is possible, but I'm used to you," she said. "It's as if you and I are together, while the little sisters and the Genaros are in a different world."

2

Seeing Together

For several weeks after my return to Los Angeles I had a sense of mild discomfort which I explained away as a dizziness or a sudden loss of breath due to physical exertion. It reached a climax one night when I woke up terrified, unable to breathe. The physician I went to see diagnosed my trouble as hyperventilation, most likely caused by tension. He prescribed a tranquilizer and suggested breathing into a paper bag if the attack should ever occur again.

I decided to return to Mexico to seek la Gorda's counsel. After I had told her the doctor's diagnosis, she calmly assured me that no illness was involved, that I was finally losing my shields, and that what I was experiencing was the "loss of my human form" and the entrance into a new state of separation from human affairs.

"Don't fight it," she said. "Our natural reaction is to struggle against it. In doing so we dispel it. Let go of your fear and follow the loss of your human form step by step."

She added that in her case the disintegration of her human form began in her womb, with a severe pain and an inordinate pressure that shifted slowly in two directions, down her legs and up to her throat. She also said that the effects are felt immediately.

I wanted to record every nuance of my entrance into that new state. I prepared myself to write down a detailed account of whatever took place, but to my utter chagrin nothing more happened. After a few days of fruitless expectation I gave up on la Gorda's explanation and concluded that the doctor had correctly diagnosed my condition. It was perfectly understandable to me. I was carrying a responsibility that generated unbearable tension. I had accepted the leadership that the apprentices believed belonged to me, but I had no idea how to lead.

The pressure in my life also showed in a more serious way. My usual level of energy was dropping steadily. Don Juan would have said that I was losing my personal power and that eventually I would lose my life. Don Juan had set me up to live exclusively by means of personal power, which I understood to be a state of being, a relationship of order between the subject and the universe, a relationship that cannot be disrupted without resulting in the subject's death. Since there was no foreseeable way to change my situation, I had concluded that my life was coming to an end. My feeling of being doomed seemed to infuriate all the apprentices. I decided to get away from them for a couple of days to dispel my gloom and their tension.

When I came back I found them standing outside the front door of the little sisters' house as if they had been waiting for me. Nestor ran to my car and before I even turned the motor off he blurted out that Pablito had run away. He had gone to die, Nestor said, in the city of Tula, the place of his ancestors. I was appalled. I felt guilty.

La Gorda did not share my concern. She was beaming, exuding contentment.

"That little pimp is better off dead," she said. "All of us are going to live together harmoniously now, as we should. The Nagual told us that you were going to bring change into our lives. Well, you did. Pablito is not bugging us any longer. You got rid of him. Look how happy we are. We are better off without him."

I was outraged by her callousness. I stated as forcefully as I could that don Juan had given all of us, in a most painstaking manner, the format of a warrior's life. I stressed that the warrior's impeccability demanded that I not let Pablito die just like that.

"And what do you think you're going to do?" la Gorda asked.

"I'm going to take one of you to live with him," I said, "until the day when all of you, including Pablito, can move out of here."

They laughed at me, even Nestor and Benigno, who I thought were closest to Pablito. La Gorda laughed longer than anyone else, obviously challenging me.

I turned to Nestor and Benigno for moral support. They looked away.

I appealed to la Gorda's superior understanding. I pleaded with her. I used all the arguments I could think of. She looked at me with utter contempt.

"Let's get going," she said to the others.

She gave me the most vacuous smile. She shrugged her shoulders and made a vague puckering gesture with her lips.

"You're welcome to come with us," she said to me, "providing that you don't ask questions or talk about that little pimp."

"You are a formless warrior, Gorda," I said. "You told me that yourself. Why, then, do you judge Pablito?"

La Gorda did not answer. But she acknowledged the blow. She frowned and avoided my gaze.

"La Gorda is with us!" Josefina yelled in a high-pitched voice.

The three little sisters gathered around la Gorda and pulled her inside the house. I followed them. Nestor and Benigno also went inside.

"What are you going to do, take one of us by force?" la Gorda asked me.

I told all of them that I considered it my duty to help Pablito and that I would do the same for any one of them.

"You really think you can pull this off?" la Gorda asked me, her eyes flaring with anger.

I wanted to roar with rage as I had once done in their presence, but the circumstances were different. I could not do it.

"I'm going to take Josefina with me," I said. "I am the Nagual."

La Gorda gathered the three little sisters and shielded them with her body. They were about to join hands. Something in me knew that if they did, their combined strength would have been awesome and my efforts to take Josefina would have been useless. My only chance was to strike before they had a chance to group. I pushed Josefina with the palms of my hands and sent her reeling to the center of the room. Before they had time to regroup themselves, I hit Lydia and Rosa. They bent over with pain. La Gorda came at me with a fury I had never witnessed in her. It was like the attack of a savage beast. Her whole concentration was on a single thrust of her body. If she had struck me, I would have been killed. She missed my chest by inches. I grabbed her from behind in a bear hug and we tumbled down. We rolled over and over until we were utterly exhausted. Her body relaxed. She began to caress the back of my hands, which were tightly clasped around her stomach.

I noticed then that Nestor and Benigno were standing by the door. They both seemed to be on the verge of becoming physically ill.

La Gorda smiled shyly and whispered in my ear that she was glad I had overcome her.

I took Josefina to Pablito. I felt that she was the only one of the apprentices who genuinely needed someone to look after

her and Pablito resented her the least. I was sure that his sense
of chivalry would force him to reach out to her since she
would be in need of help.

A month later I returned once more to Mexico. Pablito and
Josefina had returned. They were living together at don Genaro's house and shared it with Benigno and Rosa. Nestor and
Lydia lived at Soledad's place, and la Gorda lived alone in the
little sisters' house.

"Do our new living arrangements surprise you?" la Gorda
asked.

My surprise was more than evident. I wanted to know all
the implications of this new organization.

La Gorda let me know in a dry tone that there were no
implications that she knew of. They had chosen to live in
couples but not as couples. She added that, contrary to what
I might think, they were impeccable warriors.

The new format was rather pleasant. Everybody seemed to
be completely relaxed. There was no more bickering or outbursts of competitive behavior among them. They had also
taken to dressing in the Indian apparel typical of that region.
The women wore dresses with full gathered skirts that almost
touched the ground. They wore dark shawls and their hair in
braids, except for Josefina, who always wore a hat. The men
wore thin, white pajama-like pants and shirts, and straw hats.
All of them wore homemade sandals.

I asked la Gorda the reason for their new way of dressing.
She said that they were getting ready to leave. Sooner or later,
with my help or by themselves, they were going to leave that
valley. They would be going into a new world, a new life.
When they did that they would acknowledge the change; the
longer they wore their Indian clothes, the more drastic the
change would be when they put on city clothes. She added
that they had been taught to be fluid, at ease in whatever
situation they found themselves, and that I had been taught

38

the same. My challenge was to deal with them with ease regardless of what they did to me. Their challenge in turn was to leave their valley and settle down elsewhere to find out if they could be as fluid as warriors should be.

I asked for her honest opinion about our chances of succeeding. She said that failure was written all over our faces.

La Gorda changed the subject abruptly and told me that in her *dreaming* she had found herself staring at a gigantic narrow gorge between two enormous round mountains; she thought that the two mountains were familiar to her, and wanted me to drive her to a nearby town. She believed, without knowing why, that the two mountains were located there, and that the message from her *dreaming* was that both of us should go there.

We left at the crack of dawn. I had driven through that town before. It was very small and I had never noticed anything in its surroundings that even came close to la Gorda's vision. There were only eroded hills around it. It turned out that the two mountains were not there, or if they were, we could not find them.

During the two hours that we spent in that town, however, both of us had a feeling that we knew something undefined, a feeling which turned at times into a certainty and then receded again into the darkness to become merely annoyance and frustration. Visiting that town unsettled us in mysterious ways; or rather, for unknown reasons we became very agitated. I was in the throes of a most illogical conflict. I did not remember having ever stopped in that town, and yet I could have sworn that I had not only been there, but had lived there for a time. It was not a clear memory; I did not remember the streets or the houses. What I felt was a vague but strong apprehension that something was going to become clear in my mind. I was not sure what, a memory perhaps. At moments that vague apprehension became paramount, especially when

I saw a particular house. I parked in front of it. La Gorda and I looked at it from the car for perhaps an hour, yet neither of us suggested leaving the car to go into it.

Both of us were very edgy. We began to talk about her vision of the two mountains; our conversation soon turned into an argument. She thought I had not taken her *dreaming* seriously. Our tempers flared and we ended up yelling at each other, not so much out of anger as out of nervousness. I caught myself and stopped.

On our way back, I parked the car on the side of the dirt road. We got out to stretch our legs. We walked for a while; it was too windy to enjoy it. La Gorda still seemed to be agitated. We went back to the car and sat inside.

"If you would only rally your knowledge," la Gorda said in a pleading tone. "You would know that losing the human form . . ."

She stopped in midsentence; my frown must have brought her up short. She was cognizant of my struggle. If there was any knowledge in me that I could have consciously rallied, I would have done it already.

"But we are luminous beings," she said in the same pleading tone. "There is so much more to us. You are the Nagual. There is even more to you."

"What do you think I should do?" I asked.

"You must let go of your desire to cling," she said. "The very same thing happened to me. I held on to things, such as the food I liked, the mountains where I lived, the people I used to enjoy talking to. But most of all I clung to the desire to be liked."

I told her that her advice was meaningless to me, for I was not aware of holding on to anything. She insisted that somehow I knew that I was putting up barriers to losing my human form.

"Our attention is trained to focus doggedly," she went on. "That is the way we maintain the world. Your first attention has been taught to focus on something that's quite strange to me, but very familiar to you."

I told her that my mind dwells on abstractions—not abstractions like mathematics, for instance, but rather propositions of reasonableness.

"Now is the time to let go of all that," she said. "In order to lose your human form you should let go of all that ballast. You counterbalance so hard that you paralyze yourself."

I was in no mood to argue. What she called losing the human form was a concept too vague for immediate consideration. I was concerned with what we had experienced in that town. La Gorda did not want to talk about it.

"The only thing that counts is that you rally your knowledge," she said. "You can do it if you need to, like that day when Pablito ran away and you and I came to blows."

La Gorda said that what had happened on that day was an example of "rallying one's knowledge." Without being thoroughly aware of what I was doing, I had performed complex maneuvers which required *seeing*.

"You did not just attack us," she said. "You *saw*."

She was right, in a manner of speaking. Something quite out of the ordinary had taken place on that occasion. I had considered it in great detail, confining it, however, to purely personal speculation. I had no adequate explanation for it, outside of saying that the emotional charge of the moment had affected me in inconceivable ways.

When I stepped inside their house and faced the four women I became aware in one split second that I was able to shift my ordinary way of perceiving. I saw four amorphous blobs of very intense amber light in front of me. One of them was more mellow, more pleasing. The other three were unfriendly, sharp, whitish-amber glows. The mellow glow was la Gorda. And at that moment the three unfriendly glows were looming menacingly over her.

The blob of whitish luminosity closest to me, which was

Josefina, was a bit off-balance. It was leaning over, so I gave it a push. I kicked the other two in a depression they each had on their right side. I had no conscious idea that I should kick them there. I simply found the indentation convenient— somehow it invited me to put my foot in it. The result was devastating. Lydia and Rosa fainted on the spot. I had kicked each of them on their right thigh. It was not a kick that could have broken any bones, I only pushed the blobs of light in front of me with my foot. Nonetheless, it was as if I had given them a ferocious blow in the most vulnerable part of their bodies.

La Gorda was right, I had rallied some knowledge I was not aware of. If that was called *seeing*, the logical conclusion for my intellect would be to say that *seeing* is a bodily knowledge. The predominance of the visual sense in us influences this bodily knowledge and makes it seem to be eye-related. What I experienced was not altogether visual. I *saw* the blobs of light with something else besides my eyes, since I was conscious that the four women were in my field of vision during the entire time I dealt with them. The blobs of light were not even superimposed on them. The two sets of images were separate. What complicated the issue for me was the matter of time. Everything was compressed into a few seconds. If I did shift from one scene to the other, the shift must have been so fast that it became meaningless, thus I can only recall perceiving two separate scenes simultaneously.

After I had kicked the two blobs of light, the mellow one —la Gorda—came toward me. It did not come straight at me, but angled to my left from the moment it started to move; it obviously intended to miss me, so when the glow passed by I grabbed it. As I rolled over and over on the floor with it, I felt I was melting into it. That was the only time I really lost the sense of continuity. I again became aware of myself while la Gorda was caressing the backs of my hands.

"In our *dreaming*, the little sisters and I have learned to join hands," la Gorda said. "We know how to make a line. Our problem that day was that we had never made that line outside our room. That was why they dragged me inside. Your body knew what it meant for us to join hands. If we had done it, I would have been under their control. They are more fierce than I am. Their bodies are tightly sealed; they are not concerned with sex. I am. That makes me weaker. I'm sure that your concern with sex is what makes it very difficult for you to rally your knowledge."

She went on talking about the debilitating effects of having sex. I felt ill at ease. I tried to steer the conversation away from that topic, but she seemed determined to go back to it regardless of my discomfort.

"Let's you and I drive to Mexico City," I said in desperation.

I thought I would shock her. She did not answer. She puckered her lips, squinting her eyes. She contracted the muscles of her chin, pushing her upper lip until it bulged under her nose. Her face became so contorted that I was taken aback. She reacted to my surprise and relaxed her facial muscles.

"Come on, Gorda," I said. "Let's go to Mexico City."

"Sure. Why not?" she said. "What do I need?"

I did not expect that reaction and ended up shocked myself.

"Nothing," I said. "We'll go as we are."

Without saying another word, she slumped on the seat and we drove off toward Mexico City. It was still early, not even midday. I asked her if she would dare to go to Los Angeles with me. She was pensive for a moment.

"I've just asked my luminous body that question," she said.

"What did it say?"

"It said only if power permits it."

There was such a wealth of feeling in her voice that I stopped the car and hugged her. My affection for her at that moment was so deep that I got frightened. It had nothing to do with sex or the need of psychological reinforcement; it was a feeling that transcended everything I knew.

Embracing la Gorda brought back the sense I had had earlier, that something in me which was bottled up, pushed into recesses I could not consciously reach, was about to come out. I almost knew then what it was, but I lost it when I reached for it.

La Gorda and I arrived in the city of Oaxaca in the early evening. I parked my car on a side street and then we walked to the center of town, to the plaza. We looked for the bench where don Juan and don Genaro used to sit. It was unoccupied. We sat there in reverent silence. Finally la Gorda said that she had been there with don Juan many times as well as with someone else she could not remember. She was not sure whether that was something she had merely dreamed.

"What did you do with don Juan on this bench?" I asked.

"Nothing. We just sat waiting for the bus, or for the lumber truck that would give us a ride up the mountains," she replied.

I told her that when I sat on that bench with don Juan we would talk for hours.

I recounted for her the great predilection that he had for poetry, and how I used to read it to him when we had nothing else to do. He would listen to poems on the premise that only the first or sometimes the second stanza was worthwhile reading; the rest he found to be indulgence on the poet's part. There were very few poems, of the hundreds I must have read to him, that he listened to all the way through. At first I read to him what I liked; my preference was for abstract, convoluted, cerebral poetry. Later he made me read over and over what he liked. In his opinion a poem had to be compact, preferably short. And it had to be made up of precise poignant images of great simplicity.

In the late afternoon, sitting on that bench in Oaxaca, a poem by Cesar Vallejo always seemed to sum up for him a special feeling of longing. I recited it to la Gorda from memory, not so much for her benefit as for mine.

I wonder what she is doing at this hour
my Andean and sweet Rita
of reeds and wild cherry trees.
Now that this weariness chokes me, and blood dozes off,
    like lazy brandy inside me.

I wonder what she is doing with those hands
that in attitude of penitence
used to iron starchy whiteness,
in the afternoons.
Now that this rain is taking away my desire to go on.

I wonder what has become of her skirt with lace;
of her toils; of her walk;
of her scent of spring sugar cane from that place.

She must be at the door,
gazing at a fast moving cloud.
A wild bird on the tile roof will let out a call;
and shivering she will say at last, "Jesus, it's cold!"

The memory of don Juan was incredibly vivid. It was not a memory on the level of my thought, nor was it on the level of my conscious feelings. It was an unknown kind of memory that made me weep. Tears were streaming from my eyes, but they were not soothing at all.

The last hour of the afternoon had always had special significance for don Juan. I had accepted his regard for that hour, and his conviction that if something of importance were to come to me, it would have to be at that time.

La Gorda put her head on my shoulder. I rested my head on her head. We remained in that position for a while. I felt relaxed; the agitation had been driven away from me. It was strange that the single act of resting my head on la Gorda's would bring such peace. I wanted to make a joke and tell her that we should tie our heads together. Then I knew that she would actually take me up on that. My body shook with laughter and I realized that I was asleep, yet my eyes were open; if I had really wanted to, I could have stood up. I did not want to move, so I remained there fully awake and yet asleep. I saw people walking by and staring at us. I did not mind that in the least. Ordinarily I would have objected to being noticed. Then all at once the people in front of me changed into very large blobs of white light. I was facing the luminous eggs in a sustained fashion for the first time in my life! Don Juan had told me that human beings appear to the seer as luminous eggs. I had experienced flashes of that perception, but never before had I focused my vision on them as I was doing that day.

The blobs of light were quite amorphous at first. It was as if my eyes were not properly focused. But then, at one moment, it was as if I had finally arranged my vision and the blobs of white light became oblong luminous eggs. They were big, in fact, they were enormous, perhaps seven feet high by four feet wide or even larger.

At one moment I noticed that the eggs were no longer moving. I saw a solid mass of luminosity in front of me. The eggs were watching me; looming dangerously over me. I moved deliberately and sat up straight. La Gorda was sound asleep on my shoulder. There was a group of adolescents around us. They must have thought that we were drunk. They were mimicking us. The most daring adolescent was feeling la Gorda's breasts. I shook her and woke her up. We stood up in a hurry and left. They followed us, taunting us and yelling obscenities. The presence of a policeman on the corner dissuaded them from continuing with their harassment. We walked in complete silence from the plaza to where I had left my car. It was almost evening. Suddenly la Gorda grabbed my arm. Her eyes were wild, her mouth open. She pointed.

"Look! Look!" she yelled. "There's the Nagual and Genaro!"

I saw two men turning the corner a long block ahead of us.

La Gorda took off in a fast run. Running after her, I asked her if she was sure. She was beside herself. She said that when she had looked up, both don Juan and don Genaro were staring at her. The moment her eyes met theirs they moved away.

When we reached the corner ourselves, the two men were still the same distance away from us. I could not distinguish their features. They were dressed like rural Mexican men. They were wearing straw hats. One was husky, like don Juan, the other was thin, like don Genaro. The two men went around another corner and we again ran noisily after them. The street they had turned onto was deserted and led to the outskirts of town. It curved slightly to the left. The two men were just where the street curved. Right then something happened that made me feel it was possible they might really be don Juan and don Genaro. It was a movement that the smaller man made. He turned three-quarter profile to us and tilted his head as if telling us to follow, something don Genaro used to do to me whenever we were out in the woods. He always walked ahead of me, daring, coaxing me with a movement of his head to catch up with him.

La Gorda began to yell at the top of her voice. "Nagual! Genaro! Wait!"

She ran ahead of me. They were walking very fast toward some shacks that were half-visible in the semi-darkness. They must have entered one of them or turned into any of a number of pathways; suddenly they were out of sight.

La Gorda stood there and bellowed their names without any bashfulness. People came out to see who was yelling. I held her until she calmed down.

"They were right in front of me," she said, crying. "Not even ten feet away. When I yelled and called your attention to them they were a block away in one instant."

I tried to appease her. She was in a high state of nervousness. She clung to me shivering. For some indiscernible reason I was absolutely sure that the two men were not don Juan and don Genaro; therefore, I could not share la Gorda's agitation. She said that we had to drive back home, that power would not permit her to go to Los Angeles or even to Mexico City with me. It was not time yet for her journey. She was convinced that seeing them had been an omen. They had disappeared pointing toward the east, toward her hometown.

I did not have any objections to starting back that very moment. After all the things that had happened to us that day I should have been dead tired. Instead I was vibrating with a most extravagant vigor, reminiscent of times with don Juan when I had felt like ramming walls with my shoulders.

On our way back to my car I was again filled with the most passionate affection for la Gorda. I could never thank her enough for her help. I thought that whatever she had done to help me *see* the luminous eggs had worked. She had been so courageous, risking ridicule and even bodily harm by sitting on that bench. I expressed my thanks to her. She looked at me as if I were crazy and then broke into a belly laugh.

"I thought the same thing about you," she said. "I thought you had done it just for me. I too *saw* luminous eggs. This was the first time for me also. We have *seen together!* Like the Nagual and Genaro used to do."

As I opened the door of the car for la Gorda, the full impact of what we had done struck me. Up to that point I had been numb, something in me had slowed down. Now my euphoria was as intense as la Gorda's agitation had been a short while before. I wanted to run in the street and shout. It was la Gorda's turn to contain me. She squatted and rubbed my calves. Strangely enough, I calmed down immediately. I found that it was difficult for me to talk. My thoughts were running ahead of my ability to verbalize them. I did not want to drive back to her hometown right away. There seemed to be still so much more to do. Since I could not explain clearly what I wanted, I practically dragged a reluctant Gorda back to the plaza, but there were no empty benches at that hour. I was famished so I pulled her into a restaurant. She thought she could not eat but when they brought the food she turned out to be as hungry as I was. Eating relaxed us completely.

We sat on the bench later that night. I had refrained from talking about what happened to us until we had a chance to sit there. La Gorda was at first unwilling to say anything. My mind was in a peculiar state of exhilaration. I had had similar moments with don Juan, but associated, as a rule, with the aftereffects of hallucinogenic plants.

I began by describing to la Gorda what I had *seen*. The feature of those luminous eggs that had impressed me the most was their movements. They did not walk. They moved in a floating manner, yet they were grounded. The way they moved was not pleasing. Their movements were stilted, wooden, and jerky. When they were in motion the whole egg shape became smaller and rounder; they seemed to jump or jerk, or shake up and down with great speed. The result was a most annoying nervous shivering. Perhaps the closest I can get to describing the physical discomfort caused by their motion would be to say that I felt as if the images on a moving picture screen had been speeded up.

Another thing that had intrigued me was that I could not detect any legs. I had once seen a ballet production in which the dancers mimicked the movement of soldiers on ice skates; for that effect they wore loose tunics that hung all the way to the floor. There was no way to see their feet: thus the illusion that they were gliding on ice. The luminous eggs that paraded in front of me gave the impression that they were sliding on a rough surface. Their luminosity shook up and down almost imperceptibly, yet enough to make me nearly ill. When the eggs were in repose they became elongated. Some of them were so long and rigid that they brought to mind the idea of a wooden icon.

Another even more disturbing feature of the luminous eggs was the absence of eyes. I had never realized so acutely how we are drawn to the eyes of living beings. The luminous eggs were thoroughly alive; they were observing me with great curiosity. I could see them jerking up and down, leaning over to watch me, but without any eyes.

Many of those luminous eggs had black spots on them, huge spots below the midsection. Others did not. La Gorda had told me that reproduction affects the bodies of both men and women by causing a hole to appear below the stomach, but the spots on those luminous eggs did not seem like holes to me. They were areas with no luminosity, but there was no depth to them. Those that had the black spots seemed to be mellow, tired; the crest of their egg shape was wilted, it looked opaque in comparison to the rest of their glow. The ones without spots, on the other hand, were dazzlingly bright. I fancied them to be dangerous. They were vibrant, filled with energy and whiteness.

La Gorda said that the instant I rested my head on her she also entered into a state that resembled *dreaming*. She was awake, yet she could not move. She was conscious that people were milling around us. Then she *saw* them turning into luminous blobs and finally into egg-shaped creatures. She did not know that I was also *seeing*. She had thought at first that I was watching over her, but at one moment the pressure of my head was so heavy that she concluded quite consciously that I too must have been *seeing*. Only after I straightened up and caught the young man fondling her as she seemed to sleep did I have an inkling of what might be happening to her.

Our visions differed in that she could distinguish men from women by the shape of some filaments that she called "roots." Women, she said, had thick bundles of filaments that resembled a lion's tail; they grew inward from the place of the genitalia. She explained that those roots were the givers of life. The embryo, in order to accomplish its growth, attaches itself to one of those nurturing roots and thoroughly consumes it, leaving only a hole. Men, on the other hand, had short filaments that were alive and floating almost separately from the luminous mass of their bodies.

I asked her what in her opinion was the reason we had *seen together*. She declined to make any comment, but she coaxed me to go ahead with my speculations. I told her that the only thing that occurred to me was the obvious: emotions must have been a factor.

After la Gorda and I had sat down on don Juan's favorite bench in the late afternoon that day, and I had recited the poem that he liked, I was highly charged with emotion. My emotions must have prepared my body. But I also had to consider the fact that from doing *dreaming* I had learned to enter into a state of total quietness. I was able to turn off my internal dialogue and remain as if I were inside a cocoon, peeking out of a hole. In that state I could either let go of some control I had and enter into *dreaming*, or I could hold on to that control and remain passive, thoughtless, and without desires. I did not think, however, that those were the significant factors. I believed the catalyst was la Gorda. I thought it was what I felt for her which had created the conditions for *seeing*.

La Gorda laughed shyly when I told her what I believed.

"I don't agree with you," she said. "I think what has happened is that your body has started to remember."

"What do you mean by that, Gorda?" I asked.

There was a long pause. She seemed to be either fighting to say something she did not want to say, or she was desperately trying to find the appropriate word.

"There are so many things that I know," she said, "and yet I don't know what I know. I remember so many things that I finally end up remembering nothing. I think you are in the same predicament yourself."

I assured her that I was not aware of it. She refused to believe me.

"At times I really believe you don't know," she said. "At other times I believe you are playing with us. The Nagual told me that he himself didn't know. A lot of things that he told me about you are coming back to me now."

"What does it mean that my body has begun to remember?"
I insisted.

"Don't ask me that," she said with a smile. "I don't know
what you are supposed to remember, or what that remembering is like. I've never done it, myself. I know that much."

"Is there anybody among the apprentices who could tell
me?" I asked.

"No one," she said. "I think I'm a courier to you, a courier
who can bring you only half a message this time."

She stood up and begged me to drive her back to her hometown. I was too exhilarated to leave then. We walked around
the plaza at my suggestion. Finally we sat down on another
bench.

"Isn't it strange to you that we could *see together* with such
ease?" la Gorda asked.

I did not know what she had in mind. I was hesitant in
answering.

"What would you say if I told you that I think we've *seen
together* before?" la Gorda asked, carefully voicing her words.

I could not understand what she meant. She repeated the
question one more time and I still could not get her meaning.

"When could we have *seen together* before?" I asked. "Your
question doesn't make sense."

"That's the point," she replied. "It doesn't make sense, and
yet I have the feeling we have *seen together* before."

I felt a chill and stood up. I remembered again the sensation
I had had in that town. La Gorda opened her mouth to say
something but stopped herself in mid-sentence. She stared at
me, bewildered, put her hand to my lips, and then practically
dragged me to the car.

I drove all night. I wanted to talk, to analyze, but she fell
asleep as if purposely avoiding any discussion. She was right,
of course. Of the two of us, she was the one who was cognizant of the danger of dissipating a mood through overanalyz-
ing it.

As she got out of the car, when we arrived at her house, she said that we could not talk at all about what happened to us in Oaxaca.

"Why is that, Gorda?" I asked.

"I don't want to waste our power," she said. "That's the sorcerer's way. Never waste your gains."

"But if we don't talk about it, we'll never know what really happened to us," I protested.

"We have to keep quiet for at least nine days," she said.

"Can we talk about it, just between the two of us?" I asked.

"A talk between the two of us is precisely what we must avoid," she said. "We're vulnerable. We must allow ourselves time to heal."

3

Quasi Memories of the Other Self

"Can you tell us what's going on?" Nestor asked me when all of us were together that night. "Where did you two go yesterday?"

I had forgotten la Gorda's recommendation that we not talk about what had happened to us. I began to tell them that we had gone first to the nearby town and we had found a most intriguing house there.

All of them seemed to have been touched by a sudden tremor. They perked up, looked at one another, and then they stared at la Gorda as if waiting for her to tell them about it.

"What kind of a house was it?" Nestor asked.

Before I had time to answer, la Gorda interrupted me. She began to talk in a hurried almost incoherent manner. It was evident to me that she was improvising. She even used words and phrases in the Mazatec language. She gave me furtive glances that spelled out a silent plea not to say anything about it.

"How about your *dreaming*, Nagual?" she asked me with the relief of someone who has found the way out. "We'd like to know everything you do. I think it's very important that you tell us."

She leaned over and as casually as she could she whispered

in my ear that because of what had happened to us in Oaxaca I had to tell them about my *dreaming*.

"Why would it be important to you?" I said loudly.

"I think we are very close to the end," la Gorda said solemnly. "Everything you say or do to us is of key importance now."

I related to them the events of what I considered my true *dreaming*. Don Juan had told me that there was no point in emphasizing the trials. He gave me a rule of thumb; if I should have the same vision three times, he said, I had to pay extraordinary attention to it; otherwise, a neophyte's attempts were merely a stepping stone to building the second attention.

I *dreamed* once that I woke up and jumped out of bed only to be confronted by myself still sleeping in bed. I watched myself asleep and had the self-control to remember that I was *dreaming*. I followed then the directions don Juan had given me, which were to avoid sudden jolts or surprises, and to take everything with a grain of salt. The *dreamer* has to get involved, don Juan said, in dispassionate experimentations. Rather than examining his sleeping body, the *dreamer* walks out of the room. I suddenly found myself, without knowing how, outside my room. I had the absolutely clear sensation that I had been placed there instantaneously. When I first stood outside my door, the hall and the staircase were monumental. If anything really scared me that night, it was the size of those structures, which in real life were thoroughly commonplace; the hall was about fifty feet long and the staircase had sixteen steps.

I could not conceive how to cover the enormous distances I was perceiving. I vacillated, then something made me move. I did not walk, though. I did not feel my steps. Suddenly I was holding on to the railing. I could see my hands and forearms but I did not feel them. I was holding on by the force of something that had nothing to do with my musculature as I know it. The same thing happened when I tried to go down the stairs. I did not know how to walk. I just could not take a step. It was as if my legs were welded together. I could see my legs by leaning over, but I could not move them forward or laterally, nor could I lift them up toward my chest. I seemed to be stuck to the top step. I felt I was like those inflated plastic dolls that can lean in any direction until they are horizontal, only to be pulled upright again by the weight of their heavy rounded bases.

I made a supreme effort to walk and bounced from step to step like a clumsy ball. It took an incredible degree of attention to get to the ground floor. I could not describe it in any other way. Some form of attentiveness was required to maintain the bounds of my vision, to prevent it from disintegrating into the fleeting images of an ordinary dream.

When I finally got to the street door I could not open it. I tried desperately, but to no avail; then I recalled that I had gotten out of my room by gliding out of it as if the door had been open. All I needed was to recall that feeling of gliding and suddenly I was out in the street. It looked dark—a peculiarly lead-gray darkness that did not permit me to perceive any colors. My interest was drawn immediately to an enormous lagoon of brightness right in front of me, at my eye level. I deduced rather than perceived that it was the street light, since I knew there was one right on the corner, twenty feet above the ground. I knew then that I could not make the perceptual arrangements needed in order to judge up, or down, or here, or there. Everything seemed to be extraordinarily present. I had no mechanism, as in ordinary life, to arrange my perception. Everything was there in the foreground and I had no volition to construct an adequate screening procedure.

I stayed in the street, bewildered, until I began to have the sensation that I was levitating. I held on to the metal pole that supported the light and the street sign on the corner. A strong breeze was lifting me up. I was sliding up the pole until I could plainly see the name of the street: Ashton.

Months later, when I again found myself in a *dream* looking at my sleeping body, I already had a repertoire of things to do. In the course of my regular *dreaming* I had learned that what matters in that state was volition, the corporeality of the body has no significance. It is simply a memory that slows down the *dreamer*. I glided out of the room without hesitation, since I did not have to act out the motions of opening a door or walking in order to move. The hall and staircase were not as enormous as they appeared to be the first time. I glided through with great ease and ended up in the street where I willed myself to move three blocks. I became aware then that the lights were still very disturbing sights. If I focused my attention on them, they became pools of immeasurable size. The other elements of that *dream* were easy to control. The buildings were extraordinarily large, but their features were familiar. I pondered what to do. And then, quite casually, I realized that if I did not stare at things but only glanced at them, just as we do in our daily world, I could arrange my perception. In other words, if I followed don Juan's sugges- tions to the letter and took my *dreaming* for granted, I could use the perceptual biases of my everyday life. After a few moments the scenery became, if not completely familiar, con- trollable.

The next time I had a similar *dream* I went to my favorite coffee shop on the corner. The reason I selected it was because I was used to going there all the time in the very early hours of the morning. In my *dreaming* I saw the usual waitresses who worked the graveyard shift; I saw a row of people eating at the counter, and right at the very end of the counter I saw a peculiar character, a man I saw nearly every day walking aimlessly around the UCLA campus. He was the only person who actually looked at me. The instant I came in he seemed to sense me. He turned around and stared at me.

I found the same man in my waking hours a few days later in the same coffee shop in the early hours of the morning. He took one look at me and seemed to recognize me. He looked horrified and ran away without giving me a chance to talk to him.

I came back once more to the same coffee shop and that was when the course of my *dreaming* changed. As I was watching the restaurant from across the street, the scene altered. I could not see the familiar buildings any more. Instead I saw primeval scenery. It was no longer night. It was bright daylight and I was looking at a lush valley. Swampy, deep-green, reedlike plants grew all over. Next to me there was a rock ledge eight to ten feet high. A huge saber-toothed tiger was sitting there. I was petrified. We looked at each other fixedly for a long time. The size of that beast was striking, yet it was not grotesque or out of proportion. It had a splendid head, big eyes the color of dark honey, massive paws, an enormous rib cage. What impressed me the most was the color of its fur. It was uniformly dark brown, almost chocolate. Its color reminded me of roasted coffee beans, only lustrous; it had strangely longish fur, not matted or ratty. It did not look like a puma's fur, or a wolf's or a polar bear's either. It looked like something I had never seen before.

From that time on, it became routine for me to see the tiger. At times the scenery was cloudy and chilly. I could see rain in the valley, thick, copious rain. At other times the valley was bathed in sunlight. Quite often I would see other saber-toothed tigers in the valley. I could hear their unique squeaking roar—a most nauseating sound to me.

The tiger never touched me. We stared at each other from ten to twelve feet away. Yet I could tell what he wanted. He was showing me how to breathe in a specific manner. It got to the point in my *dreaming* where I could imitate the tiger's breathing so well that I felt I was turning into one. I told the apprentices that a tangible result of my *dreaming* was that my body became more muscular.

After listening to my account, Nestor marveled at how different their *dreaming* was from mine. They had particular *dreaming* tasks. His was to find cures for anything that ailed the human body. Benigno's task was to predict, foresee, find a solution for anything that was of human concern. Pablito's task was to find ways to build. Nestor said that those tasks were the reason why he dealt with medicinal plants, Benigno had an oracle, and Pablito was a carpenter. He added that, so far, they had only scratched the surface of their *dreaming* and that they had nothing of substance to report.

"You may think that we've done a great deal," he went on, "but we haven't. Genaro and the Nagual did everything for us and for these four women. We've done nothing on our own yet."

"It seems to me that the Nagual set you up differently," Benigno said, speaking very slowly and deliberately. "You must've been a tiger and you are definitely going to turn into one again. That's what happened to the Nagual, he had been a crow already and while in this life he turned into one again."

"The problem is that that kind of tiger doesn't exist any more," Nestor said. "We never heard what happens in that case."

He swept his head around to include all of them with his gesture.

"I know what happens," la Gorda said. "I remember that the Nagual Juan Matus called that *ghost dreaming*. He said that none of us has ever done *ghost dreaming* because we are not violent or destructive. He never did it himself. And he said that whoever does it is marked by fate to have ghost helpers and allies."

"What does that mean, Gorda?" I asked.

"It means that you're not like us," she replied somberly.

La Gorda seemed to be very agitated. She stood up and paced up and down the room four or five times before she sat down again by my side.

There was a gap of silence in the conversation. Josefina mumbled something unintelligible. She also seemed to be very nervous. La Gorda tried to calm her down, hugging her and patting her back.

"Josefina has something to tell you about Eligio," la Gorda said to me.

Everyone looked at Josefina without saying a word, a question in their eyes.

"In spite of the fact that Eligio has disappeared from the face of the earth," la Gorda went on, "he is still one of us. And Josefina talks to him all the time."

The rest of them suddenly became attentive. They looked at one another and then they looked at me.

"They meet in *dreaming*," la Gorda said dramatically.

Josefina took a deep breath, she seemed to be the epitome of nervousness. Her body shook convulsively. Pablito lay on top of her on the floor and began breathing hard with his diaphragm, pushing it in and out, forcing her to breathe in unison with him.

"What's he doing?" I asked la Gorda.

"What's he doing! Can't you see?" she replied sharply.

I whispered to her that I was aware that he was trying to make her relax, but that his procedure was novel to me. She said that Pablito was giving Josefina energy by placing his midsection, where men have a surplus of it, over Josefina's womb, where women store their energy.

Josefina sat up and smiled at me. She seemed to be perfectly relaxed.

"I do meet Eligio all the time," she said. "He waits for me every day."

"How come you've never told us that?" Pablito asked in a huffy tone.

"She told me," la Gorda interrupted, and then went into a lengthy explanation of what it meant to all of us that Eligio was available. She added that she had been waiting for a sign from me to disclose Eligio's words.

"Don't beat around the bush, woman!" Pablito yelled. "Tell us his words."

"They are not for you!" la Gorda yelled back.

"Who are they for, then?" Pablito asked.

"They are for the Nagual," la Gorda yelled, pointing at me.

La Gorda apologized for raising her voice. She said that whatever Eligio had said was complex and mysterious and she could not make heads or tails of it.

"I just listened to him. That's all I was able to do, listen to him," she continued.

"Do you mean you also meet Eligio?" Pablito asked in a tone that was a mixture of anger and expectation.

"I do," la Gorda replied in almost a whisper. "I couldn't talk about it because I had to wait for him."

She pointed to me and then pushed me with both hands. I momentarily lost my balance and tumbled down on my side.

"What is this? What are you doing to him?" Pablito asked in a very angry voice. "Was that a display of Indian love?"

I turned to la Gorda. She made a gesture with her lips to tell me to be quiet.

"Eligio says that you are the Nagual, but you are not for us," Josefina said to me.

There was dead silence in the room. I did not know what to make of Josefina's statement. I had to wait until someone else talked.

"Do you feel relieved?" la Gorda prodded me.

I said to all of them that I did not have any opinions one way or the other. They looked like children, bewildered children. La Gorda had the air of a mistress of ceremonies who is thoroughly embarrassed.

Nestor stood up and faced la Gorda. He spoke a phrase in Mazatec to her. It had the sound of a command or a reproach.

"Tell us everything you know, Gorda," he went on in Spanish. "You have no right to play with us, to hold back something so important, just for yourself."

La Gorda protested vehemently. She explained that she was holding on to what she knew because Eligio had asked her to do so. Josefina assented with a nod of her head.

"Did he tell all this to you or to Josefina?" Pablito asked.

"We were together," la Gorda said in a barely audible whisper.

"You mean you and Josefina *dream together!*" Pablito exclaimed breathlessly.

The surprise in his voice corresponded to the shock wave that seemed to go through the rest of them.

"What exactly has Eligio said to you two?" Nestor asked when the shock had subsided.

"He said that I should try to help the Nagual remember his left side," la Gorda said.

"Do you know what she's talking about?" Nestor asked me.

There was no possibility that I would have known. I told them that they should turn to themselves for answers. But none of them voiced any suggestions.

"He told Josefina other things which she can't remember," la Gorda said. "So we are in a real fix. Eligio said that you are definitely the Nagual and you have to help us, but that you are not for us. Only upon remembering your left side can you take us to where we have to go."

Nestor spoke to Josefina in a fatherly manner and urged her to remember what Eligio had said, rather than insisting that I should remember something which must have been in some sort of code, since none of us could make sense of it.

Josefina winced and frowned as if she were under a heavy weight that was pushing her down. She actually looked like a rag doll that was being compressed. I watched in true fascination.

"I can't," she finally said. "I know what he's talking about when he speaks to me, but I can't say now what it is. It doesn't come out."

"Do you remember any words?" Nestor asked. "Any single words?"

She stuck her tongue out, shook her head from side to side, and screamed at the same time.

"No. I can't," she said after a moment.

"What kind of *dreaming* do you do, Josefina?" I asked.

"The only kind I know," she snapped.

"I've told you how I do mine," I said. "Now tell me how you do yours."

"I close my eyes and I see this wall," she said. "It's like a wall of fog. Eligio waits for me there. He takes me through it and shows me things, I suppose. I don't know what we do, but we do things together. Then he brings me back to the wall and lets me go. And I come back and forget what I've seen."

"How did you happen to go with la Gorda?" I asked.

"Eligio told me to get her," she said. "The two of us waited for la Gorda, and when she went into her *dreaming* we snatched her and pulled her behind that wall. We've done that twice."

"How did you snatch her?" I asked.

"I don't know!" Josefina replied. "But I'll wait for you and when you do your *dreaming* I'll snatch you and then you'll know."

"Can you snatch anyone?" I asked.

"Sure," she said, smiling. "But I don't do it because it's a waste. I snatched la Gorda because Eligio told me that he wanted to tell her something on account of her being more levelheaded than I am."

"Then Eligio must have told you the same things, Gorda," Nestor said with a firmness that was not familiar to me.

La Gorda made an unusual gesture of lowering her head, opening her mouth on the sides, shrugging her shoulders, and lifting her arms above her head.

"Josefina has just told you what happened," she said. "There is no way for me to remember. Eligio speaks with a different speed. He speaks but my body cannot understand him. No. No. My body cannot remember, that's what it is. I know he said that the Nagual here will remember and will take us to where we have to go. He couldn't tell me more because there was so much to tell and so little time. He said that somebody, and I don't remember who, is waiting for me in particular."

"Is that all he said?" Nestor insisted.

"The second time I saw him, he told me that all of us will have to remember our left side, sooner or later, if we want to get to where we have to go. But he is the one who has to remember first."

She pointed to me and pushed me again as she had done earlier. The force of her shove sent me tumbling like a ball.

"What are you doing this for, Gorda?" I asked, a bit annoyed at her.

"I'm trying to help you remember," she said. "The Nagual Juan Matus told me that I should give you a push from time to time in order to jolt you."

La Gorda hugged me in a very abrupt movement.

"Help us, Nagual," she pleaded. "We are worse off than dead if you don't."

I was close to tears. Not because of their dilemma, but because I felt something stirring inside me. It was something that had been edging its way out ever since we visited that town.

La Gorda's pleading was heartbreaking. I then had another attack of what seemed to be hyperventilation. A cold sweat enveloped me and then I got sick to my stomach. La Gorda tended to me with absolute kindness.

True to her practice of waiting before revealing a finding, la Gorda would not consider discussing our *seeing together* in Oaxaca. For days she remained aloof and determinedly uninterested. She would not even discuss my getting ill. Neither would the other women. Don Juan used to stress the need for waiting for the most appropriate time to let go of something that we hold. I understood the mechanics of la Gorda's actions, although I found her insistence on waiting rather annoying and not in accord with our needs. I could not stay with them too long, so I demanded that all of us should get together and share everything we knew. She was inflexible.

"We have to wait," she said. "We have to give our bodies a chance to come up with a solution. Our task is the task of remembering, not with our minds but with our bodies. Everybody understands it like that."

She looked at me inquisitively. She seemed to be looking for a clue that would tell her that I too had understood the task. I admitted to being thoroughly mystified, since I was the outsider. I was alone, while they had one another for support.

"This is the silence of warriors," she said, laughing, and then added in a conciliatory tone, "This silence doesn't mean that we can't talk about something else."

"Maybe we should go back to our old discussion of losing the human form," I said.

There was a look of annoyance in her eyes. I explained at length that, especially when foreign concepts were involved, meaning had to be continually clarified for me.

"What exactly do you want to know?" she asked.

"Anything that you may want to tell me," I said.

"The Nagual told me that losing the human form brings freedom," she said. "I believe it. But I haven't felt that freedom, not yet."

There was a moment of silence. She was obviously assessing my reaction.

"What kind of freedom is it, Gorda?" I asked.

"The freedom to remember your self," she said. "The Nagual said that losing the human form is like a spiral. It gives you the freedom to remember and this in turn makes you even freer."

"Why haven't you felt that freedom yet?" I asked.

She clicked her tongue, shrugged her shoulders. She seemed confused or reluctant to go on with our conversation.

"I'm tied to you," she said. "Until you lose your human form in order to remember, I won't be able to know what that freedom is. But perhaps you won't be able to lose your human form unless you remember first. We shouldn't be talking about this anyway. Why don't you go and talk to the Genaros?"

She sounded like a mother sending her child out to play. I did not mind it in the least. From someone else, I could easily have taken the same attitude as arrogance or contempt. I liked being with her, that was the difference.

I found Pablito, Nestor, and Benigno in Genaro's house playing a strange game. Pablito was dangling about four feet above the ground inside something that seemed to be a dark leather harness strapped to his chest under his armpits. The harness resembled a thick leather vest. As I focused my attention on it, I noticed that Pablito was actually standing on some thick straps that looped down from the harness like stirrups. He was suspended in the center of the room by two ropes strung over a thick round transverse beam that supported the roof. Each rope was attached to the harness itself, over Pablito's shoulders, by a metal ring.

Nestor and Benigno each held a rope. They were standing, facing each other, holding Pablito in midair by the strength of their pull. Pablito was holding on with all his strength to two long thin poles that were planted in the ground and fitted comfortably in his clasped hands. Nestor was to Pablito's left and Benigno to his right.

The game seemed to be a three-sided tug-of-war, a ferocious battle between the ones who were tugging and the one who was suspended.

When I walked into the room, all I could hear was the heavy breathing of Nestor and Benigno. The muscles of their arms and necks were bulging with the strain of pulling.

Pablito kept an eye on both of them, focusing on each one, one at a time, with a split-second glance. All three were so absorbed in their game that they did not even notice my presence, or if they did, they could not afford to break their concentration to greet me.

Nestor and Benigno stared at each other for ten to fifteen minutes in total silence. Then Nestor faked letting his rope go. Benigno did not fall for it, but Pablito did. He tightened the grip of his left hand and braced his feet on the poles in order to strengthen his hold. Benigno used the moment to strike and gave a mighty tug at the precise instant that Pablito eased his grip.

Benigno's pull caught Pablito and Nestor by surprise. Benigno hung from the rope with all his weight. Nestor was outmaneuvered. Pablito fought desperately to balance himself. It was useless. Benigno won the round.

Pablito got out of the harness and came to where I was. I asked him about their extraordinary game. He seemed somehow reluctant to talk. Nestor and Benigno joined us after putting their gear away. Nestor said that their game had been designed by Pablito, who found the structure in *dreaming* and then constructed it as a game. At first it was a device for tensing the muscles of two of them at the same time. They used to take turns at being hoisted. But then Benigno's *dreaming* gave them the entry into a game where all three of them tensed their muscles, and they sharpened their visual prowess by remaining in a state of alertness, sometimes for hours.

"Benigno thinks now that it is helping our bodies to remember," Nestor went on. "La Gorda, for instance, plays it in a weird way. She wins every time, no matter what position she plays. Benigno thinks that's because her body remembers."

I asked them if they also had the silence rule. They laughed. Pablito said that la Gorda wanted more than anything else to be like the Nagual Juan Matus. She deliberately imitated him, up to the most absurd detail.

"Do you mean we can talk about what happened the other night?" I asked, almost bewildered, since la Gorda had been so emphatically against it.

"We don't care," Pablito said. "You're the Nagual!"

"Benigno here remembered something real, real weird," Nestor said without looking at me.

"I think it was a mixed-up dream, myself," Benigno said. "But Nestor thinks it wasn't."

I waited impatiently. With a movement of my head, I urged them to go on.

"The other day he remembered you teaching him how to look for tracks in soft dirt," Nestor said.

"It must have been a dream," I said.

I wanted to laugh at the absurdity, but all three of them looked at me with pleading eyes.

"It's absurd," I said.

"Anyway, I better tell you now that I have a similar recollection," Nestor said. "You took me to some rocks and showed me how to hide. Mine was not a mixed-up dream. I was awake. I was walking with Benigno one day, looking for plants, and suddenly I remembered you teaching me, so I hid as you taught me and scared Benigno out of his wits."

"I taught you! How could that be? When?" I asked.

I was beginning to get nervous. They did not seem to be joking.

"When? That's the point," Nestor said. "We can't figure out when. But Benigno and I know it was you."

I felt heavy, oppressed. My breathing became difficult. I feared I was going to get ill again. I decided right then to tell them about what la Gorda and I had *seen together*. Talking about it relaxed me. At the end of my recounting I was again in control of myself.

"The Nagual Juan Matus left us a little bit open," Nestor said. "All of us can *see* a little. We *see* holes in people who have had children and also, from time to time, we *see* a little glow in people. Since you don't *see* at all, it looks like the Nagual left you completely closed so that you will open yourself from within. Now you've helped la Gorda and she either *sees* from within or she's merely riding on your back."

I told them that what had happened in Oaxaca may have been a fluke.

Pablito thought that we should go to Genaro's favorite rock

and sit there with our heads together. The other two found his idea brilliant. I had no objections. Although we sat there for a long time, nothing happened. We did get very relaxed, however.

While we were still sitting on the rock I told them about the two men la Gorda had believed to be don Juan and don Genaro. They slid down and practically dragged me back to la Gorda's house. Nestor was the most agitated. He was almost incoherent. All I got out of them was that they had been waiting for a sign of that nature.

La Gorda was waiting for us at the door. She knew what I had told them.

"I just wanted to give my body time," she said before we had said anything. "I have to be dead sure, which I am. It was the Nagual and Genaro."

"What's in those shacks?" Nestor asked.

"They didn't go inside them," la Gorda said. "They walked away toward the open fields, toward the east. In the direction of this town."

She seemed bent on appeasing them. She asked them to stay; they did not want to. They excused themselves and left. I was sure that they felt ill at ease in her presence. She seemed to be very angry. I rather enjoyed her explosions of temper, and this was quite contrary to my normal reactions. I had always felt edgy in the presence of anyone who was upset, with the mysterious exception of la Gorda.

During the early hours of the evening all of us congregated in la Gorda's room. All of them seemed preoccupied. They sat in silence, staring at the floor. La Gorda tried to start a conversation. She said that she had not been idle, that she had put two and two together and had come up with some solutions.

"This is not a matter of putting two and two together," Nestor said. "This is a task of remembering with the body."

It seemed that they had talked about it among themselves, judging by the nods of agreement Nestor had from the others. That left la Gorda and myself as the outsiders.

"Lydia also remembers something," Nestor went on. "She thought it was her stupidity, but upon hearing what I've remembered she told us that this Nagual here took her to a curer and left her there to have her eyes cured."

La Gorda and I turned to Lydia. She lowered her head as if embarrassed. She mumbled. The memory seemed too painful for her. She said that when don Juan first found her, her eyes were infected and she could not see. Someone drove her in a car over a great distance to the curer who healed her. She had always been convinced that don Juan had done that, but upon hearing my voice she realized that it was I who had taken her there. The incongruity of such a memory threw her into agony from the first day she met me.

"My ears don't lie to me," Lydia added after a long silence. "It was you who took me there."

"Impossible! Impossible!" I yelled.

My body began to shake, out of control. I had a sense of duality. Perhaps what I call my rational self, incapable of controlling the rest of me, took the seat of a spectator. Some part of me was watching as another part of me shook.

4

Crossing the Boundaries of Affection

"What's happening to us, Gorda?" I asked after the others had gone home.

"Our bodies are remembering, but I just can't figure out what," she said.

"Do you believe the memories of Lydia, Nestor, and Benigno?"

"Sure. They're very serious people. They don't just say things like that for the hell of it."

"But what they say is impossible. You believe me, don't you, Gorda?"

"I believe that you don't remember, but then . . ."

She did not finish. She came to my side and began to whisper in my ear. She said that there was something that the Nagual Juan Matus had made her promise to keep to herself until the time was right, a trump card to be used only when there was no other way out. She added in a dramatic whisper that the Nagual had foreseen their new living arrangement, which was the result of my taking Josefina to Tula to be with Pablito. She said that there was a faint chance that we might succeed as a group if we followed the natural order of that organization. La Gorda explained that since we were divided into couples, we formed a living organism. We were a snake, a rattlesnake. The snake had four sections and was divided into two longitudinal halves, male and female. She said that she and I made up the first section of the snake, the head. It was a cold, calculating, poisonous head. The second section, formed by Nestor and Lydia, was the firm and fair heart of the snake. The third was the belly—a shifty, moody, untrustworthy belly made up by Pablito and Josefina. And the fourth section, the tail, where the rattle was located, was formed by the couple who in real life could rattle on in their Tzotzil language for hours on end, Benigno and Rosa.

La Gorda straightened herself up from the position she had adopted to whisper in my ear. She smiled at me and patted me on the back.

"Eligio said one word that finally came back to me," she went on. "Josefina agrees with me that he said the word 'trail' over and over. We are going to go on a trail!"

Without giving me a chance to ask her any questions, she said that she was going to sleep for a while and then assemble everyone to go on a trip.

We started out before midnight, hiking in bright moonlight. Everyone of the others had been reluctant to go at first, but la Gorda very skillfully sketched out for them don Juan's alleged description of the snake. Before we started, Lydia suggested that we provide ourselves with supplies in case the trip turned out to be a long one. La Gorda dismissed her suggestion on the grounds that we had no idea about the nature of the trip. She said that the Nagual Juan Matus had once pointed out to her the beginning of a pathway and said that at the right opportunity we should place ourselves on that spot and let the power of the trail reveal itself to us. La Gorda added that it was not an ordinary goats' path but a natural line on the earth which the Nagual had said would give us strength and knowledge if we could follow it and become one with it.

We moved under mixed leadership. La Gorda supplied the

impetus and Nestor knew the actual terrain. She led us to a place in the mountains. Nestor took over then and located a pathway. Our formation was evident, the head taking the lead and the others arranging themselves according to the anatomical model of a snake: heart, intestines, and tail. The men were to the right of the women. Each couple was five feet behind the one in front of them.

We hiked as quickly and as quietly as we could. There were dogs barking for a time; as we got higher into the mountains there was only the sound of crickets. We walked for a long while. All of a sudden la Gorda stopped and grabbed my arm. She pointed ahead of us. Twenty or thirty yards away, right in the middle of the trail, there was the bulky silhouette of an enormous man, over seven feet tall. He was blocking our way. We grouped together in a tight bunch. Our eyes were fixed on the dark shape. He did not move. After a while, Nestor alone advanced a few steps toward him. Only then did the figure move. He came toward us. Gigantic as he was, he moved nimbly.

Nestor came back running. The moment he joined us, the man stopped. Boldly, la Gorda took a step toward him. The man took a step toward us. It was evident that if we kept on moving forward, we were going to clash with the giant. We were no match for whatever it was. Without waiting to prove it, I took the initiative and pulled everyone back and quickly steered them away from that place.

We walked back to la Gorda's house in total silence. It took us hours to get there. We were utterly exhausted. When we were safely sitting in her room, la Gorda spoke.

"We are doomed," she said to me. "You didn't want us to move on. That thing we saw on the trail was one of your allies, wasn't it? They come out of their hiding place when you pull them out."

I did not answer. There was no point in protesting. I remembered the countless times I had believed that don Juan and don Genaro were in cahoots with each other. I thought that while don Juan talked to me in the darkness, don Genaro would put on a disguise in order to scare me, and don Juan would insist that it was an ally. The idea that there were allies or entities at large that escape our everyday attention had been too farfetched for me. But then I had lived to find out that the allies of don Juan's description existed in fact; there were, as he had said, entities at large in the world.

In an authoritarian outburst, rare to me in my everyday life, I stood up and told la Gorda and the rest of them that I had a proposition for them and they could take it or leave it. If they were ready to move out of there, I was willing to take the responsibility of taking them somewhere else. If they were not ready, I would feel exonerated from any further commitment to them.

I felt a surge of optimism and certainty. None of them said anything. They looked at me silently, as if they were internally assessing my statements.

"How long would it take you to get your gear?" I asked.

"We have no gear," la Gorda said. "We'll go as we are. And we can go right this minute if it is necessary. But if we can wait three more days, everything will be better for us."

"What about the houses that you have?" I asked.

"Soledad will take care of that," she said.

That was the first time doña Soledad's name had been mentioned since I last saw her. I was so intrigued that I momentarily forgot the drama of the moment. I sat down. La Gorda was hesitant to answer my questions about doña Soledad. Nestor took over and said that doña Soledad was around but that none of them knew much about her activities. She came and went without giving anyone notice, the agreement between them being that they would look after her house and vice versa. Doña Soledad knew that they had to leave sooner or later, and she would assume the responsibility of doing whatever was necessary to dispose of their property.

"How will you let her know?" I asked.

"That's la Gorda's department," Nestor said. "We don't know where she is."

"Where is doña Soledad, Gorda?" I asked.

"How in the hell would I know?" la Gorda snapped at me.

"But you're the one who calls her," Nestor said.

La Gorda looked at me. It was a casual look, yet it gave me a shiver. I recognized that look, but from where? The depths of my body stirred; my solar plexus had a solidity I had never felt before. My diaphragm seemed to be pushing up on its own. I was pondering whether I should lie down when suddenly I found myself standing.

"La Gorda doesn't know," I said. "Only I know where she is."

Everyone was shocked—I perhaps more than anyone else. I had made the statement with no rational foundation whatsoever. At the moment I was voicing it, nevertheless, I had had the perfect conviction that I knew where she was. It was like a flash that crossed my consciousness. I saw a mountainous area with very rugged, arid peaks; a scraggy terrain, desolate and cold. As soon as I had spoken, my next conscious thought was that I must have seen that landscape in a movie and that the pressure of being with these people was causing me to have a breakdown.

I apologized to them for mystifying them in such a blatant although unintentional manner. I sat down again.

"You mean you don't know why you said that?" Nestor asked me.

He had chosen his words carefully. The natural thing to say, at least for me, would have been, "So you really don't know where she is." I told them that something unknown had come upon me. I described the terrain I had seen and the certainty I had had that doña Soledad was there.

"That happens to us quite often," Nestor said.

I turned to la Gorda and she nodded her head. I asked for an explanation.

"These crazy mixed-up things keep coming to our minds," la Gorda said. "Ask Lydia, or Rosa, or Josefina."

Since they had entered into their new living arrangement Lydia, Rosa, and Josefina had not said much to me. They had confined themselves to greetings and casual comments about food or the weather.

Lydia avoided my eyes. She mumbled that she thought at times that she remembered other things.

"Sometimes I can really hate you," she said to me. "I think you are pretending to be stupid. Then I remember that you were very ill because of us. Was it you?"

"Of course it was him," Rosa said. "I too remember things. I remember a lady who was kind to me. She taught me how to keep myself clean, and this Nagual cut my hair for the first time, while the lady held me, because I was scared. That lady loved me. She hugged me all the time. She was very tall. I remember my face was on her bosom when she used to hug me. She was the only person who ever cared for me. I would've gladly gone to my death for her."

"Who was that lady, Rosa?" la Gorda asked with bated breath.

Rosa pointed to me with a movement of her chin, a gesture heavy with dejection and contempt.

"He knows," she said.

All of them stared at me, waiting for an answer. I became angry and yelled at Rosa that she had no business making statements that were really accusations. I was not in any way lying to them.

Rosa was not flustered by my outburst. She calmly explained that she remembered the lady telling her that I would come back some day, after I had recovered from my illness. Rosa understood that the lady was taking care of me, nursing me back to health; therefore, I had to know who she was and where she was, since I seemed to have recovered.

"What kind of illness did I have, Rosa?" I asked.

"You got ill because you couldn't hold your world," she

said with utter conviction. "Someone told me, I think a very long time ago, that you were not made for us, just like Eligio told la Gorda in *dreaming*. You left us because of it and Lydia never forgave you. She'll hate you beyond this world."

Lydia protested that her feelings for me had nothing to do with what Rosa was saying. She was merely short-tempered and easily got angry at my stupidities.

I asked Josefina if she also remembered me.

"I sure do," she said with a grin. "But you know me, I'm crazy. You can't trust me. I'm not dependable."

La Gorda insisted on hearing what Josefina remembered. Josefina was set not to say anything and they argued back and forth; finally Josefina spoke to me.

"What's the use of all this talk about remembering? It's just talk," she said. "And it isn't worth a fig."

Josefina seemed to have scored a point with all of us. There was no more to be said. They were getting up to leave after having sat in polite silence for a few minutes.

"I remember you bought me beautiful clothes," Josefina suddenly said to me. "Don't you remember when I fell down the stairs in one store? I nearly broke my leg and you had to carry me out."

Everybody sat down again and kept their eyes fixed on Josefina.

"I also remember a crazy woman," she went on. "She wanted to beat me and used to chase me all over the place until you got angry and stopped her."

I felt exasperated. Everyone seemed to be hanging on Josefina's words when she herself had told us not to trust her because she was crazy. She was right. Her remembering was sheer aberration to me.

"I know why you got ill, too," she went on. "I was there. But I can't remember where. They took you beyond that wall of fog to find this stupid Gorda. I suppose she must have gotten lost. You couldn't make it back. When they brought you out you were almost dead."

The silence that followed her revelations was oppressive. I was afraid to ask anything.

"I can't remember why on earth she went in there, or who brought you back," Josefina continued. "I do remember that you were ill and didn't recognize me any more. This stupid Gorda swears that she didn't know you when you first came to this house a few months ago. I knew you right away. I remembered you were the Nagual that got ill. You want to know something? I think these women are just indulging. And so are the men, especially that stupid Pablito. They've got to remember, they were there, too."

"Can you remember where we were?" I asked.

"No. I can't," Josefina said. "I'll know it if you take me there, though. When we all were there, they used to call us the drunkards because we were groggy. I was the least dizzy of all, so I remember pretty well."

"Who called us drunkards?" I asked.

"Not you, just us," Josefina replied. "I don't know who. The Nagual Juan Matus, I suppose."

I looked at them and each one of them avoided my eyes.

"We are coming to the end," Nestor muttered, as if talking to himself. "Our ending is staring us in the eye."

He seemed to be on the verge of tears.

"I should be glad and proud that we have arrived at the end," he went on. "Yet I'm sad. Can you explain that, Nagual?"

Suddenly all of them were sad. Even defiant Lydia was sad.

"What's wrong with all of you?" I asked in a convivial tone. "What ending are you talking about?"

"I think everyone knows what ending it is," Nestor said. "Lately, I've been having strange feelings. Something is calling us. And we don't let go as we should. We cling."

Pablito had a true moment of gallantry and said that la Gorda was the only one among them who did not cling to anything. The rest of them, he assured me, were nearly hopeless egotists.

"The Nagual Juan Matus said that when it's time to go we will have a sign," Nestor said. "Something we truly like will come forth and take us."

"He said it doesn't have to be something great," Benigno added. "Anything we like will do."

"For me the sign will come in the form of the lead soldiers I never had," Nestor said to me. "A row of Hussars on horseback will come to take me. What will it be for you?"

I remembered don Juan telling me once that death might be behind anything imaginable, even behind a dot on my writing pad. He gave me then the definitive metaphor of my death. I had told him that once while walking on Hollywood Boulevard in Los Angeles I had heard the sound of a trumpet playing an old, idiotic popular tune. The music was coming from a record shop across the street. Never had I heard a more beautiful sound. I became enraptured by it. I had to sit down on the curb. The limpid brass sound of that trumpet was going directly to my brain. I felt it just above my right temple. It soothed me until I was drunk with it. When it concluded, I knew that there would be no way of ever repeating that experience, and I had enough detachment not to rush into the store and buy the record and a stereo set to play it on.

Don Juan said that it had been a sign given to me by the powers that rule the destiny of men. When the time comes for me to leave the world, in whatever form, I will hear the same sound of that trumpet, the same idiotic tune, the same peerless trumpeter.

The next day was a frantic day for them. They seemed to have endless things to do. La Gorda said that all their chores were personal and had to be performed by each one of them without any help. I welcomed being alone. I too had things to work out. I drove to the nearby town that had disturbed me so thoroughly. I went directly to the house that had held such fascination for la Gorda and myself; I knocked on the door. A lady answered. I made up a story that I had lived in that house as a child and wanted to look at it again. She was a very gracious woman. She let me go through the house, apologizing profusely for a nonexistent disorder.

There was a wealth of hidden memories in that house. They were there, I could feel them, but I could not remember anything.

The following day la Gorda left at dawn; I expected her to be gone all day but she came back at noon. She seemed very upset.

"Soledad has come back and wants to see you," she said flatly.

Without any word of explanation, she took me to doña Soledad's house. Doña Soledad was standing by the door. She looked younger and stronger than the last time I had seen her. She bore only the slightest resemblance to the lady I had known years before.

La Gorda seemed to be on the verge of crying. The tension we were going through made her mood perfectly understandable to me. She left without saying a word.

Doña Soledad said that she had only a little time to talk to me and that she was going to use every minute of it. She was strangely deferential. There was a tone of politeness in every word she said.

I made a gesture to interrupt her to ask a question. I wanted to know where she had been. She rebuffed me in a most delicate manner. She said that she had chosen her words carefully and that the lack of time would permit her only to say what was essential.

She peered into my eyes for a moment that seemed unnaturally long. That annoyed me. She could have talked to me and answered some questions in the same length of time. She broke her silence and spoke what I thought were absurdities. She said that she had attacked me as I had requested her to, the day we crossed the parallel lines for the first time, and that she only hoped her attack had been effective and served its purpose. I wanted to shout that I had never asked her to do anything of the sort. I did not know about parallel lines and what she was saying was nonsense. She pressed my lips with her hand. I recoiled automatically. She seemed sad. She said that there was no way for us to talk because at that moment we were on two parallel lines and neither of us had the energy to cross over; only her eyes could tell me her mood.

For no reason, I began to feel relaxed, something inside me felt at ease. I noticed that tears were rolling down my cheeks. And then a most incredible sensation took possession of me for a moment, a short moment but long enough to jolt the foundations of my consciousness, or of my person, or of what I think and feel is myself. During that brief moment I knew that we were very close to each other in purpose and temperament. Our circumstances were alike. I wanted to acknowledge to her that it had been an arduous struggle, but the struggle was not over yet. It would never be over. She was saying goodbye because being the impeccable warrior she was, she knew that our paths would never cross again. We had come to the end of a trail. A lost wave of affiliation, of kinship, burst out from some unimaginable dark corner of myself. That flash was like an electric charge in my body. I embraced her; my mouth was moving, saying things that had no meaning to me. Her eyes lit up. She was also saying something I could not understand. The only sensation that was clear to me, that I had crossed the parallel lines, had no pragmatic significance. There was a welled-up anguish inside me pushing outward. Some inexplicable force was splitting me apart. I could not breathe and everything went black.

I felt someone moving me, shaking me gently. La Gorda's face came into focus. I was lying in doña Soledad's bed and la Gorda was sitting by my side. We were alone.

"Where is she?" I asked.

"She's gone," la Gorda replied.

I wanted to tell la Gorda everything. She stopped me. She opened the door. All the apprentices were outside waiting for me. They had put on their raunchiest clothes. La Gorda explained that they had torn up everything they had. It was late afternoon. I had been asleep for hours. Without talking, we walked to la Gorda's house, where I had my car parked. They crammed inside like children going on a Sunday drive.

Before I got into the car I stood gazing at the valley. My body rotated slowly and made a complete circle, as if it had a volition and purpose of its own. I felt I was capturing the essence of that place. I wanted to keep it with me because I knew unequivocally that never in this life would I see it again.

The others must have done that already. They were free of melancholy, they were laughing, teasing one another.

I started the car and drove away. When we reached the last bend in the road the sun was setting, and la Gorda yelled at me to stop. She got out and ran to a small hill at the side of the road. She climbed it and took a last look at her valley. She extended her arms toward it and breathed it in.

The ride down those mountains was strangely short and thoroughly uneventful. Everybody was quiet. I tried to get la Gorda into a conversation, but she flatly refused. She said that the mountains, being possessive, claimed ownership of them, and that if they did not save their energy, the mountains would never let them go.

Once we got to the lowlands they became more animated, especially la Gorda. She seemed to be bubbling with energy. She even volunteered information without any coaxing on my part. One of her statements was that the Nagual Juan Matus had told her, and Soledad had confirmed, that there was another side to us. Upon hearing it, the rest of them joined in with questions and comments. They were baffled by their strange memories of events that could not logically have taken place. Since some of them had first met me only months before, remembering me in the remote past was something beyond the bounds of their reason.

I told them then about my meeting with doña Soledad. I described my feeling of having known her intimately before, and my sense of having unmistakably crossed what she called the parallel lines. They reacted with confusion to my statement; it seemed that they had heard the term before but I was not sure they all understood what it meant. For me it was a metaphor. I could not vouch that it was the same for them.

When we were coming into the city of Oaxaca they expressed the desire to visit the place where la Gorda had said don Juan and don Genaro disappeared. I drove directly to the spot. They rushed out of the car and seemed to be orienting themselves, sniffing at something, looking for clues. La Gorda pointed in the direction she thought they had gone.

"You've made a terrible mistake, Gorda," Nestor said loudly. "That's not the east, that's the north."

La Gorda protested and defended her opinion. The women backed her, and so did Pablito. Benigno was noncommittal; he kept on looking at me as if I were going to furnish the answer, which I did. I referred to a map of the city of Oaxaca that I had in the car. The direction la Gorda was pointing was indeed north.

Nestor remarked that he had felt all along that their departure from their town was not premature or forced in any way; the timing was right. The others had not, and their hesitation arose from la Gorda's misjudgment. They had believed, as she herself had, that the Nagual had pointed toward their hometown, meaning that they had to stay put. I admitted, as an afterthought, that in the final analysis I was the one to blame because, although I had had the map, I had failed to use it at the time.

I then mentioned that I had forgotten to tell them that one of the men, the one I had thought for a moment was don

Genaro, had beckoned us with a movement of his head. La Gorda's eyes widened with genuine surprise, or even alarm. She had not detected the gesture, she said. The beckoning had been only for me.

"That's it!" Nestor exclaimed. "Our fates are sealed!"

He turned to address the others. All of them were talking at once. He made frantic gestures with his hands to calm them.

"I only hope that all of you did whatever you had to do as if you were never coming back," he said. "Because we are never going back."

"Are you telling us the truth?" Lydia asked me with a fierce look in her eyes, as the others peered expectantly at me.

I assured them that I had no reason to make it up. The fact that I saw that man gesturing to me with his head had no significance whatsoever for me. Besides, I was not even convinced that those men were don Juan and don Genaro.

"You're very crafty," Lydia said. "You may just be telling us this so that we will follow you meekly."

"Now, wait a minute," la Gorda said. "This Nagual may be as crafty as you like, but he'd never do anything like that."

They all began talking at once. I tried to mediate and had to shout over their voices that what I had seen did not make any difference anyway.

Nestor very politely explained that Genaro had told them that when the time came for them to leave their valley he would somehow let them know with a movement of his head. They quieted down when I said that if their fates were sealed by that event, so was mine; all of us were going north.

Nestor then led us to a place of lodging, a boardinghouse where he stayed when doing business in the city. Their spirits were high, in fact too high for my comfort. Even Lydia embraced me, apologizing for being so difficult. She explained that she had believed la Gorda and therefore had not bothered to cut her ties effectively. Josefina and Rosa were ebullient and patted me on the back over and over. I wanted to talk with la Gorda. I needed to discuss our course of action. But there was no way to be alone with her that night.

Nestor, Pablito, and Benigno left in the early morning to do some errands. Lydia, Rosa, and Josefina also went out to go shopping. La Gorda requested that I help her buy her new clothes. She wanted me to pick out one dress for her, the perfect one to give her the self-confidence she needed to be a fluid warrior. I not only found a dress but an entire outfit, shoes, nylons, and lingerie.

I took her for a stroll. We meandered in the center of town like two tourists, staring at the Indians in their regional garments. Being a formless warrior, she was already perfectly at ease in her elegant outfit. She looked ravishing. It was as if she had never dressed any other way. It was I who could not get used to it.

The questions that I wanted to ask la Gorda, which should have poured out of me, were impossible to formulate. I had no idea what to ask her. I told her in true seriousness that her new appearance was affecting me. Very soberly, she said that the crossing of boundaries was what had affected me.

"We crossed some boundaries last night," she said. "Soledad told me what to expect, so I was prepared. But you were not."

She began to explain softly and slowly that we had crossed some boundaries of affection the night before. She was enunciating every syllable as if she were talking to a child or a foreigner. But I could not concentrate. We went back to our lodgings. I needed to rest, yet I ended up going out again. Lydia, Rosa, and Josefina had not been able to find anything and wanted something like la Gorda's outfit.

By midafternoon I was back in the boardinghouse admiring the little sisters. Rosa had difficulty walking with high-heeled shoes. We were joking about her feet when the door opened slowly and Nestor made a dramatic entrance. He was wearing a tailored dark-blue suit, light-pink shirt, and blue necktie. His hair was neatly combed and a bit fluffy, as if it had been blown dry. He looked at the women and the women looked at him. Pablito came in, followed by Benigno. Both were dashing. Their shoes were brand new and their suits looked custom made.

I could not get over everyone's adaptation to city clothes. They reminded me so much of don Juan. I was perhaps as shocked seeing the three Genaros in city clothes as I had been when I saw don Juan wearing a suit, yet I accepted their change instantly. On the other hand, while I was not surprised at the women's transformation, for some reason I could not get accustomed to it.

I thought that the Genaros must have had a streak of sorcerers' luck in order to find such perfect fits. They laughed when they heard me raving about their luck. Nestor said that a tailor had made their suits months before.

"We each have another suit," he said to me. "We even have leather suitcases. We knew our time in these mountains was up. We are ready to go! Of course, you first have to tell us where. And also how long we are going to stay here."

He explained that he had old business accounts he had to close and needed time. La Gorda stepped in and with great certainty and authority stated that that night we were going to go as far away as power permitted; consequently they had until the end of the day to settle their business. Nestor and Pablito hesitated by the door. They looked at me, waiting for confirmation. I thought the least I could do was to be honest with them, but la Gorda interrupted me just as I was about to say that I was in limbo as to what exactly we were going to do.

"We will meet at the Nagual's bench at dusk," she said. "We'll leave from there. We should do whatever we have to or want to, until then, knowing that never again in this life will we be back."

La Gorda and I were alone after everybody left. In an

abrupt and clumsy movement, she sat on my lap. She was so light, I could make her thin body shake by contracting the muscles of my calves. Her hair had a peculiar perfume. I joked that the smell was unbearable. She was laughing and shaking when out of nowhere a feeling came to me—a memory? All of a sudden I had another Gorda on my lap, fat, twice the size of the Gorda I knew. Her face was round and I was teasing her about the perfume in her hair. I had the sensation that I was taking care of her.

The impact of that spurious memory made me stand up. La Gorda fell noisily to the floor. I described what I had "remembered." I told her that I had seen her as a fat woman only once, and so briefly that I had no idea of her features, and yet I had just had a vision of her face when she was fat.

She did not make any comments. She took off her clothes and put on her old dress again.

"I am not yet ready for it," she said, pointing at her new outfit. "We still have one more thing to do before we are free. According to the Nagual Juan Matus' instructions, all of us must sit together on a power spot of his choice."

"Where's that spot?"

"Somewhere in the mountains around here. It's like a door. The Nagual told me that there was a natural crack on that spot. He said that certain power spots are holes in this world; if you are formless you can go through one of those holes into the unknown, into another world. That world and this world we live in are on two parallel lines. Chances are that all of us have been taken across those lines at one time or another, but we don't remember. Eligio is in that other world. Sometimes we reach it through *dreaming*. Josefina, of course, is the best *dreamer* among us. She crosses those lines every day, but being crazy makes her indifferent, even dumb, so Eligio helped me to cross those lines thinking I was more intelligent, and I turned out to be just as dumb. Eligio wants us to remember our left side. Soledad told me that the left side is the parallel line to the one we are living in now. So if he wants us to remember it, we must have been there. And not in *dreaming*, either. That's why all of us remember weird things now and then."

Her conclusions were logical given the premises she was working with. I knew what she was talking about; those occasional unsolicited memories reeked of the reality of everyday life and yet we could find no time sequence for them, no opening in the continuum of our lives where we could fit them.

La Gorda reclined on the bed. There was a worried look in her eyes.

"What bothers me is what to do to find that power spot," she said. "Without it there is no possible journey for us."

"What worries me is where I'm going to take all of you and what I'm going to do with you," I said.

"Soledad told me that we will go as far north as the border," la Gorda said. "Some of us even further north perhaps. But you won't go all the way through with us. You have another fate."

La Gorda was pensive for a moment. She frowned with the apparent effort of arranging her thoughts.

"Soledad said that you will take me to fulfill my destiny," la Gorda said. "I am the only one of us who is in your charge."

Alarm must have been written all over my face. She smiled.

"Soledad also told me that you are plugged up," la Gorda went on. "You have moments, though, when you are a Nagual. The rest of the time, Soledad says, you are like a crazy man who is lucid only for a few moments and then reverts back to his madness."

Doña Soledad had used an appropriate image to describe me, one I could understand. I must have had a moment of lucidity for her when I knew I had crossed the parallel lines. That same moment, by my standards, was the most incongruous of all. Doña Soledad and I were certainly on two different lines of thought.

"What else did she tell you?" I asked.

"She told me I should force myself to remember," la Gorda said. "She exhausted herself trying to bring out my memory; that was why she couldn't deal with you."

La Gorda got up; she was ready to leave. I took her for a walk around the city. She seemed very happy. She went from place to place watching everything, feasting her eyes on the world. Don Juan had given me that image. He had said that a warrior knows that he is waiting and knows also what he is waiting for, and while he waits he feasts his eyes on the world. For him the ultimate accomplishment of a warrior was joy. That day in Oaxaca la Gorda was following don Juan's teachings to the letter.

In the late afternoon, before dusk, we sat down on don Juan's bench. Benigno, Pablito, and Josefina showed up first. After a few minutes the other three joined us. Pablito sat down between Josefina and Lydia and put his arms around them. They had changed back into their old clothes. La Gorda stood up and began to tell them about the power spot.

Nestor laughed at her and the rest of them joined him.

"Never again will you get us to fall for your bossiness," Nestor said. "We are free of you. We crossed the boundaries last night."

La Gorda was unruffled but the others were angry. I had to intervene. I said loudly that I wanted to know more about the boundaries we had crossed the night before. Nestor explained that that pertained only to them. La Gorda disagreed. They seemed to be on the verge of fighting. I pulled Nestor to the side and ordered him to tell me about the boundaries.

"Our feelings make boundaries around anything," he said. "The more we love, the stronger the boundary is. In this case we loved our home; before we left it we had to lift up our feelings. Our feelings for our home went up to the top of the mountains to the west from our valley. That was the boundary and when we crossed the top of those mountains, knowing that we'll never be back, we broke it."

"But I also knew that I'd never be back," I said.

"You didn't love those mountains the way we did," Nestor replied.

"That remains to be seen," la Gorda said cryptically.

"We were under her influence," Pablito said, standing up and pointing to la Gorda. "She had us by the napes of our necks. Now I see how stupid we've been on account of her. We can't cry over spilled milk, but we'll never fall for it again."

Lydia and Josefina joined Nestor and Pablito. Benigno and Rosa looked on as if the struggle did not concern them any more.

I had right then another moment of certainty and authoritarian behavior. I stood up and, without any conscious volition, announced that I was taking charge and that I relieved la Gorda of any further obligation to make comments or to present her ideas as the only solution. When I finished talking I was shocked at my boldness. Everyone, including la Gorda, was delighted.

The force behind my explosion had been first a physical sensation that my sinuses were opening, and second the certainty that I knew what don Juan had meant, and exactly where the place was that we had to visit before we could be free. As my sinuses opened I had had a vision of the house that had intrigued me.

I told them where we had to go. They accepted my directions without any arguments or even comments. We checked out of the boardinghouse and went to eat dinner. Afterward we strolled around the plaza until about eleven o'clock. I brought the car around, they piled noisily inside, and we were off. La Gorda remained awake to keep me company while the rest of them went to sleep, and then Nestor drove while la Gorda and I slept.

5

A Horde of Angry Sorcerers

We were in the town at the crack of dawn. At that point I took the wheel and drove toward the house. A couple of blocks before we got there, la Gorda asked me to stop. She got out of the car and began to walk on the high sidewalk. One by one, all of them got out. They followed la Gorda. Pablito came to my side and said that I should park on the plaza, which was a block away. I did that.

The moment I saw la Gorda turning the corner I knew that something was wrong with her. She was extraordinarily pale. She came to me and said in a whisper that she was going to go to hear early mass. Lydia also wanted to do that. Both of them walked across the plaza and went inside the church.

Pablito, Nestor, and Benigno were as somber as I had ever seen them. Rosa was frightened, her mouth open, her eyes fixed, unblinking, looking in the direction of the house. Only Josefina was beaming. She gave me a buddy-buddy slap on the back.

"You've done it, you son of a gun!" she exclaimed. "You've knocked the tar out of these sons of bitches."

She laughed until she was nearly out of breath.

"Is this the place, Josefina?" I asked.

"It surely is," she said. "La Gorda used to go to church all the time. She was a real churchgoer at that time."

"Do you remember that house over there?" I asked, pointing to it.

"That's Silvio Manuel's house," she said.

All of us jumped upon hearing the name. I felt something similar to a mild shock of electric current going through my knees. The name was definitely not familiar to me, yet my body jumped upon hearing it. Silvio Manuel was such a rare name; so liquid a sound.

The three Genaros and Rosa were as perturbed as I was. I noticed that they were pale. Judging by what I felt, I must have been just as pale as they were.

"Who is Silvio Manuel?" I finally managed to ask Josefina.

"Now you got me," she said. "I don't know."

She reiterated that she was crazy and nothing that she said should be taken seriously. Nestor begged her to tell us whatever she remembered.

Josefina tried to think but she was not the person to perform well under pressure. I knew that she would do better if no one asked her. I proposed that we look for a bakery or a place to eat.

"They didn't let me do much in that house, that's what I remember," Josefina said all of a sudden.

She turned around as if looking for something, or as if she were orienting herself.

"Something is missing here!" she exclaimed. "This is not quite the way it used to be."

I attempted to help her by asking questions that I deemed appropriate, such as whether houses were missing or had been painted, or new ones built. But Josefina could not figure out how it was different.

We walked to the bakery and bought sweet rolls. As we were heading back to the plaza to wait for la Gorda and Lydia, Josefina suddenly hit her forehead as if an idea had just struck her.

"I know what's missing!" she shouted. "That stupid wall of fog! It used to be here then. It's gone now."

All of us spoke at once, asking her about the wall, but Josefina went on talking undisturbed, as if we were not there.

"It was a wall of fog that went all the way up to the sky," she said. "It was right here. Every time I turned my head, there it was. It drove me crazy. That's right, damn it. I wasn't nuts until I was driven crazy by that wall. I saw it with my eyes closed or with my eyes open. I thought that wall was after me."

For a moment Josefina lost her natural vivaciousness. A desperate look appeared in her eyes. I had seen that look in people who were going through a psychotic episode. I hurriedly suggested that she eat her sweet roll. She calmed down immediately and began to eat it.

"What do you think of all this, Nestor?" I asked.

"I'm scared," he said softly.

"Do you remember anything?" I asked him.

He shook his head negatively. I questioned Pablito and Benigno with a movement of my brows. They also shook their heads to say no.

"How about you, Rosa?" I asked.

Rosa jumped when she heard me addressing her. She seemed to have lost her speech. She held a sweet roll in her hand and stared at it, seemingly undecided as to what to do with it.

"Of course she remembers," Josefina said, laughing, "but she's frightened to death. Can't you see that piss is even coming out her ears?"

Josefina seemed to think her statement was the ultimate joke. She doubled up laughing and dropped her roll on the ground. She picked it up, dusted it off, and ate it.

"Crazy people eat anything," she said, slapping me on the back.

Nestor and Benigno seemed uncomfortable with Josefina's antics. Pablito was delighted. There was a look of admiration

93

in his eyes. He shook his head and clicked his tongue as if he could not believe such grace.

"Let's go to the house," Josefina urged us. "I'll tell you all kinds of things there."

I said that we should wait for la Gorda and Lydia; besides, it was still too early to bother the charming lady who lived there. Pablito said that in the course of his carpentry business he had been in the town and knew a house where a family prepared food for transient people. Josefina did not want to wait; for her, it was either going to the house or going to eat. I opted for having breakfast and told Rosa to go into the church to get la Gorda and Lydia, but Benigno gallantly volunteered to wait for them and take them to the breakfast place. Apparently he too knew where the place was.

Pablito did not take us directly there. Instead, at my request, we made a long detour. There was an old bridge at the edge of town that I wanted to examine. I had seen it from my car the day I had come with la Gorda. Its structure seemed to be colonial. We went out on the bridge and then stopped abruptly in the middle of it. I asked a man who was standing there if the bridge was very old. He said that he had seen it all his life and he was over fifty. I thought that the bridge held a unique fascination for me alone, but watching the others, I had to conclude that they too had been affected by it. Nestor and Rosa were panting, out of breath. Pablito was holding on to Josefina; she in turn was holding on to me.

"Do you remember anything, Josefina?" I asked.

"That devil Silvio Manuel is on the other side of this bridge," she said, pointing to the other end, some thirty feet away.

I looked Rosa in the eyes. She nodded her head affirmatively and whispered that she had once crossed that bridge in great fear and that something had been waiting to devour her at the other end.

The two men were no help. They looked at me, bewildered. Each said that he was afraid for no reason. I had to agree with them. I felt I would not dare cross that bridge at night for all the money in the world. I did not know why.

"What else do you remember, Josefina?" I asked.

"My body is very frightened now," she said. "I can't remember anything else. That devil Silvio Manuel is always in the darkness. Ask Rosa."

With a movement of my head, I invited Rosa to talk. She nodded affirmatively three or four times but could not vocalize her words. The tension I myself was experiencing was uncalled for, yet real. All of us were standing on that bridge, midway across, incapable of taking one more step in the direction Josefina had pointed. At last Josefina took the initiative and turned around. We walked back to the center of town. Pablito guided us then to a large house. La Gorda, Lydia, and Benigno were already eating; they had even ordered food for us. I was not hungry. Pablito, Nestor, and Rosa were in a daze; Josefina ate heartily. There was an ominous silence at the table. Everybody avoided my eyes when I tried to start a conversation.

After breakfast we walked to the house. No one said a word. I knocked and when the lady came out I explained to her that I wanted to show her house to my friends. She hesitated for a moment. La Gorda gave her some money and apologized for inconveniencing her.

Josefina led us directly to the back. I had not seen that part of the house when I was there before. There was a cobbled courtyard with rooms arranged around it. Bulky farming equipment was stored away in the roofed corridors. I had the feeling I had seen that courtyard when there was no clutter in it. There were eight rooms, two on each of the four sides of the courtyard. Nestor, Pablito, and Benigno seemed to be on the brink of getting physically ill. La Gorda was perspiring profusely. She sat down with Josefina in an alcove in one of the walls, while Lydia and Rosa went inside one of the rooms.

Suddenly Nestor seemed to have an urge to find something and disappeared into another of those rooms. So did Pablito and Benigno.

I was left alone with the lady. I wanted to talk to her, ask her questions, see if she knew Silvio Manuel, but I could not muster the energy to talk. My stomach was in knots. My hands were dripping perspiration. What oppressed me was an intangible sadness, a longing for something not present, unformulated.

I could not stand it. I was about to say goodbye to the lady and walk out of the house when la Gorda came to my side. She whispered that we should sit down in a large room off a hall separate from the courtyard. The room was visible from where we were standing. We went there and stepped inside. It was a very large, empty room with a high beamed ceiling, dark but airy.

La Gorda called everyone to the room. The lady just looked at us but did not come in herself. Everyone seemed to know precisely where to sit. The Genaros sat to the right of the door, on one side of the room, and la Gorda and the three little sisters sat to the left, on the other side. They sat close to the walls. Although I would have liked to sit next to la Gorda, I sat near the center of the room. The place seemed right to me. I did not know why, but an ulterior order seemed to have determined our places.

While I sat there, a wave of strange feelings rolled over me. I was passive and relaxed. I fancied myself to be like a moving picture screen on which alien feelings of sadness and longing were being projected. But there was nothing I could recognize as a precise memory. We stayed in that room for over an hour. Toward the end I felt I was about to uncover the source of the unearthly sadness that was making me weep almost without control. But then, as involuntarily as we had sat there, we stood up and left the house. We did not even thank the lady or say goodbye to her.

We congregated in the plaza. La Gorda stated right away

that because she was formless she was still in charge. She said that she was taking this stand because of conclusions she had reached in Silvio Manuel's house. La Gorda seemed to be waiting for comments. The silence of the others was unbearable to me. I finally had to say something.

"What are the conclusions you reached in that house, Gorda?" I asked.

"I think we all know what they are," she replied in a haughty tone.

"We don't know that," I said. "Nobody has said anything yet."

"We don't have to talk, we know," la Gorda said.

I insisted that I could not take such an important event for granted. We needed to talk about our feelings. As far as I was concerned, all I had gotten out of it was a devastating sense of sadness and despair.

"The Nagual Juan Matus was right," la Gorda said. "We had to sit on that place of power to be free. I am free now. I don't know how it happened but something was lifted off me as I sat there."

The three women agreed with her. The three men did not. Nestor said that he had been about to remember actual faces, but that no matter how hard he had tried to clear his view, something thwarted him. All he had experienced was a sense of longing and sadness at finding himself still in the world. Pablito and Benigno said more or less the same thing.

"See what I mean, Gorda?" I said.

She seemed displeased; she puffed up as I had never seen her. Or had I seen her all puffed-up before, somewhere? She harangued the group. I could not pay attention to what she was saying. I was immersed in a memory that was formless, but almost within my grasp. To keep it going it seemed I needed a continuous flow from la Gorda. I was fixed on the sound of her voice, her anger. At a certain moment, when she was becoming more subdued, I yelled at her that she was bossy. She got truly upset. I watched her for a while. I was remembering another Gorda, another time; an angry, fat Gorda, pounding her fists on my chest. I remembered laughing at seeing her angry, humoring her like a child. The memory ended the moment la Gorda's voice stopped. She seemed to have realized what I was doing.

I addressed all of them and told them that we were in a precarious position—something unknown was looming over us.

"It's not looming over us," la Gorda said dryly. "It's hit us already. And I think you know what it is."

"I don't, and I think I'm also speaking for the rest of the men," I said.

The three Genaros assented with a nod.

"We have lived in that house, while we were on the left side," la Gorda explained. "I used to sit in that alcove to cry because I couldn't figure out what to do. I think if I could have stayed in that room a bit longer today, I would've remembered it all. But something pushed me out of there. I also used to sit in that room when there were more people in there. I couldn't remember their faces, though. Yet other things became clear as I sat there today. I'm formless. Things come to me, good and bad. I, for instance, picked up my old arrogance and my desire to brood. But I also picked up other things, good things."

"Me too," Lydia said in a raspy voice.

"What are the good things?" I asked.

"I think I'm wrong in hating you," Lydia said. "My hatred will keep me from flying away. They told me that in that room, the men there and the women."

"What men and what women?" Nestor asked in a tone of fright.

"I was there when they were there, that's all I know," Lydia said. "You also were there. All of us were there."

"Who were those men and women, Lydia?" I asked.

"I was there when they were there, that's all I know," she repeated.

"How about you, Gorda?" I asked.

"I've told you already that I can't remember any faces or anything specific," she said. "But I know one thing: whatever we did in that house was on the left side. We crossed, or somebody made us cross, over the parallel lines. The weird memories we have come from that time, from that world."

Without any verbal agreement, we left the plaza and headed for the bridge. La Gorda and Lydia ran ahead of us. When we got there we found both of them standing exactly where we ourselves had stopped earlier.

"Silvio Manuel is the darkness," la Gorda whispered to me, her eyes fixed on the other end of the bridge.

Lydia was shaking. She also tried to talk to me. I could not understand what she was mouthing.

I pulled everyone back away from the bridge. I thought that perhaps if we could piece together what we knew about that place, we might have a composite that would help us understand our dilemma.

We sat on the ground a few yards away from the bridge. There were lots of people milling around but no one paid any attention to us.

"Who's Silvio Manuel, Gorda?" I asked.

"I never heard the name until now," she said. "I don't know the man, yet I know him. Something like waves came upon me when I heard that name. Josefina told me the name when we were in the house. From that moment on, things have started to come to my mind and to my mouth, just like Josefina. I never thought I would live to find myself being like Josefina."

"Why did you say that Silvio Manuel is the darkness?" I asked.

"I have no idea," she said. "Yet all of us here know that that is the truth."

She urged the women to speak up. No one uttered a word. I picked on Rosa. She had been about to say something three or four times. I accused her of holding out on us. Her little body convulsed.

"We crossed this bridge and Silvio Manuel waited for us at the other end," she said in a voice barely audible. "I went last. When he devoured the others I heard their screams. I wanted to run away but the devil Silvio Manuel was at both ends of the bridge. There was no way to escape."

La Gorda, Lydia, and Josefina agreed. I asked whether it was just a feeling that they had had or an actual moment-to-moment memory of something. La Gorda said that for her it had been exactly as Rosa had described it, a moment-to-moment memory. The other two agreed with her.

I wondered aloud what had happened with the people who lived around the bridge. If the women were screaming as Rosa said they were, the passersby must have heard them; screaming would have caused a commotion. For a moment I felt that the whole town must have collaborated in some plot. A chill ran through me. I turned to Nestor and bluntly expressed the full scope of my fear.

Nestor said that the Nagual Juan Matus and Genaro were indeed warriors of supreme accomplishment and as such they were solitary beings. Their contacts with people were one-to-one. There was no possibility that the entire town or even the people who lived around the bridge were in collusion with them. For that to happen, Nestor said, all those people would have to be warriors, a most unlikely possibility.

Josefina began to circle me, looking me up and down with a sneer.

"You certainly have gall," she said. "Pretending that you don't know anything, when you were here yourself. You brought us here! You pushed us onto this bridge!"

The eyes of the women became menacing. I turned to Nestor for assistance.

"I don't remember a thing," he said. "This place scares me, that's all I know."

Turning to Nestor was an excellent maneuver on my part. The women lashed out at him.

"Of course you remember!" Josefina yelled. "All of us were here. What kind of stupid ass are you?"

My inquiry required a sense of order. I moved them away from the bridge. I thought that, being the active persons they were, they would find it more relaxing to stroll and talk things out, rather than sitting, as I would have preferred.

As we walked, the women's anger vanished as quickly as it had come. Lydia and Josefina became even more talkative. They stated over and over the sense they had had that Silvio Manuel was awesome. Nevertheless, neither of them could remember being physically hurt; they only remembered being paralyzed by fear. Rosa did not say a word, but gestured her agreement with everything the others said. I asked them if it had been night when they tried to cross the bridge. Both Lydia and Josefina said that it was daytime. Rosa cleared her throat and whispered that it was at night. La Gorda clarified the discrepancy, explaining that it had been the morning twilight, or just before.

We reached the end of a short street and automatically turned back toward the bridge.

"It's simplicity itself," la Gorda said suddenly, as if she had just thought it through. "We were crossing, or rather Silvio Manuel was making us cross, the parallel lines. That bridge is a power spot, a hole in this world, a door to the other. We went through it. It must have hurt us to go through, because my body is scared. Silvio Manuel was waiting for us on the other side. None of us remembers his face, because Silvio Manuel is the darkness and never would he show his face. We could see only his eyes."

"One eye," Rosa said quietly, and looked away.

"Everyone here, including you," la Gorda said to me, "knows that Silvio Manuel's face is in darkness. One could only hear his voice—soft, like muffled coughing."

La Gorda stopped talking and began scrutinizing me in a way that made me feel self-conscious. Her eyes were cagey; she gave me the impression that she was holding back something she knew. I asked her. She denied it, but she admitted having scores of feelings with no foundation that she did not care to explain. I urged and then demanded that the women make an effort to recollect what had happened to them on the other side of that bridge. Each of them could remember only hearing the screams of the others.

The three Genaros remained outside our discussion. I asked Nestor if he had any idea of what had happened. His somber answer was that all of it was beyond his understanding.

I came then to a quick decision. It seemed to me that the only avenue open for us was to cross that bridge. I rallied them to walk back to the bridge and go over it as a group. The men agreed instantaneously, the women did not. After exhausting all my reasonings I finally had to push and drag Lydia, Rosa, and Josefina. La Gorda was reluctant to go but seemed intrigued by the prospect. She moved along without helping me with the women, and so did the Genaros; they giggled nervously at my efforts to herd the little sisters, but they did not move a finger to help. We walked up to the point where we had stopped earlier. I felt there that I was suddenly too weak to hold the three women. I yelled at la Gorda to help. She made a halfhearted attempt to catch Lydia as the group lost its cohesion and everyone of them except la Gorda scrambled, stumping and puffing, to the safety of the street. La Gorda and I stayed as if we were glued to that bridge, incapable of going forward and begrudging having to retreat.

La Gorda whispered in my ear that I should not be afraid at all because it had actually been I who had been waiting for them on the other side. She added that she was convinced I knew I was Silvio Manuel's helper but that I did not dare to reveal it to anyone.

Right then a fury beyond my control shook my body. I felt that la Gorda had no business making those remarks or having those feelings. I grabbed her by the hair and twirled her around. I caught myself at the apex of my wrath and stopped. I apologized and hugged her. A sober thought came to my rescue. I said to her that being a leader was getting on my nerves; the tension was becoming more and more acute as we proceeded. She did not agree with me. She held on steadfastly to her interpretation that Silvio Manuel and I were utterly close, and that upon being reminded of my master I had re-acted with anger. It was lucky that she had been entrusted to my care, she said; otherwise I probably would have thrown her off the bridge.

We turned back. The rest of them were safely off the bridge, staring at us with unmistakable fear. A very peculiar state of timelessness seemed to prevail. There were no people around. We must have been on that bridge for at least five minutes and not a single person had crossed it or even come in sight. Then all of a sudden people were moving around as on any thoroughfare during the busy hours.

Without a word, we walked back to the plaza. We were dangerously weak. I had a vague desire to remain in the town a bit longer, but we got in the car and drove east, toward the Atlantic coast. Nestor and I took turns driving, stopping only for gasoline and to eat, until we reached Veracruz. That city was neutral ground for us. I had been there only once; none of the others had ever been there. La Gorda believed that such an unknown city was the proper place to shed their old wrap-pings. We checked into a hotel and there they proceeded to rip their old clothes to shreds. The excitation of a new city did wonders for their morale and their feeling of well-being.

Our next stop was Mexico City. We stayed at a hotel by the Alameda Park where don Juan and I had once stayed. For two days we were perfect tourists. We shopped and visited as many tourist spots as possible. The women looked simply stunning. Benigno bought a camera in a pawn shop. He took four hundred and twenty-five shots without any film. At one place, while we were admiring the stupendous mosaics on the walls, a security guard asked me where those gorgeous foreign women were from. He assumed I was a tourist guide. I told him that they were from Sri Lanka. He believed me and marveled at the fact that they almost looked Mexican.

The following day at ten o'clock in the morning we were at the airline office into which don Juan had once pushed me. When he shoved me I had gone in through one door and come out through another, not to the street, as I should have, but to a market at least a mile away, where I had watched the activities of the people there.

La Gorda speculated that the airline office was also, like that bridge, a power spot, a door to cross from one parallel line to the other. She said that evidently the Nagual had pushed me through that opening but I got caught midway between the two worlds, in between the lines; thus I had watched the activity in the market without being part of it. She said that the Nagual, of course, had intended to push me all the way through, but my willfulness thwarted him and I ended back on the line I came from, this world.

We walked from the airline office to the market and from there to the Alameda Park, where don Juan and I had sat after our experience at the office. I had been in that park with don Juan many times. I felt it was the most appropriate place to talk about the course of our future actions.

It was my intention to summarize everything we had done in order to let the power of that place decide what our next step would be. After our deliberate attempt at crossing the bridge, I had tried unsuccessfully to think out a way to handle my companions as a group. We sat on some stone steps and I started off with the idea that for me knowledge was fused with words. I told them that it was my earnest belief that if an event or experience was not formulated into a concept, it was condemned to dissipate; I asked them therefore to give me their individual assessments of our situation.

Pablito was the first one to talk. I found that odd, since he had been extraordinarily quiet up until now. He apologized because what he was going to say was not something he had remembered or felt but a conclusion based on everything he knew. He said that he saw no problem in understanding what the women said had happened on that bridge. It had been, Pablito maintained, a matter of being compelled to cross from the right side, the *tonal*, to the left side, the *nagual*. What had scared everyone was the fact that someone else was in control, forcing the crossing. He saw no problem either in accepting that I had been the one who had then helped Silvio Manuel. He backed up his conclusion with the statement that only two days earlier he had seen me doing the same thing, pushing everyone onto the bridge. That time I had had no one to help me on the other side, no Silvio Manuel to pull them.

I tried to change the topic and began to explain to them that to forget the way we had forgotten was called amnesia. The little I knew about amnesia was not enough to shed any light on our case, but enough to make me believe that we could not forget as if on command. I told them that someone, possibly don Juan, must have done something unfathomable to us. I wanted to find out exactly what that had been.

Pablito insisted that it was important for me to understand that it was I who had been in cahoots with Silvio Manuel. He intimated then that Lydia and Josefina had talked to him about the role I had played in forcing them to cross the parallel lines.

I did not feel comfortable discussing that subject. I commented that I had never heard about the parallel lines until the day I spoke with doña Soledad; yet I had had no qualms about immediately adopting the idea. I told them that I knew in a flash what she meant. I even became convinced I had crossed them myself when I thought I remembered her. Every one of the others, with the exception of la Gorda, said that the first time they had heard about parallel lines was when I spoke of them. La Gorda said that she had first learned about them from doña Soledad, just before I did.

Pablito made an attempt to talk about my relationship with Silvio Manuel. I interrupted him. I said that while all of us were at the bridge trying to cross it, I had failed to recognize that I—and presumably all of them—had entered into a state of non-ordinary reality. I only became aware of the change when I realized that there were no other people on the bridge. Only the eight of us had stood there. It had been a clear day, but suddenly the skies became cloudy and the light of the midmorning turned to dusk. I had been so busy with my fears and personalistic interpretations then that I had failed to notice the awesome change. When we retreated from the bridge I perceived that other people were again walking around. But what had happened to them when we were attempting our crossing?

La Gorda and the rest of them had not noticed anything—in fact they had not been aware of any changes until the very moment I described them. All of them stared at me with a mixture of annoyance and fear. Pablito again took the lead and accused me of trying to railroad them into something they did not want. He was not specific about what that might be, but his eloquence was enough to rally the others behind him. Suddenly I had a horde of angry sorcerers on me. It took me a long time to explain my need to examine from every possible point of view something so strange and engulfing as our experience on the bridge. They finally calmed down, not so much because they were convinced, but from emotional fatigue. All of them, la Gorda included, had vehemently supported Pablito's stand.

Nestor advanced another line of reasoning. He suggested that I was possibly an unwilling envoy who did not fully realize the scope of my actions. He added that he could not bring himself to believe, as the others did, that I was aware that I had been left with the task of misleading them. He felt that I did not really know that I was leading them to their destruction, yet I was doing just that. He thought that there were two ways of crossing the parallel lines, one by means of someone else's power, and the other by one's own power. His final conclusion was that Silvio Manuel had made them cross by frightening them so intensely that some of them did not even remember having done it. The task left for them to accomplish was to cross on their own power; mine was to thwart them.

Benigno spoke then. He said that in his opinion the last thing don Juan did to the male apprentices was to help us cross the parallel lines by making us jump into an abyss. Benigno believed that we already had a great deal of knowledge about the crossing but that it was not yet time to accomplish it again. At the bridge they were incapable of taking one more step because the time was not right. They were correct, therefore, in believing that I had tried to destroy them by forcing them to cross. He thought that going over the parallel lines in full awareness meant a final step for all of them, a step to be taken only when they were ready to disappear from this earth.

Lydia faced me next. She did not make any assessments but challenged me to remember how I had first lured her to the bridge. She blatantly stated that I was not the Nagual Juan Matus's apprentice but Silvio Manuel's; that Silvio Manuel and I had devoured each other's bodies.

I had another attack of rage, as with la Gorda on the bridge. I caught myself in time. A logical thought calmed me. I said to myself over and over that I was interested in analyses.

I explained to Lydia that it was useless to taunt me like that. She did not want to stop. She yelled that Silvio Manuel was my master and that this was the reason I was not part of them at all. Rosa added that Silvio Manuel gave me everything I was.

I questioned Rosa's choice of words. I told her that she should have said that Silvio Manuel gave me everything I had. She defended her wording. Silvio Manuel had given me what I *was*. Even la Gorda backed her up and said that she remembered a time when I had gotten so ill that I had no resources

left, everything in me was exhausted; it was then that Silvio
Manuel had taken over and pumped new life into my body.
La Gorda said that I was indeed better off knowing my true
origins than proceeding, as I had done so far, on the assump-
tion that it was the Nagual Juan Matus who had helped me.
She insisted that I was fixed on the Nagual because of his
predilection for words. Silvio Manuel, on the other hand, was
the silent darkness. She explained that in order to follow him
I would need to cross the parallel lines. But to follow the
Nagual Juan Matus, all I needed to do was to talk about him.

What they were saying was nothing but nonsense to me. I
was about to make what I thought was a very good point
about it when my line of reasoning became literally scrambled. I could not think what my point had been, although
only a second before, it was clarity itself. Instead, a most
curious memory beset me. It was not a feeling of something,
but the actual hard memory of an event. I remembered that
once I was with don Juan and another man whose face I could
not remember. The three of us were talking about something
I was perceiving as a feature of the world. It was three or four
yards to my right and it was an inconceivable bank of yellowish fog that, as far as I could tell, divided the world in two. It
went from the ground up to the sky, to infinity. While I talked
to the two men, the half of the world to my left was intact and
the half to my right was veiled in fog. I remembered that I
had oriented myself with the aid of landmarks and realized
that the axis of the bank of fog went from east to west. Everything to the north of that line was the world as I knew it. I
remembered asking don Juan what had happened to the world
south of the line. Don Juan made me turn a few degrees to my
right, and I saw that the wall of fog moved as I turned my
head. The world was divided in two at a level my intellect
could not comprehend. The division seemed real, but the
boundary was not on a physical plane; it had to be somehow
in myself. Or was it?

There was still one more facet to this memory. The other

man said that it was a great accomplishment to divide the world in two, but it was an even greater accomplishment when a warrior had the serenity and control to stop the rotation of that wall. He said that the wall was not inside us; it was certainly out in the world, dividing it in two, and rotating when we moved our heads, as if it were stuck to our right temples. The great accomplishment of keeping the wall from turning enabled the warrior to face the wall and gave him the power to go through it anytime he so desired.

When I told the apprentices what I had just remembered, the women were convinced that the other man was Silvio Manuel. Josefina, as a connoisseur of the wall of fog, explained that the advantage Eligio had over everyone else was his capacity to make the wall stand still so he could go through it at will. She added that it is easier to pierce the wall of fog in *dreaming* because then it does not move.

La Gorda seemed to be touched by a series of perhaps painful memories. Her body jumped involuntarily until finally she exploded into words. She said that it was no longer possible for her to deny the fact that I was Silvio Manuel's helper. The Nagual himself had warned her that I would enslave her if she was not careful. Even Soledad had told her to watch me because my spirit took prisoners and kept them as servants, a thing only Silvio Manuel would do. He had enslaved me and I in turn would enslave anyone who came close to me. She asserted that she had lived under my spell up to the moment she sat in that room in Silvio Manuel's house, when something was suddenly lifted off her shoulders.

I stood up and literally staggered under the impact of la Gorda's words. There was a vacuum in my stomach. I had been convinced that I could count on her for support under any conditions. I felt betrayed. I thought it would be appropriate to let them know my feelings, but a sense of sobriety came to my rescue. I told them instead that it had been my dispassionate conclusion, as a warrior, that don Juan had changed the course of my life for the better. I had assessed over and over what he had done to me and the conclusion had always been the same. He had brought me freedom. Freedom was all I knew, all I could bring to anyone who might come to me.

Nestor made a gesture of solidarity with me. He exhorted the women to abandon their animosity toward me. He looked at me with the eyes of one who does not understand but wants to. He said that I did not belong with them, that I was indeed a solitary bird. They had needed me for a moment in order to break their boundaries of affection and routine. Now that they were free, the sky was their limit. To remain with me would doubtlessly be pleasant but deadly for them.

He seemed to be deeply moved. He came to my side and put his hand on my shoulder. He said that he had the feeling we were not going to see each other ever again on this earth. He regretted that we were going to part like petty people, bickering, complaining, accusing. He told me that speaking on behalf of the others, but not for himself, he was going to ask me to leave, for we had no more possibilities in being together. He added that he had laughed at la Gorda for telling us about the snake we had formed. He had changed his mind and no longer found the idea ridiculous. It had been our last opportunity to succeed as a group.

Don Juan had taught me to accept my fate in humbleness.

"The course of a warrior's destiny is unalterable," he once said to me. "The challenge is how far he can go within those rigid bounds, how impeccable he can be within those rigid bounds. If there are obstacles in his path, the warrior strives impeccably to overcome them. If he finds unbearable hardship and pain on his path, he weeps, but all his tears put together could not move the line of his destiny the breadth of one hair."

My original decision to let the power of that place point out our next step had been correct. I stood up. The others turned their heads away. La Gorda came to my side and said, as if nothing had happened, that I should leave and that she would catch up with me and join me at a later time. I wanted to retort that I saw no reason for her to join me. She had chosen to join the others. She seemed to read my feeling of having been betrayed. She calmly assured me that we had to fulfill our fate together as warriors and not as the petty people we were.

Part Two

THE ART OF DREAMING

6

Losing the Human Form

A few months later, after helping everyone to resettle in different parts of Mexico, la Gorda took up residence in Arizona. We began then to unravel the strangest and most engulfing part of our apprenticeship. At first our relationship was rather strained. It was very difficult for me to overcome my feelings about the way we had parted in the Alameda Park. Although la Gorda knew the whereabouts of the others, she never said anything to me. She felt that it would have been superfluous for me to know about their activities.

On the surface everything seemed to be all right between la Gorda and me. Nevertheless, I held a bitter resentment toward her for siding with the others against me. I did not express it but it was always there. I helped her and did everything for her as if nothing had happened, but that entered under the heading of impeccability. It was my duty; to fulfill it, I would have gladly gone to my death. I purposely absorbed myself in guiding and coaching her in the intricacies of modern city living; she was even learning English. Her progress was phenomenal.

Three months went by almost unnoticed. But one day, while I was in Los Angeles, I woke up in the early morning hours with an unbearable pressure in my head. It was not a headache; it was rather a very intense weight in my ears. I felt it also on my eyelids and the roof of my mouth. I knew I was feverish, but the heat was only in my head. I made a feeble attempt to sit up. The thought crossed my mind that I was having a stroke. My first reaction was to call for help, but somehow I calmed down and tried to let go of my fear. After a while the pressure in my head began to diminish but it also began to shift to my throat. I gasped for air, gagging and coughing for some time; then the pressure moved slowly to my chest, then to my stomach, to my groin, to my legs, and to my feet before it finally left my body.

Whatever had happened to me had taken about two hours to unfold. During the course of those two grueling hours it was as if something inside my body was actually moving downward, moving out of me. I fancied it to be rolling up like a carpet. Another image that occurred to me was of a blob moving inside the cavity of my body. I discarded that image in favor of the first, because the feeling was of something being coiled within itself. Just like a carpet being rolled up, it became heavier, thus more painful, as it went down. The two areas where the pain became excruciating were my knees and my feet, especially my right foot, which remained hot for thirty-five minutes after all the pain and pressure had vanished.

La Gorda, upon hearing my report, said that this time for certain I had lost my human form, that I had dropped all my shields, or most of them. She was right. Without knowing how or even realizing what had happened, I found myself in a most unfamiliar state. I felt detached, unbiased. It did not matter what la Gorda had done to me. It was not that I had forgiven her for her reproachable behavior with me; it was as if there had never been any betrayal. There was no overt or covert rancor left in me, for la Gorda or for anyone else. What I felt was not a willed indifference, or negligence to act; neither was it alienation or even the desire to be alone. It was rather an alien feeling of aloofness, a capability of immersing myself in the moment and having no thoughts whatever about anything else. People's actions no longer affected me, for I had no more expectations of any kind. A strange peace had become the ruling force in my life. I felt I had somehow adopted one of the concepts of a warrior's life—detachment. La Gorda said that I had done more than adopt it; I had actually embodied it.

Don Juan and I had had long discussions on the possibility that someday I would do just that. He had said that detachment did not automatically mean wisdom, but that it was, nonetheless, an advantage because it allowed the warrior to pause momentarily to reassess situations, to reconsider positions. In order to use that extra moment consistently and correctly, however, he said that a warrior had to struggle unyieldingly for a lifetime.

I had despaired that I would ever experience that feeling. As far as I could determine, there was no way to improvise it. It had been useless for me to think about its benefits, or to reason out the possibilities of its advent. During the years I knew don Juan I had certainly experienced a steady lessening of personal ties with the world, but that had taken place on an intellectual plane; in my everyday life I was unchanged until the moment I lost my human form.

I speculated with la Gorda that the concept of losing the human form refers to a bodily condition that besets the apprentice upon his reaching a certain threshold in the course of training. Be that as it may, the end result of losing the human form for la Gorda and myself, oddly enough, was not only the sought-after and coveted sense of detachment, but also the fulfillment of our elusive task of remembering. And again in this case, the intellect played a minimal part.

One night la Gorda and I were discussing a movie. She had gone to see an X-rated movie and I was eager to hear her description of it. She had not liked it at all. She maintained that it was a weakening experience because being a warrior entailed leading an austere life in total celibacy, like the Nagual Juan Matus.

I told her that I knew for a fact that don Juan liked women and was not celibate, and that I found that delightful.

"You're insane!" she exclaimed with a tinge of amusement in her voice. "The Nagual was a perfect warrior. He was not caught up in any webs of sensuality."

She wanted to know why I thought don Juan was not celibate. I told her about an incident that had taken place in Arizona at the beginning of my apprenticeship. I was resting at don Juan's house one day after an exhausting hike. Don Juan appeared to be strangely nervous. He kept getting up to look out the door. He seemed to be waiting for someone. Then, quite abruptly, he told me that a car had just come around the bend in the road and was heading for the house. He said that it was a girl, a friend of his, who was bringing him some blankets. I had never seen don Juan embarrassed, and I felt terribly sad to see him so upset that he did not know what to do. I thought that he did not want me to meet the girl. I suggested that I might hide, but there was no place to conceal myself in the room, so he made me lie down on the floor and covered me with a straw mat. I heard the sound of a car motor being turned off and then, through the slits in the mat, I saw a girl standing at the door. She was tall, slender, and very young. I thought she was beautiful. Don Juan was saying something to her in a low, intimate voice. Then he turned and pointed at me.

"Carlos is hiding under the mat," he said to the girl in a loud clear voice. "Say hello to him."

The girl waved at me and said hello with the friendliest smile. I felt stupid and angry at don Juan for putting me in that embarrassing position. It seemed obvious to me that he was trying to alleviate his nervousness, or even worse, that he was showing off in front of me.

When the girl left I angrily asked for an explanation. He

candidly said that he had gotten carried away because my feet were showing and he did not know what else to do. When I heard this, his whole maneuver became clear; he had been showing off his young friend to me. I could not possibly have had my feet uncovered because they were tucked under my thighs. I laughed knowingly and don Juan felt obligated to explain that he liked women, especially that girl.

I never forgot the incident. Don Juan never discussed it. Whenever I brought it up he always made me stop. I wondered almost obsessively about that young woman. I had hopes that someday she might look me up after reading my books.

La Gorda had become very agitated. She was pacing back and forth in the room while I talked. She was about to weep. I imagined all sorts of intricate networks of relationships that might be at stake. I thought la Gorda was possessive and was reacting like a woman threatened by another woman.

"Are you jealous, Gorda?" I asked.

"Don't be stupid," she said angrily. "I'm a formless warrior. I've no envy or jealousy left in me."

I brought up something that the Genaros had told me, that la Gorda was the Nagual's woman. Her voice became barely audible.

"I think I was," she said, and with a vague look, she sat on her bed. "I have a feeling that I was. I don't know how, though. In this life, the Nagual Juan Matus was to me what he was to you. He was not a man. He was the Nagual. He had no interest in sex."

I assured her that I had heard don Juan express his liking for that girl.

"Did he say that he had sex with her?" la Gorda asked.

"No, he didn't, but it was obvious from the way he talked," I said.

"You would like the Nagual to be like you, wouldn't you?" she asked with a sneer. "The Nagual was an impeccable warrior."

I thought I was right and did not need to review my opinion. Just to humor la Gorda, I said that perhaps the young woman was don Juan's apprentice if not his mistress.

There was a long pause. What I had said had a disturbing effect on me. Until that moment I had never thought about such a possibility. I had been locked into a prejudgment, allowing myself no room for revision.

La Gorda asked me to describe the young woman. I could not do it. I had not really looked at her features. I had been too annoyed, too embarrassed, to examine her in detail. She also seemed to have been struck by the awkwardness of the situation and had hurried out of the house.

La Gorda said that without any logical reason she felt that the young woman was a key figure in the Nagual's life. Her statement led us to talking about don Juan's known friends. We struggled for hours trying to piece together all the information we had about his associates. I told her about the different times don Juan had taken me to participate in peyote ceremonies. I described everyone who was there. She recognized none of them. I realized then that I might know more people associated with don Juan than she did. But something I had said triggered her recollection of a time when she had seen a young woman driving the Nagual and Genaro in a small white car. The woman let the two men off at the door of la Gorda's house, and she stared at la Gorda before she drove away. La Gorda thought that the young woman was someone who had given the Nagual and Genaro a lift. I remembered then that I had gotten up from under the straw mat at don Juan's house just in time to see a white Volkswagen driving away.

I mentioned one more incident involving another of don Juan's friends, a man who had given me some peyote plants once in the market of a city in northern Mexico. He had also obsessed me for years. His name was Vicente. Upon hearing that name la Gorda's body reacted as if a nerve had been touched. Her voice became shrill. She asked me to repeat the name and describe the man. Again, I could not come up with any description. I had seen the man only once, for a few minutes, more than ten years before.

La Gorda and I went through a period of almost being angry, not at one another but at whatever was keeping us imprisoned.

The final incident that precipitated our full-fledged remembering came one day when I had a cold and was running a high fever. I had stayed in bed, dozing off and on, with thoughts rambling aimlessly in my mind. The melody of an old Mexican song had been running through my head all day. At one moment I was dreaming that someone was playing it on a guitar. I complained about the monotony of it, and whoever I was protesting to thrust the guitar toward my stomach. I jumped back to avoid being hit, and bumped my head on the wall and woke up. It had not been a vivid dream, only the tune had been haunting. I could not dispel the sound of the guitar; it kept running through my mind. I remained half awake, listening to the tune. It seemed as if I were entering into a state of *dreaming*—a complete and detailed *dreaming* scene appeared in front of my eyes. In the scene there was a young woman sitting next to me. I could distinguish every detail of her features. I did not know who she was, but seeing her shocked me. I was fully awake in one instant. The anxiety that that face created in me was so intense that I got up and quite automatically began to pace back and forth. I was perspiring profusely and I dreaded to leave my room. I could not call la Gorda for help either. She had gone back to Mexico for a few days to see Josefina. I tied a sheet around my waist to brace my midsection. It helped to subdue some ripples of nervous energy that went through me.

As I paced back and forth the image in my mind began to dissolve, not into peaceful oblivion, as I would have liked, but into an intricate, full-fledged memory. I remembered that once I was sitting on some sacks of wheat or barley stacked up in a grain bin. The young woman was singing the old Mexican song that had been running in my mind, while she played a guitar. When I joked about her playing, she nudged me in the ribs with the butt of the guitar. There had been other people sitting with me, la Gorda and two men. I knew those men very well, but I still could not remember who the young woman was. I tried but it seemed hopeless.

I lay down again drenched in a cold sweat. I wanted to rest for a moment before I got out of my soaked pajamas. As I rested my head on a high pillow, my memory seemed to clear up further and then I knew who the guitar player was. She was the Nagual woman; the most important being on earth for la Gorda and myself. She was the feminine analogue of the Nagual man; not his wife or his woman, but his counterpart. She had the serenity and command of a true leader. Being a woman, she nurtured us.

I did not dare to push my memory too far. I knew intuitively that I did not have the strength to withstand the full recollection. I stopped on the level of abstract feelings. I knew that she was the embodiment of the purest, most unbiased and profound affection. It would be most appropriate to say that la Gorda and I loved the Nagual woman more than life itself. What on earth had happened to us to have forgotten her?

That night lying on my bed I became so agitated that I feared for my very life. I began to chant some words which became a guiding force to me. And only when I had calmed down did I remember that the words I had said to myself over and over were also a memory that had come back to me that night; the memory of a formula, an incantation to pull me through an upheaval, such as the one I had experienced.

I am already given to the power that rules my fate.
And I cling to nothing, so I will have nothing to defend.

I have no thoughts, so I will see.
I fear nothing, so I will remember myself.

The formula had one more line, which at the time was incomprehensible to me.

Detached and at ease,
I will dart past the Eagle to be free.

Being sick and feverish may have served as a cushion of sorts; it may have been enough to deviate the main impact of what I had done, or rather, of what had come upon me, since I had not intentionally done anything.

Up to that night, if my inventory of experience had been examined, I could have accounted for the continuity of my existence. The nebulous memories I had of la Gorda, or the presentiment of having lived in that house in the mountains of central Mexico were in a way real threats to the idea of my continuity, but nothing in comparison to remembering the Nagual woman. Not so much because of the emotions that the memory itself brought back, but because I had forgotten her; and not as one forgets a name or a tune. There had been nothing about her in my mind prior to that moment of revelation. Nothing! Then something came upon me, or something fell off me, and I found myself remembering a most important being who, from the point of view of my experiential self prior to that moment, I had never met.

I had to wait two more days for la Gorda's return before I could tell her about my recollection. The moment I described the Nagual woman la Gorda remembered her; her awareness was somehow dependent on mine.

"The girl I saw in the white car was the Nagual woman!" la Gorda exclaimed. "She came back to me and I couldn't remember her."

I heard the words and understood their meaning, but it

took a long time for my mind to focus on what she had said. My attention wavered; it was as if a light was actually placed in front of my eyes and was being dimmed. I had the notion that if I did not stop the dimming I would die. Suddenly I felt a convulsion and I knew that I had put together two pieces of myself that had become separated; I realized that the young woman I had seen at don Juan's house was the Nagual woman.

In that moment of emotional upheaval la Gorda was no help to me. Her mood was contagious. She was weeping without restraint. The emotional shock of remembering the Nagual woman had been traumatic to her.

"How could I have forgotten her?" la Gorda sighed.

I caught a glint of suspicion in her eyes as she faced me.

"You had no idea that she existed, did you?" she asked.

Under any other conditions I would have thought that her question was impertinent, insulting, but I was wondering the same about her. It had occurred to me that she might have known more than she was revealing.

"No. I didn't," I said. "But how about you, Gorda? Did you know that she existed?"

Her face had such a look of innocence and perplexity that my doubts were dispelled.

"No," she replied. "Not until today. I know now for a fact that I used to sit with her and the Nagual Juan Matus on that bench in the plaza in Oaxaca. I always remembered having done that, and I remembered her features, but I thought I had dreamed it all. I knew everything and yet I didn't. But why did I think it was a dream?"

I had a moment of panic. Then I had the perfect physical certainty that as she spoke a channel opened somewhere in my body. Suddenly I knew that I also used to sit on that bench with don Juan and the Nagual woman. I remembered then a sensation I had experienced on every one of those occasions. It was a sense of physical contentment, happiness, plenitude, that would be impossible to imagine. I thought that don Juan and the Nagual woman were perfect beings, and that to be in their company was indeed my great fortune. Sitting on that bench, flanked by the most exquisite beings on earth, I experienced perhaps the epitome of my human sentiments. One time I told don Juan, and I meant it, that I wanted to die then, so as to keep that feeling pure, intact, free from disruption.

I told la Gorda about my memory. She said that she understood what I meant. We were quiet for a moment and then the thrust of our remembering swayed us dangerously toward sadness, even despair. I had to exert the most extraordinary control over my emotions not to weep. La Gorda was sobbing, covering her face with her forearm.

After a while we became more calm. La Gorda stared into my eyes. I knew what she was thinking. It was as if I could read her questions in her eyes. They were the same questions that had obsessed me for days. Who was the Nagual woman? Where had we met her? Where did she fit? Did the others know her too?

I was just about to voice my questions when la Gorda interrupted me.

"I really don't know," she said quickly, beating me to the question. "I was counting on you to tell me. I don't know why, but I feel that you can tell me what's what."

She was counting on me and I was counting on her. We laughed at the irony of our situation. I asked her to tell me everything she remembered about the Nagual woman. La Gorda made efforts to say something two or three times but seemed to be unable to organize her thoughts.

"I really don't know where to start," she said. "I only know that I loved her."

I told her that I had the same feeling. An unearthly sadness gripped me every time I thought of the Nagual woman. As I was talking my body began to shake.

"You and I loved her," la Gorda said. "I don't know why I'm saying this, but I know that she owned us."

I prodded her to explain that statement. She could not determine why she had said it. She was talking nervously, elaborating on her feelings. I could no longer pay attention to her. I felt a fluttering in my solar plexus. A vague memory of the Nagual woman started to form. I urged la Gorda to keep on talking, to repeat herself if she had nothing else to say, but not to stop. The sound of her voice seemed to act for me as a conduit into another dimension, another kind of time. It was as if blood was rushing through my body with an unusual pressure. I felt a prickling all over, and then I had an odd bodily memory. I knew in my body that the Nagual woman was the being who made the Nagual complete. She brought to the Nagual peace, plenitude, a sense of being protected, delivered.

I told la Gorda that I had the insight that the Nagual woman was don Juan's partner. La Gorda looked at me aghast. She slowly shook her head from side to side.

"She had nothing to do with the Nagual Juan Matus, you idiot," she said with a tone of ultimate authority. "She was for you. That's why you and I belonged to her."

La Gorda and I stared into each other's eyes. I was certain that she was involuntarily voicing thoughts which rationally did not mean anything to her.

"What do you mean, she was for me, Gorda?" I asked after a long silence.

"She was your partner," she said. "You two were a team. And I was her ward. And she entrusted you to deliver me to her someday."

I begged la Gorda to tell me all she knew, but she did not seem to know anything else. I felt exhausted.

"Where did she go?" la Gorda said suddenly. "I just can't figure that out. She was with you, not with the Nagual. She should be here with us now."

She had then another attack of disbelief and fear. She accused me of hiding the Nagual woman in Los Angeles. I tried to ease her apprehensions. I surprised myself by talking to la

Gorda as if she were a child. She listened to me with all the outward signs of complete attention; her eyes, however, were vacant, out of focus. It occurred to me then that she was using the sound of my voice just as I had used hers, as a conduit. I knew that she was also aware of it. I kept on talking until I had run out of things to say within the bounds of our topic. Something else took place then, and I found myself half listening to the sound of my own voice. I was talking to la Gorda without any volition on my part. Words that seemed to have been bottled up inside me, now free, reached indescribable levels of absurdity. I talked and talked until something made me stop. I had remembered that don Juan told the Nagual woman and me, on that bench in Oaxaca, about a particular human being whose presence had synthesized for him all that he could aspire or expect from human companionship. It was a woman who had been for him what the Nagual woman was for me, a partner, a counterpart. She left him, just as the Nagual woman left me. His feelings for her were unchanged and were rekindled by the melancholy that certain poems evoked in him.

I also remembered that it was the Nagual woman who used to supply me with books of poetry. She kept stacks of them in the trunk of her car. It was at her instigation that I read poems to don Juan. Suddenly the physical memory of the Nagual woman sitting with me on that bench was so clear that I took an involuntary gasp of air, my chest swelled. An oppressive sense of loss, greater than any feeling I had ever had, took possession of me. I bent over with a ripping pain in my right shoulder blade. There was something else I knew, a memory which part of me did not want to release.

I became involved with whatever was left of my shield of intellectuality, as the only means to recover my equanimity. I said to myself over and over that la Gorda and I had been operating all along on two absolutely different planes. She remembered a great deal more than I did, but she was not inquisitive. She had not been trained to ask questions of others or of herself. But then the thought struck me that I was no better off; I still was as sloppy as don Juan had once said I was. I had never forgotten reading poetry to don Juan, and yet it had never occurred to me to examine the fact that I had never owned a book of Spanish poetry, nor did I ever carry one in my car.

La Gorda brought me out of my ruminations. She was almost hysterical. She shouted that she had just figured out that the Nagual woman had to be somewhere very near us. Just as we had been left to find one another, the Nagual woman had been left to find us. The force of her reasoning almost convinced me. Something in me knew, nevertheless, that it was not so. That was the memory that was inside me, which I did not dare to bring out.

I wanted to start a debate with la Gorda, but there was no reason, my shield of intellect and words was insufficient to absorb the impact of remembering the Nagual woman. Its effect was staggering to me, more devastating than even the fear of dying.

"The Nagual woman is shipwrecked somewhere," la Gorda said meekly. "She's probably marooned and we're doing nothing to help her."

"No! No!" I yelled. "She's not here any more."

I did not exactly know why I had said that, yet I knew that it was true. We sank for a moment into depths of melancholy that would be impossible to fathom rationally. For the first time in the memory of the me I know, I felt a true, boundless sadness, a dreadful incompleteness. There was a wound somewhere in me that had been opened again. This time I could not take refuge, as I had done so many times in the past, behind a veil of mystery and not knowing. Not to know had been bliss to me. For a moment, I was dangerously sliding into despondency. La Gorda stopped me.

"A warrior is someone who seeks freedom," she said in my ear. "Sadness is not freedom. We must snap out of it."

Having a sense of detachment, as don Juan had said, entails having a moment's pause to reassess situations. At the depth of my sadness I understood what he meant. I had the detachment; it was up to me to strive to use that pause correctly.

I could not be sure whether or not my volition played a role, but all of a sudden my sadness vanished; it was as if it had never existed. The speed of my change of mood and its thoroughness alarmed me.

"Now you are where I am!" la Gorda exclaimed when I described what had happened. "After all these years I still haven't learned how to handle formlessness. I shift helplessly from one feeling to another in one instant. Because of my formlessness I could help the little sisters, but I was also at their mercy. Any one of them was strong enough to make me sway from one extreme to the other.

"The problem was that I lost my human form before you did. If you and I had lost it together, we could have helped each other; as it was, I went up and down faster than I care to remember."

I had to admit that her claim of being formless had always seemed spurious to me. In my understanding, losing the human form included a necessary concomitant, a consistency of character, which was, in light of her emotional ups and downs, beyond her reach. On account of that, I had judged her harshly and unjustly. Having lost my human form, I was now in a position to understand that formlessness is, if anything, a detriment to sobriety and levelheadedness. There is no automatic emotional strength involved in it. An aspect of being detached, the capacity to become immersed in whatever one is doing, naturally extends to everything one does, including being inconsistent, and outright petty. The advantage of being formless is that it allows us a moment's pause, providing that we have the self-discipline and courage to utilize it.

At last la Gorda's past behavior became comprehensible to me. She had been formless for years but without the self-discipline required. Thus she had been at the mercy of drastic shifts of mood, and incredible discrepancies between her actions and her purposes.

After our initial recollection of the Nagual woman, la Gorda and I summoned all our forces and tried for days to elicit more memories, but there seemed to be none. I myself was back where I had been before I had begun to remember. I intuited that there should be a great deal more somehow buried in me, but I could not get to it. My mind was void of even the vaguest inkling of any other memories.

La Gorda and I went through a period of tremendous confusion and doubt. In our case, being formless meant to be ravaged by the worst distrust imaginable. We felt that we were guinea pigs in the hands of don Juan, a being supposedly familiar to us, but about whom in reality we knew nothing. We fueled each other with doubts and fears. The most serious issue was of course the Nagual woman. When we would focus our attention on her, our memory of her became so keen that it was past comprehension that we could have forgotten her. This would give rise over and over to speculations of what don Juan had really done to us. These conjectures led very easily to the feeling that we had been used. We became enraged by the unavoidable conclusion that he had manipulated us, rendered us helpless and unknown to ourselves.

When our rage was exhausted, fear began to loom over us —for we were faced with the awesome possibility that don Juan might have done still more deleterious things to us.

7

Dreaming Together

One day, in order to alleviate our distress momentarily, I suggested that we immerse ourselves in *dreaming*. As soon as I voiced my suggestion, I became aware that a gloom which had been haunting me for days could be drastically altered by willing the change. I clearly understood then that the problem with la Gorda and myself had been that we had unwittingly focused on fear and distrust, as if those were the only possible options available to us, while all along we had had, without consciously knowing it, the alternative of deliberately centering our attention on the opposite, the mystery, the wonder of what had happened to us.

I told la Gorda my realization. She agreed immediately. She became instantly animated, the pall of her gloom dispelled in a matter of seconds.

"What kind of *dreaming* do you propose we should do?" she asked.

"How many kinds are there?" I asked.

"We could do *dreaming together*," she replied. "My body tells me that we have done this already. We have gone into *dreaming* as a team. It'll be a cinch for us, as it was for us to *see together*."

"But we don't know what the procedure is to do *dreaming together*," I said.

"We didn't know how to *see together* and yet we *saw*," she said. "I'm sure that if we try we can do it, because there are no steps to anything a warrior does. There is only personal power. And right now we have it.

"We should start out *dreaming* from two different places, as far away as possible from each other. The one who goes into *dreaming* first waits for the other. Once we find each other we interlock our arms and go deeper in together."

I told her that I had no idea how to wait for her if I went into *dreaming* ahead of her. She herself could not explain what was involved, but she said that to wait for the other *dreamer* was what Josefina had described as "snatching" them. La Gorda had been snatched by Josefina twice.

"The reason Josefina called it snatching was because one of us had to grab the other by the arm," she explained.

She demonstrated then a procedure of interlocking her left forearm with my right forearm by each of us grabbing hold of the area below each other's elbows.

"How can we do that in *dreaming?*" I asked.

I personally considered *dreaming* one of the most private states imaginable.

"I don't know how, but I'll grab you," la Gorda said. "I think my body knows how. The more we talk about it, though, the more difficult it seems to be."

We started off our *dreaming* from two distant locations. We could agree only on the time to lie down, since the entrance into *dreaming* was something impossible to prearrange. The foreseeable possibility that I might have to wait for la Gorda gave me a great deal of anxiety, and I could not enter into *dreaming* with my customary ease. After some ten to fifteen minutes of restlessness I finally succeeded in going into a state I call *restful vigil*.

Years before, when I had acquired a degree of experience in *dreaming*, I had asked don Juan if there were any known steps which were common to all of us. He had told me that in the final analysis every *dreamer* was different. But in talking with la Gorda I discovered such similarities in our experiences of *dreaming* that I ventured a possible classificatory scheme of the different stages.

Restful vigil is the preliminary state, a state in which the senses become dormant and yet one is aware. In my case, I had always perceived in this state a flood of reddish light, a light exactly like what one sees facing the sun with the eyelids tightly closed.

The second state of *dreaming* I called *dynamic vigil*. In this state the reddish light dissipates, as fog dissipates, and one is left looking at a scene, a tableau of sorts, which is static. One sees a three-dimensional picture, a frozen bit of something— a landscape, a street, a house, a person, a face, anything.

I called the third state *passive witnessing*. In it the *dreamer* is no longer viewing a frozen bit of the world but is observing, eyewitnessing, an event as it occurs. It is as if the primacy of the visual and auditory senses makes this state of *dreaming* mainly an affair of the eyes and ears.

The fourth state was the one in which I was drawn to act. In it one is compelled to enterprise, to take steps, to make the most of one's time. I called this state *dynamic initiative*.

La Gorda's proposition of waiting for me had to do with affecting the second and third states of our *dreaming together*. When I entered into the second state, *dynamic vigil*, I saw a *dreaming* scene of don Juan and various other persons, including a fat Gorda. Before I even had time to consider what I was viewing, I felt a tremendous pull on my arm and I realized that the "real" Gorda was by my side. She was to my left and had gripped my right forearm with her left hand. I clearly felt her lifting my hand to her forearm so that we were gripping each other's forearms. Next, I found myself in the third state of *dreaming, passive witnessing*. Don Juan was telling me that I had to look after la Gorda and take care of her in a most selfish fashion—that is, as if she were my own self.

His play on words delighted me. I felt an unearthly happiness in being there with him and the others. Don Juan went on explaining that my selfishness could be put to a grand use, and that to harness it was not impossible.

There was a general feeling of comradeship among all the people gathered there. They were laughing at what don Juan was saying to me, but without making fun. Don Juan said that the surest way to harness selfishness was through the daily activities of our lives, that I was efficient in whatever I did because I had no one to bug the devil out of me, and that it was no challenge to me to soar like an arrow by myself. If I were given the task of taking care of la Gorda, however, my independent effectiveness would go to pieces, and in order to survive I would have to extend my selfish concern for myself to include la Gorda. Only through helping her, don Juan was saying in the most emphatic tone, would I find the clues for the fulfillment of my true task.

La Gorda put her fat arms around my neck. Don Juan had to stop talking. He was laughing so hard he could not go on. All of them were roaring.

I felt embarrassed and annoyed with la Gorda. I tried to get out of her embrace but her arms were tightly fastened around my neck. Don Juan made a sign with his hands to make me stop. He said that the minimal embarrassment I was experiencing then was nothing in comparison with what was in store for me.

The sound of laughter was deafening. I felt very happy, although I was worried about having to deal with la Gorda, for I did not know what it would entail.

At that moment in my *dreaming* I changed my point of view —or rather, something pulled me out of the scene and I began to look around as a spectator. We were in a house in northern Mexico; I could tell by the surroundings, which were partially visible from where I stood. I could see the mountains in the distance. I also remembered the paraphernalia of the house.

We were at the back, under a roofed, open porch. Some of the people were sitting on some bulky chairs; most of them, however, were either standing or sitting on the floor. I recognized every one of them. There were sixteen people. La Gorda was standing by my side facing don Juan.

I became aware that I could have two different feelings at the same time. I could either go into the *dreaming* scene and feel that I was recovering a long-lost sentiment, or I could witness the scene with the mood that was current in my life. When I plunged into the *dreaming* scene I felt secure and protected; when I witnessed it with my current mood I felt lost, insecure, anguished. I did not like my current mood, so I plunged into my *dreaming* scene.

A fat Gorda asked don Juan, in a voice which could be heard above everyone's laughter, if I was going to be her husband. There was a moment's silence. Don Juan seemed to be calculating what to say. He patted her on the head and said that he could speak for me and that I would be delighted to be her husband. People were laughing riotously. I laughed with them. My body convulsed with a most genuine enjoyment, yet I did not feel I was laughing at la Gorda. I did not regard her as a clown, or as stupid. She was a child. Don Juan turned to me and said that I had to honor la Gorda regardless of what she did to me, and that I had to train my body, through my interaction with her, to feel at ease in the face of the most trying situations. Don Juan addressed the whole group and said that it was much easier to fare well under conditions of maximum stress than to be impeccable under normal circumstances, such as in the interplay with someone like la Gorda. Don Juan added that I could not under any circumstances get angry with la Gorda, because she was indeed my benefactress; only through her would I be capable of harnessing my selfishness.

I had become so thoroughly immersed in the *dreaming* scene that I had forgotten I was a *dreamer*. A sudden pressure on my arm reminded me that I was *dreaming*. I felt la Gorda's presence next to me, but without seeing her. She was there only as a touch, a tactile sensation on my forearm. I focused my attention on it; it felt like a solid grip on me, and then la Gorda as a whole person materialized, as if she were made of superimposed frames of photographic film. It was like trick photography in a movie. The *dreaming* scene dissolved. Instead, la Gorda and I were looking at each other with our forearms interlocked.

In unison, we again focused our attention on the *dreaming* scene we had been witnessing. At that moment I knew beyond the shadow of a doubt that both of us had been viewing the same thing. Now don Juan was saying something to la Gorda, but I could not hear him. My attention was being pulled back and forth between the third state of *dreaming*, *passive witnessing*, and the second, *dynamic vigil*. I was for a moment with don Juan, a fat Gorda, and sixteen other people, and the next moment I was with the current Gorda watching a frozen scene.

Then a drastic jolt in my body brought me to still another level of attention: I felt something like the cracking of a dry piece of wood. It was a minor explosion, yet it sounded more like an extraordinarily loud cracking of knuckles. I found myself in the first state of *dreaming*, *restful vigil*. I was asleep and yet thoroughly aware. I wanted to stay for as long as I could in that peaceful stage, but another jolt made me wake up instantly. I had suddenly realized that la Gorda and I had *dreamed together*.

I was more than eager to speak with her. She felt the same. We rushed to talk to each other. When we had calmed down, I asked her to describe to me everything that had happened to her in our *dreaming together*.

"I waited for you for a long time," she said. "Some part of me thought I had missed you, but another part thought that you were nervous and were having problems, so I waited."

"Where did you wait, Gorda?" I asked.

"I don't know," she replied. "I know that I was out of the reddish light, but I couldn't see anything. Come to think of it, I had no sight, I was feeling my way around. Perhaps I was still in the reddish light; it wasn't red, though. The place where I was, was tinted with a light peach color. Then I opened my eyes and there you were. You seemed to be ready to leave, so I grabbed you by the arm. Then I looked and saw the Nagual Juan Matus, you, me, and other people in Vicente's house. You were younger and I was fat."

The mention of Vicente's house brought a sudden realization to me. I told la Gorda that once while driving through Zacatecas, in northern Mexico, I had had a strange urge and gone to visit one of don Juan's friends, Vicente, not understanding that in doing so I had unwittingly crossed into an excluded domain, for don Juan had never introduced me to him. Vicente, like the Nagual woman, belonged to another area, another world. It was no wonder that la Gorda was so shaken when I told her about the visit. We knew him so very well; he was as close to us as don Genaro, perhaps even closer. Yet we had forgotten him, just as we had forgotten the Nagual woman.

At that point la Gorda and I made a huge digression. We remembered together that Vicente, Genaro, and Silvio Manuel were don Juan's friends, his cohorts. They were bound together by a vow of sorts. La Gorda and I could not remember what it was that had united them. Vicente was not an Indian. He had been a pharmacist as a young man. He was the scholar of the group, and the real healer who kept all of them healthy. He had a passion for botany. I was convinced beyond any doubt that he knew more about plants than any human being alive. La Gorda and I remembered that it was Vicente who had taught everyone, including don Juan, about medicinal plants. He took special interest in Nestor, and all of us thought that Nestor was going to be like him.

"Remembering Vicente makes me think about myself," la Gorda said. "It makes me think what an unbearable woman I've been. The worst thing that can happen to a woman is to have children, to have holes in her body, and still act like a little girl. That was my problem. I wanted to be cute and I was empty. And they let me make a fool out of myself, they encouraged me to be a jackass."

"Who are they, Gorda?" I asked.

"The Nagual and Vicente and all those people who were in Vicente's house when I acted like such an ass with you."

La Gorda and I had a realization in unison. They had allowed her to be unbearable only with me. No one else put up with her nonsense, although she tried it on everyone.

"Vicente did put up with me," la Gorda said. "He played along with me. I even called him uncle. When I tried to call Silvio Manuel uncle he nearly ripped the skin off my armpits with his clawlike hands."

We tried to focus our attention on Silvio Manuel but we could not remember what he looked like. We could feel his presence in our memories but he was not a person, he was only a feeling.

As far as the *dreaming* scene was concerned, we remembered that it had been a faithful replica of what really did occur in our lives at a certain place and time; it still was not possible for us to recall when. I knew, however, that I took care of la Gorda as a means of training myself for the hardship of interacting with people. It was imperative that I internalize a mood of ease in the face of difficult social situations, and no one could have been a better coach than la Gorda. The flashes of faint memories I had had of a fat Gorda stemmed from those circumstances, for I had followed don Juan's orders to the letter.

La Gorda said that she had not liked the mood of the *dreaming* scene. She would have preferred just to watch it, but I pulled her in to feel her old feelings, which were abhorrent to her. Her discomfort was so acute that she deliberately squeezed my arm to force me to end our participation in something so odious to her.

The next day we arranged a time for another session of *dreaming together*. She started from her bedroom and I from my study, but nothing happened. We became exhausted merely trying to enter into *dreaming*. For weeks after that we tried to achieve again the effectiveness of our first performance, but without any success. With every failure we became more desperate and greedy.

In the face of our impasse, I decided that we should postpone our *dreaming together* for the time being and take a closer look at the process of *dreaming* and analyze its concepts and procedures. La Gorda did not agree with me at first. For her, the idea of reviewing what we knew about *dreaming* was another way of succumbing to despair and greed. She preferred to keep on trying even if we did not succeed. I persisted and she finally accepted my point of view out of the sheer sense of being lost.

One night we sat down and, as casually as we could, we began to discuss what we knew about *dreaming*. It quickly became obvious that there were some core topics which don Juan had given special emphasis.

First was the act itself. It seemed to begin as a unique state of awareness arrived at by focusing the residue of consciousness, which one still has when asleep, on the elements, or the features, of one's dreams.

The residue of consciousness, which don Juan called the second attention, was brought into action, or was harnessed, through exercises of *not-doing*. We thought that the essential aid to *dreaming* was a state of mental quietness, which don Juan had called "stopping the internal dialogue," or the "*not doing* of talking to oneself." To teach me how to master it, he used to make me walk for miles with my eyes held fixed and out of focus at a level just above the horizon so as to emphasize the peripheral view. His method was effective on two counts. It allowed me to stop my internal dialogue after years of trying, and it trained my attention. By forcing me to concentrate on the peripheral view, don Juan reinforced my capacity to concentrate for long periods of time on one single activity.

Later on, when I had succeeded in controlling my attention and could work for hours at a chore without distraction—a thing I had never before been able to do—he told me that the best way to enter into *dreaming* was to concentrate on the area just at the tip of the sternum, at the top of the belly. He said that the attention needed for *dreaming* stems from that area. The energy needed in order to move and to seek in *dreaming* stems from the area an inch or two below the belly button. He called that energy the *will*, or the power to select, to assemble. In a woman both the attention and the energy for *dreaming* originate from the womb.

"A woman's *dreaming* has to come from her womb because that's her center," la Gorda said. "In order for me to start *dreaming* or to stop it all I have to do is place my attention on my womb. I've learned to feel the inside of it. I see a reddish glow for an instant and then I'm off."

"How long does it take you to get to see that reddish glow?" I asked.

"A few seconds. The moment my attention is on my womb I'm already into *dreaming*," she continued. "I never toil, not ever. Women are like that. The most difficult part for a woman is to learn how to begin; it took me a couple of years to stop my internal dialogue by concentrating my attention on my womb. Perhaps that's why a woman always needs someone else to prod her.

"The Nagual Juan Matus used to put cold, wet river pebbles on my belly to get me to feel that area. Or he would place a weight on it; I had a chunk of lead that he got for me. He would make me close my eyes and focus my attention on the spot where the weight was. I used to fall asleep every time. But that didn't bother him. It doesn't really matter what one does as long as the attention is on the womb. Finally I learned to concentrate on that spot without anything being placed on it. I went into *dreaming* one day all by myself. I was feeling my belly, at the spot where the Nagual had placed the weight so many times, when all of a sudden I fell asleep as usual, except that something pulled me right into my womb. I saw the reddish glow and I then had a most beautiful dream. But as soon as I tried to tell it to the Nagual, I knew that it had not been an ordinary dream. There was no way of telling him what the dream was; I had just felt very happy and strong. He said it had been *dreaming*.

"From then on he never put a weight on me. He let me do *dreaming* without interfering. He asked me from time to time to tell him about it, then he would give me pointers. That's the way the instruction in *dreaming* should be conducted."

La Gorda said that don Juan told her that anything may suffice as a *not-doing* to help *dreaming*, providing that it forces the attention to remain fixed. For instance, he made her and all the other apprentices gaze at leaves and rocks, and encouraged Pablito to construct his own *not-doing* device. Pablito started off with the *not-doing* of walking backwards. He would move by taking short glances to his sides in order to direct his path and to avoid obstacles on the way. I gave him the idea of using a rearview mirror, and he expanded it into the construction of a wooden helmet with an attachment that held two small mirrors, about six inches away from his face and two inches below his eye level. The two mirrors did not interfere with his frontal view, and due to the lateral angle at which they were set, they covered the whole range behind him. Pablito boasted that he had a 360-degree peripheral view of the world. Aided by this artifact, Pablito could walk backwards for any distance, or any length of time.

The position one assumes to do *dreaming* was also a very important topic.

"I don't know why the Nagual didn't tell me from the very beginning," la Gorda said, "that the best position for a woman to start from is to sit with her legs crossed and then let the body fall, as it may do once the attention is on *dreaming*. The Nagual told me about this perhaps a year after I had begun. Now I sit in that position for a moment, I feel my womb, and right away I'm *dreaming*."

In the beginning, just like la Gorda, I had done it while lying on my back, until one day when don Juan told me that for the best results I should sit up on a soft, thin mat, with the soles of my feet placed together and my thighs touching the mat. He pointed out that, since I had elastic hip joints, I should exercise them to the fullest, aiming at having my thighs completely flat against the mat. He added that if I were to enter into *dreaming* in that sitting position, my body would not slide or fall to either side, but my trunk would bend forward and my forehead would rest on my feet.

Another topic of great significance was the time to do *dreaming*. Don Juan had told us that the late night or early morning hours were by far the best. His reason for favoring those hours was what he called a practical application of the sorcerers' knowledge. He said that since one has to do *dreaming* within a social milieu, one has to seek the best possible conditions of solitude and lack of interference. The interference he was referring to had to do with the attention of people, and not their physical presence. For don Juan it was meaningless to retreat from the world and hide, for even if one were alone in an isolated, deserted place, the interference of our fellow men is prevalent because the fixation of their first attention cannot be shut off. Only locally, at the hours when most people are asleep, can one avert part of that fixation for a short period of time. It is at those times that the first attention of those around us is dormant.

This led to his description of the second attention. Don Juan explained to us that the attention one needs in the beginning of *dreaming* has to be forcibly made to stay on any given item in a dream. Only through immobilizing our attention can one turn an ordinary dream into *dreaming*.

He explained, furthermore, that in *dreaming* one has to use the same mechanisms of attention as in everyday life, that our first attention had been taught to focus on the items of the world with great force in order to turn the amorphous and chaotic realm of perception into the orderly world of awareness.

Don Juan also told us that the second attention served the function of a beckoner, a caller of chances. The more it is exercised, the greater the possibility of getting the desired result. But that was also the function of attention in general, a function so taken for granted in our daily life that it has become unnoticeable; if we encounter a fortuitous occurrence, we talk about it in terms of accident or coincidence, rather than in terms of our attention having beckoned the event.

Our discussion of the second attention prepared the ground for another key topic, the *dreaming body*. As a means of guiding la Gorda to it, don Juan gave her the task of immobilizing her second attention as steadily as she could on the components of the feeling of flying in *dreaming*.

"How did you learn to fly in *dreaming?*" I asked her. "Did someone teach you?"

"The Nagual Juan Matus taught me on this earth," she replied. "And in *dreaming*, someone I could never see taught me. It was only a voice telling me what to do. The Nagual gave me the task of learning to fly in *dreaming*, and the voice taught me how to do it. Then it took me years to teach myself to shift from my regular body, the one you can touch, to my *dreaming body*."

"You have to explain this to me, Gorda," I said.

"You were learning to get to your *dreaming body* when you *dreamed* that you got out of your body," she continued. "But, the way I see it, the Nagual did not give you any specific task, so you went any old way you could. I, on the other hand, was given the task of using my *dreaming body*. The little sisters had the same task. In my case, I once had a dream where I flew like a kite. I told the Nagual about it because I had liked the feeling of gliding. He took it very seriously and turned it into a task. He said that as soon as one learns to do *dreaming*, any dream that one can remember is no longer a dream, it's *dreaming*.

"I began then to seek flying in *dreaming*. But I couldn't set it up; the more I tried to influence my *dreaming*, the more difficult it got. The Nagual finally told me to stop trying and let it come of its own accord. Little by little I started to fly in *dreaming*. That was when some voice began to tell me what to do. I've always felt it was a woman's voice.

"When I had learned to fly perfectly, the Nagual told me that every movement of flying which I did in *dreaming* I had to repeat while I was awake. You had the same chance when the saber-toothed tiger was showing you how to breathe. But you never changed into a tiger in *dreaming*, so you couldn't properly try to do it while you were awake. But I did learn to fly in *dreaming*. By shifting my attention to my *dreaming body*, I could fly like a kite while I was awake. I showed you my flying once, because I wanted you to see that I had learned to use my *dreaming body*, but you didn't know what was going on."

She was referring to a time she had scared me with the incomprehensible act of actually bobbing up and down in the air like a kite. The event was so farfetched for me that I could not begin to understand it in any logical way. As usual when things of that nature confronted me, I would lump them into an amorphous category of "perceptions under conditions of severe stress." I argued that in cases of severe stress, perception could be greatly distorted by the senses. My explanation did not explain anything but seemed to keep my reason pacified.

I told la Gorda that there must have been more to what she had called her shift into her *dreaming body* than merely repeating the action of flying.

She thought for a while before answering.

"I think the Nagual must have told you, too," she said,

"that the only thing that really counts in making that shift is anchoring the second attention. The Nagual said that attention is what makes the world; he was of course absolutely right. He had reasons to say that. He was the master of attention. I suppose he left it up to me to find out that all I needed to shift into my *dreaming body* was to focus my attention on flying. What was important was to store attention in *dreaming*, to observe everything I did in flying. That was the only way of grooming my second attention. Once it was solid, just to focus it lightly on the details and feeling of flying brought more *dreaming* of flying, until it was routine for me to *dream* I was soaring through the air.

"In the matter of flying, then, my second attention was keen. When the Nagual gave me the task of shifting to my *dreaming body* he meant for me to turn on my second attention while I was awake. This is the way I understand it. The first attention, the attention that makes the world, can never be completely overcome; it can only be turned off for a moment and replaced with the second attention, providing that the body has stored enough of it. *Dreaming* is naturally a way of storing the second attention. So, I would say that in order to shift into your *dreaming body* when awake you have to practice *dreaming* until it comes out your ears."

"Can you get to your *dreaming body* any time you want?" I asked.

"No. It's not that easy," she replied. "I've learned to repeat the movements and feelings of flying while I'm awake, and yet I can't fly every time I want to. There is always a barrier to my *dreaming body*. Sometimes I feel that the barrier is down; my body is free at those times and I can fly as if I were *dreaming*."

I told la Gorda that in my case don Juan gave me three tasks to train my second attention. The first was to find my hands in *dreaming*. Next he recommended that I should choose a locale, focus my attention on it, and then do daytime *dreaming* and find out if I could really go there. He suggested that I should place someone I knew at the site, preferably a woman, in order to do two things: first to check subtle changes that might indicate that I was there in *dreaming*, and second, to isolate unobtrusive detail, which would be precisely what my second attention would zero in on.

The most serious problem the *dreamer* has in this respect is the unbending fixation of the second attention on detail that would be thoroughly undetected by the attention of everyday life, creating in this manner a nearly insurmountable obstacle to validation. What one seeks in *dreaming* is not what one would pay attention to in everyday life.

Don Juan said that one strives to immobilize the second attention only in the learning period. After that, one has to fight the almost invincible pull of the second attention and give only cursory glances at everything. In *dreaming* one has to be satisfied with the briefest possible views of everything. As soon as one focuses on anything, one loses control.

The last generalized task he gave me was to get out of my body. I had partially succeeded, and all along I had considered it my only real accomplishment in *dreaming*. Don Juan left before I had perfected the feeling in *dreaming* that I could handle the world of ordinary affairs while I was *dreaming*. His departure interrupted what I thought was going to be an unavoidable overlapping of my *dreaming* time into my world of everyday life.

To elucidate the control of the second attention, don Juan presented the idea of *will*. He said that *will* can be described as the maximum control of the luminosity of the body as a field of energy; or it can be described as a level of proficiency, or a state of being that comes abruptly into the daily life of a warrior at any given time. It is experienced as a force that radiates out of the middle part of the body following a moment of the most absolute silence, or a moment of sheer terror, or profound sadness; but not after a moment of happiness, because happiness is too disruptive to afford the warrior the concentration needed to use the luminosity of the body and turn it into silence.

"The Nagual told me that for a human being sadness is as powerful as terror," la Gorda said. "Sadness makes a warrior shed tears of blood. Both can bring the moment of silence. Or the silence comes of itself, because the warrior tries for it throughout his life."

"Have you ever felt that moment of silence yourself?" I asked.

"I have, by all means, but I can't remember what it is like," she said. "You and I have both felt it before and neither of us can remember anything about it. The Nagual said that it is a moment of blackness, a moment still more silent than the moment of shutting off the internal dialogue. That blackness, that silence, gives rise to the *intent* to direct the second attention, to command it, to make it do things. This is why it's called *will*. The *intent* and the effect are *will*; the Nagual said that they are tied together. He told me all this when I was trying to learn flying in *dreaming*. The *intent* of flying produces the effect of flying."

I told her that I had nearly written off the possibility of ever experiencing *will*.

"You'll experience it," la Gorda said. "The trouble is that you and I are not keen enough to know what's happening to us. We don't feel our *will* because we think that it should be something we know for sure that we are doing or feeling, like getting angry, for instance. *Will* is very quiet, unnoticeable. *Will* belongs to the other self."

"What other self, Gorda?" I asked.

"You know what I'm talking about," she replied briskly. "We are in our other selves when we do *dreaming*. We have entered into our other selves countless times by now, but we are not complete yet."

There was a long silence. I conceded to myself that she was right in saying that we were not complete yet. I understood that as meaning that we were merely apprentices of an inexhaustible art. But then the thought crossed my mind that perhaps she was referring to something else. It was not a rational thought. I felt first something like a prickling sensation in my solar plexus and then I had the thought that perhaps she was talking about something else. Next I felt the answer. It came to me in a block, a clump of sorts. I knew that all of it was there, first at the tip of my sternum and then in my mind. My problem was that I could not disentangle what I knew fast enough to verbalize it.

La Gorda did not interrupt my thought processes with further comments or gestures. She was perfectly quiet, waiting. She seemed to be internally connected to me to such a degree that there was no need for us to say anything.

We sustained the feeling of communality with each other for a moment longer and then it overwhelmed us both. La Gorda and I calmed down by degrees. I finally began to speak. Not that I needed to reiterate what we had felt and known in common, but just to reestablish our grounds for discussion, I told her that I knew in what way we were incomplete, but that I could not put my knowledge into words.

"There are lots and lots of things we know," she said. "And yet we can't get them to work for us because we really don't know how to bring them out of us. You've just begun to feel that pressure. I've had it for years. I know and yet I don't know. Most of the time I trip over myself and sound like an imbecile when I try to say what I know."

I understood what she meant and I understood her at a physical level. I knew something thoroughly practical and self-evident about *will* and what la Gorda had called the other self and yet I could not utter a single word about what I knew, not because I was reticent or bashful, but because I did not know where to begin, or how to organize my knowledge.

"*Will* is such a complete control of the second attention that it is called the other self," la Gorda said after a long pause. "In spite of all we've done, we know only a tiny bit of the other self. The Nagual left it up to us to complete our knowledge. That's our task of remembering."

She smacked her forehead with the palm of her hand, as if something had just come to her mind.

"Holy Jesus! We are remembering the other self!" she exclaimed, her voice almost bordering on hysteria. Then she calmed down and went on talking in a subdued tone. "Evidently we've already been there and the only way of remembering it is the way we're doing it, by shooting off our *dreaming bodies* while *dreaming together*."

"What do you mean, shooting off our *dreaming bodies?*" I asked.

"You yourself have witnessed when Genaro used to shoot off his *dreaming body*," she said. "It pops off like a slow bullet; it actually glues and unglues itself from the physical body with a loud crack. The Nagual told me that Genaro's *dreaming body* could do most of the things we normally do; he used to come to you that way in order to jolt you. I know now what the Nagual and Genaro were after. They wanted you to remember, and for that effect Genaro used to perform incredible feats in front of your very eyes by shooting off his *dreaming body*. But to no avail."

"I never knew that he was in his *dreaming body*," I said.

"You never knew because you weren't watching," she said. "Genaro tried to let you know by attempting to do things that the *dreaming body* cannot do, like eating, drinking, and so forth. The Nagual told me that Genaro used to joke with you that he was going to shit and make the mountains tremble."

"Why can't the *dreaming body* do those things?" I asked.

"Because the *dreaming body* cannot handle the *intent* of eating, or drinking," she replied.

"What do you mean by that, Gorda?" I asked.

"Genaro's great accomplishment was that in his *dreaming* he learned the *intent* of the body," she explained. "He finished what you had started to do. He could *dream* his whole body as perfectly as it could be. But the *dreaming body* has a different *intent* from the *intent* of the physical body. For instance, the *dreaming body* can go through a wall, because it knows the *intent* of disappearing into thin air. The physical body knows the *intent* of eating, but not the one of disappearing. For Genaro's physical body to go through a wall would be as impossible as for his *dreaming body* to eat."

La Gorda was silent for a while as if measuring what she had just said. I wanted to wait before asking her any questions.

"Genaro had mastered only the *intent* of the *dreaming body*," she said in a soft voice. "Silvio Manuel, on the other hand, was the ultimate master of *intent*. I know now that the reason we can't remember his face is because he was not like everybody else."

"What makes you say that, Gorda?" I asked.

She started to explain what she meant, but she was incapable of speaking coherently. Suddenly she smiled. Her eyes lit up.

"I've got it!" she exclaimed. "The Nagual told me that Silvio Manuel was the master of *intent* because he was permanently in his other self. He was the real chief. He was behind everything the Nagual did. In fact, he's the one who made the Nagual take care of you."

I experienced a great physical discomfort upon hearing la Gorda say that. I nearly became sick to my stomach and made extraordinary efforts to hide it from her. I turned my back to her and began to gag. She stopped talking for an instant and then proceeded as if she had made up her mind not to acknowledge my state. Instead, she began to yell at me. She said that it was time that we air our grievances. She confronted me with my feelings of resentment after what happened in Mexico City. She added that my rancor was not because she had sided with the other apprentices against me, but because she had taken part in unmasking me. I explained to her that all of those feelings had vanished from me. She was adamant. She maintained that unless I faced them they would come back to me in some way. She insisted that my affiliation with Silvio Manuel was at the crux of the matter.

I could not believe the changes of mood I went through upon hearing that statement. I became two people—one raving, foaming at the mouth, the other calm, observing. I had a final painful spasm in my stomach and got ill. But it was not a feeling of nausea that had caused the spasm. It was rather an uncontainable wrath.

When I finally calmed down I was embarrassed at my behavior and worried that an incident of that nature might happen to me again at another time.

"As soon as you accept your true nature, you'll be free from rage," la Gorda said in a nonchalant tone.

I wanted to argue with her, but I saw the futility of it. Besides, my attack of anger had drained me of energy. I laughed at the fact that I did not know what I would do if she were right. The thought occurred to me then that if I could forget about the Nagual woman, anything was possible. I had a strange sensation of heat or irritation in my throat, as if I had eaten hot spicy food. I felt a jolt of bodily alarm, just as though I had seen someone sneaking behind my back, and I knew at that moment something I had had no idea I knew a moment before. La Gorda was right. Silvio Manuel had been in charge of me.

La Gorda laughed loudly when I told her that. She said that she had also remembered something about Silvio Manuel.

"I don't remember him as a person, as I remember the Nagual woman," she went on, "but I remember what the Nagual told me about him."

"What did he tell you?" I asked.

"He said that while Silvio Manuel was on this earth he was like Eligio. He disappeared once without leaving a trace and went into the other world. He was gone for years; then one day he returned. The Nagual said that Silvio Manuel did not remember where he'd been or what he'd done, but his body had been changed. He had come back to the world, but he had come back in his other self."

"What else did he say, Gorda?" I asked.

"I can't remember any more," she replied. "It is as if I were looking through a fog."

I knew that if we pushed ourselves hard enough, we were going to find out right then who Silvio Manuel was. I told her so.

"The Nagual said that *intent* is present everywhere," la Gorda said all of a sudden.

"What does that mean?" I asked.

"I don't know," she said. "I'm just voicing things that come to my mind. The Nagual also said that *intent* is what makes the world."

I knew that I had heard those words before. I thought that don Juan must have also told me the same thing and I had forgotten it.

"When did don Juan tell you that?" I asked.

"I can't remember when," she said. "But he told me that people, and all other living creatures for that matter, are the slaves of *intent*. We are in its clutches. It makes us do whatever it wants. It makes us act in the world. It even makes us die.

"He said that when we become warriors, though, *intent* becomes our friend. It lets us be free for a moment; at times it even comes to us, as if it had been waiting around for us. He told me that he himself was only a friend of *intent*—not like Silvio Manuel, who was the master of it."

There were barrages of hidden memories in me that fought to get out. They seemed about to surface. I experienced a tremendous frustration for a moment and then something in me gave up. I became calm. I was no longer interested in finding out about Silvio Manuel.

La Gorda interpreted my change of mood as a sign that we were not ready to face our memories of Silvio Manuel.

"The Nagual showed all of us what he could do with his

intent," she said abruptly. "He could make things appear by calling *intent*.

"He told me that if I wanted to fly, I had to summon the *intent* of flying. He showed me then how he himself could summon it, and jumped in the air and soared in a circle, like a huge kite. Or he would make things appear in his hand. He said that he knew the *intent* of many things and could call those things by *intending* them. The difference between him and Silvio Manuel was that Silvio Manuel, by being the master of *intent*, knew the *intent* of everything."

I told her that her explanation needed more explaining. She seemed to struggle arranging words in her mind.

"I learned the *intent* of flying," she said, "by repeating all the feelings I had while flying in *dreaming*. This was only one thing. The Nagual had learned in his life the *intent* of hundreds of things. But Silvio Manuel went to the source itself. He tapped it. He didn't have to learn the *intent* of anything. He was one with *intent*. The problem was that he had no more desires because *intent* has no desire of its own, so he had to rely on the Nagual for volition. In other words, Silvio Manuel could do anything the Nagual wanted. The Nagual directed Silvio Manuel's *intent*. But since the Nagual had no desires either, most of the time they didn't do anything."

8

The Right and the
Left Side Awareness

Our discussion of *dreaming* was most helpful to us, not only
because it solved our impasse in *dreaming together*, but because
it brought its concepts to an intellectual level. Talking about
it kept us busy; it allowed us to have a moment's pause in
order to ease our agitation.

One night while I was out running an errand I called la
Gorda from a telephone booth. She told me that she had been
in a department store and had had the sensation that I was
hiding there behind some mannequins on display. She was
certain I was teasing her and became furious with me. She
rushed through the store trying to catch me, to show me how
angry she was. Then she realized that she was actually remembering something she had done quite often around me,
having a tantrum.

In unison, we arrived then at the conclusion that it was time
to try again our *dreaming together*. As we talked, we felt a
renewed optimism. I went home immediately.

I very easily entered into the first state, *restful vigil*. I had a
sensation of bodily pleasure, a tingling radiating from my
solar plexus, which was transformed into the thought that we
were going to have great results. That thought turned into a
nervous anticipation. I became aware that my thoughts were

emanating from the tingling in the middle of my chest. The instant I turned my attention to it, however, the tingling stopped. It was like an electric current that I could switch on and off.

The tingling began again, even more pronounced than before, and suddenly I found myself face to face with la Gorda. It was as if I had turned a corner and bumped into her. I became immersed in watching her. She was so absolutely real, so herself, that I had the urge to touch her. The most pure, unearthly affection for her burst out of me at that moment. I began to sob uncontrollably.

La Gorda quickly tried to interlock our arms to stop my indulging, but she could not move at all. We looked around. There was no fixed tableau in front of our eyes, no static picture of any sort. I had a sudden insight and told la Gorda that it was because we had been watching each other that we had missed the appearance of the *dreaming* scene. Only after I had spoken did I realize that we were in a new situation. The sound of my voice scared me. It was a strange voice, harsh, unappealing. It gave me a feeling of physical revulsion.

La Gorda replied that we had not missed anything, that our second attention had been caught by something else. She smiled and made a puckering gesture with her mouth, a mixture of surprise and annoyance at the sound of her own voice.

I found the novelty of talking in *dreaming* spellbinding, for we were not *dreaming* of a scene in which we talked, we were actually conversing. And it required a unique effort, quite similar to my initial effort of walking down a stairway in *dreaming*.

I asked her whether she thought my voice sounded funny. She nodded and laughed out loud. The sound of her laughter was shocking. I remembered that don Genaro used to make the strangest and most frightening noises; la Gorda's laughter was in the same category. The realization struck me then that la Gorda and I had quite spontaneously entered into our *dreaming bodies*.

I wanted to hold her hand. I tried but I could not move my arm. Because I had some experience with moving in that state, I willed myself to go to la Gorda's side. My desire was to embrace her, but instead I moved in on her so close that we merged. I was aware of myself as an individual being, but at the same time I felt I was part of la Gorda. I liked that feeling immensely.

We stayed merged until something broke our hold. I felt a command to examine the environment. As I looked, I clearly remembered having seen it before. We were surrounded by small round mounds that looked exactly like sand dunes. They were all around us, in every direction, as far as we could see. They seemed to be made of something that looked like pale yellow sandstone, or rough granules of sulphur. The sky was the same color and was very low and oppressive. There were banks of yellowish fog or some sort of yellow vapor that hung from certain spots in the sky.

I noticed then that la Gorda and I seemed to be breathing normally. I could not feel my chest with my hands, but I was able to feel it expanding as I inhaled. The yellow vapors were obviously not harmful to us.

We began to move in unison, slowly, cautiously, almost as if we were walking. After a short distance I got very fatigued and so did la Gorda. We were gliding just over the ground, and apparently moving that way was very tiring to our second attention; it required an inordinate degree of concentration. We were not deliberately mimicking our ordinary walk, but the effect was much the same as if we had been. To move required outbursts of energy, something like tiny explosions, with pauses in between. We had no objective in our movement but moving itself, so finally we had to stop.

La Gorda spoke to me, her voice so faint that it was barely audible. She said that we were mindlessly going toward the heavier regions, and that if we kept on moving in that direction, the pressure would get so great that we would die.

We automatically turned around and headed back in the

direction we had come from, but the feeling of fatigue did not let up. Both of us were so exhausted that we could no longer maintain our upright posture. We collapsed and quite spontaneously adopted the *dreaming* position.

I woke up instantly in my study. La Gorda woke up in her bedroom.

The first thing I told her upon awakening was that I had been in that barren landscape several times before. I had seen at least two aspects of it, one perfectly flat, the other covered with small, sand-dune-like mounds. As I was talking, I realized that I had not even bothered to confirm that we had had the same vision. I stopped and told her that I had gotten carried away by my own excitement; I had proceeded as if I were comparing notes with her about a vacation trip.

"It's too late for that kind of talk between us," she said with a sigh, "but if it makes you happy, I'll tell you what we saw."

She patiently described everything we had seen, said, and done. She added that she too had been in that deserted place before, and that she knew for a fact that it was a no-man's land, the space between the world we know and the other world.

"It is the area between the parallel lines," she went on. "We can go to it in *dreaming*. But in order to leave this world and reach the other, the one beyond the parallel lines, we have to go through that area with our whole bodies."

I felt a chill at the thought of entering that barren place with our whole bodies.

"You and I have been there together, with our bodies," la Gorda went on. "Don't you remember?"

I told her that all I could remember was seeing that landscape twice under don Juan's guidance. Both times I had written off the experience because it had been brought about by the ingestion of hallucinogenic plants. Following the dictums of my intellect, I had regarded them as private visions and not as consensual experiences. I did not remember viewing that scene under any other circumstances.

"When did you and I get there with our bodies?" I asked.

"I don't know," she said. "The vague memory of it just popped into my mind when you mentioned being there before. I think that now it is your turn to help me finish what I have started to remember. I can't focus on it yet, but I do recall that Silvio Manuel took the Nagual woman, you, and me into that desolate place. I don't know why he took us in there, though. We were not in *dreaming*."

I did not hear what else she was saying. My mind had begun to zero in on something still inarticulate. I struggled to set my thoughts in order. They rambled aimlessly. For a moment I felt as if I had reverted back years, to a time when I could not stop my internal dialogue. Then the fog began to clear. My thoughts arranged themselves without my conscious direction, and the result was the full memory of an event which I had already partially recalled in one of those unstructured flashes of recollection that I used to have. La Gorda was right, we had been taken once to a region that don Juan had called "limbo," apparently drawing the term from religious dogma. I knew that la Gorda was also right in saying that we had not been in *dreaming*.

On that occasion, at the request of Silvio Manuel, don Juan had rounded up the Nagual woman, la Gorda, and myself. Don Juan told me that the reason for our meeting was the fact that, by my own means but without knowing how, I had entered into a special recess of awareness, which was the site of the keenest form of attention. I had previously reached that state, which don Juan had called the "left left side," but all too briefly and always aided by him. One of its main features, the one that had the greatest value for all of us involved with don Juan, was that in that state we were able to perceive a colossal bank of yellowish vapor, something which don Juan called the "wall of fog." Whenever I was capable of perceiving it, it was always to my right, extending forward to the horizon and up to infinity, thus dividing the world in two. The wall of fog would turn either to the right or to the left as I turned my head, so there was never a way for me to face it.

On the day in question, both don Juan and Silvio Manuel had talked to me about the wall of fog. I remembered that after Silvio Manuel had finished talking, he grabbed la Gorda by the nape of her neck, as if she were a kitten, and disappeared with her into the bank of fog. I had had a split second to observe their disappearance, because don Juan had somehow succeeded in making me face the wall myself. He did not pick me up by the nape of the neck but pushed me into the fog; and the next thing I knew, I was looking at the desolate plain. Don Juan, Silvio Manuel, the Nagual woman, and la Gorda were also there. I did not care what they were doing. I was concerned with a most unpleasant and threatening feeling of oppression—a fatigue, a maddening difficulty in breathing. I perceived that I was standing inside a suffocating, yellow, low-ceilinged cave. The physical sensation of pressure became so overwhelming that I could no longer breathe. It seemed that all my physical functions had stopped; I could not feel any part of my body. Yet I still could move, walk, extend my arms, rotate my head. I put my hands on my thighs; there was no feeling in my thighs, nor in the palms of my hands. My legs and arms were visibly there, but not palpably there.

Moved by the boundless fear I was feeling, I grabbed the Nagual woman by the arm and yanked her off balance. But it was not my muscle strength that had pulled her. It was a force that was stored not in my muscles or skeletal frame but in the very center of my body.

Wanting to play that force once more, I grabbed la Gorda. She was rocked by the strength of my pull. Then I realized that the energy to move them had come from a sticklike protuberance that acted upon them as a tentacle. It was balanced at the midpoint of my body.

All that had taken only an instant. The next moment I was

back again at the same point of physical anguish and fear. I looked at Silvio Manuel in a silent plea for help. The way he returned my look convinced me that I was lost. His eyes were cold and indifferent. Don Juan turned his back to me and I shook from the inside out with a physical terror beyond comprehension. I thought that the blood in my body was boiling, not because I felt heat, but because an internal pressure was mounting to the point of bursting.

Don Juan commanded me to relax and abandon myself to my death. He said that I had to remain in there until I died and that I had a chance either to die peacefully, if I would make a supreme effort and let my terror possess me, or I could die in agony, if I chose to fight it.

Silvio Manuel spoke to me, a thing he rarely did. He said that the energy I needed to accept my terror was in my middle point, and that the only way to succeed was to acquiesce, to surrender without surrendering.

The Nagual woman and la Gorda were perfectly calm. I was the only one who was dying there. Silvio Manuel said that the way I was wasting energy, my end was only moments away, and that I should consider myself already dead. Don Juan signaled the Nagual woman and la Gorda to follow him. They turned their backs to me. I did not see what else they did. I felt a powerful vibration go through me. I figured that it was my death rattle; my struggle was over. I did not care any more. I gave in to the unsurpassable terror that was killing me. My body, or the configuration I regarded as my body, relaxed, abandoned itself to its death. As I let the terror come in, or perhaps go out of me, I felt and saw a tenuous vapor— a whitish smear against the sulphur-yellow surroundings— leaving my body.

Don Juan came back to my side and examined me with curiosity. Silvio Manuel moved away and grabbed la Gorda again by the nape of her neck. I clearly saw him hurling her, like a giant rag doll, into the fog bank. Then he stepped in himself and disappeared.

The Nagual woman made a gesture to invite me to come into the fog. I moved toward her, but before I reached her, don Juan gave me a forceful shove that propelled me through the thick yellow fog. I did not stagger but glided through and ended up falling headlong onto the ground in the everyday world.

La Gorda remembered the whole affair as I narrated it to her. Then she added more details.

"The Nagual woman and I were not afraid for your life," she said. "The Nagual had told us that you had to be forced to give up your holdings, but that that was nothing new. Every male warrior has to be forced by fear.

"Silvio Manuel had already taken me behind that wall three times so that I would learn to relax. He said that if you saw me at ease, you would be affected by it, and you were. You gave up and relaxed."

"Did you also have a hard time learning to relax?" I asked.

"No. It's a cinch for a woman," she said. "That's our advantage. The only problem is that we have to be transported through the fog. We can't do it on our own."

"Why not, Gorda?" I asked.

"One needs to be very heavy to go through and a woman is light," she said. "Too light, in fact."

"What about the Nagual woman? I didn't see anyone transporting her," I said.

"The Nagual woman was special," la Gorda said. "She could do everything by herself. She could take me in there, or take you. She could even pass through that deserted plain, a thing which the Nagual said was mandatory for all travelers who journey into the unknown."

"Why did the Nagual woman go in there with me?" I asked.

"Silvio Manuel took us along to buttress you," she said. "He thought that you needed the protection of two females and two males flanking you. Silvio Manuel thought that you needed to be protected from the entities that roam and lurk in there. Allies come from that deserted plain. And other things even more fierce."

"Were you also protected?" I asked.

"I don't need protection," she said. "I'm a woman. I'm free from all that. But we all thought that you were in a terrible fix. You were the Nagual, and a very stupid one. We thought that any of those fierce allies—or if you wish, call them demons—could have blasted you, or dismembered you. That was what Silvio Manuel said. He took us to flank your four corners. But the funny part was that neither the Nagual nor Silvio Manuel knew that you didn't need us. We were supposed to walk for quite a while until you lost your energy. Then Silvio Manuel was going to frighten you by pointing out the allies to you and beckoning them to come after you. He and the Nagual planned to help you little by little. That is the rule. But something went wrong. The minute you got in there, you went crazy. You hadn't moved an inch and you were already dying. You were frightened to death and you hadn't even seen the allies yet.

"Silvio Manuel told me that he didn't know what to do, so he said in your ear the last thing he was supposed to say to you, to give in, to surrender without surrendering. You became calm at once all by yourself, and they didn't have to do any of the things that they had planned. There was nothing for the Nagual and Silvio Manuel to do except to take us out of there."

I told la Gorda that when I found myself back in the world there was someone standing by me who helped me to stand up. That was all I could recollect.

"We were in Silvio Manuel's house," she said. "I can now remember a lot about that house. Someone told me, I don't know who, that Silvio Manuel found that house and bought it because it was built on a power spot. But someone else said that Silvio Manuel found the house, liked it, bought it, and then brought the power spot to it. I personally feel that Silvio Manuel brought the power. I feel that his impeccability held the power spot on that house for as long as he and his companions lived there.

"When it was time for them to move away, the power of that spot vanished with them, and the house became what it had been before Silvio Manuel found it, an ordinary house."

As la Gorda talked, my mind seemed to clear up further, but not enough to reveal what had happened to us in that house that filled me with such sadness. Without knowing why, I was sure it had to do with the Nagual woman. Where was she?

La Gorda did not answer when I asked her that. There was a long silence. She excused herself, saying that she had to make breakfast; it was already morning. She left me by myself, with a most painful, heavy heart. I called her back. She got angry and threw her pots on the floor. I understood why.

In another session of *dreaming together* we went still deeper into the intricacies of the second attention. This took place a few days later. La Gorda and I, with no such expectation or effort, found ourselves standing together. She tried three or four times in vain to interlock her arm with mine. She spoke to me, but her speech was incomprehensible. I knew, however, that she was saying that we were again in our *dreaming bodies*. She was cautioning me that all movement should stem from our midsections.

As in our last attempt, no *dreaming* scene presented itself for our examination, but I seemed to recognize a physical locale which I had seen in *dreaming* nearly every day for over a year: it was the valley of the saber-toothed tiger.

We walked a few yards; this time our movements were not jerky or explosive. We actually walked from the belly, with no muscular action involved. The trying part was my lack of practice; it was like the first time I had ridden a bicycle. I easily got tired and lost my rhythm, became hesitant and unsure of myself. We stopped. La Gorda was out of synchronization, too.

We began then to examine what was around us. Everything had an indisputable reality, at least to the eye. We were in a rugged area with a weird vegetation. I could not identify the strange shrubs I saw. They seemed like small trees, five to six feet high. They had a few leaves, which were flat and thick, chartreuse in color, and huge, gorgeous, deep-brown flowers striped with gold. The stems were not woody, but seemed to be light and pliable, like reeds; they were covered with long, formidable-looking needlelike thorns. Some old dead plants that had dried up and fallen to the ground gave me the impression that the stems were hollow.

The ground was very dark and seemed moist. I tried to bend over to touch it, but I failed to move. La Gorda signaled me to use my midsection. When I did that I did not have to bend over to touch the ground; there was something in me like a tentacle which could feel. But I could not tell what I was feeling. There were no particular tactile qualities on which to base distinctions. The ground that I touched appeared to be soil, not to my sense of touch but to what seemed to be a visual core in me. I was plunged then into an intellectual dilemma. Why would *dreaming* seem to be the product of my visual faculty? Was it because of the predominance of the visual in daily life? The questions were meaningless. I was in no position to answer them, and all my queries did was to debilitate my second attention.

La Gorda jolted me out of my deliberations by ramming me. I experienced a sensation like a blow; a tremor ran through me. She pointed ahead of us. As usual, the saber-toothed tiger was lying on the ledge where I had always seen it. We approached until we were a mere six feet from the ledge and we had to lift our heads to see the tiger. We stopped. It stood up. Its size was stupendous, especially its breadth.

I knew that la Gorda wanted us to sneak around the tiger to the other side of the hill. I wanted to tell her that that might be dangerous, but I could not find a way to convey the message to her. The tiger seemed angry, aroused. It crouched back on its hind legs, as if it were preparing to jump on us. I was terrified.

La Gorda turned to me, smiling. I understood that she was telling me not to succumb to my panic, because the tiger was only a ghostlike image. With a movement of her head, she coaxed me to go on. Yet at an unfathomable level I knew that the tiger was an entity, perhaps not in the factual sense of our daily world, but real nonetheless. And because la Gorda and I were *dreaming*, we had lost our own factuality-in-the-world. At that moment we were on a par with the tiger: our existence also was ghostlike.

We took one more step at the nagging insistence of la Gorda. The tiger jumped from the ledge. I saw its enormous body hurtling through the air, coming directly at me. I lost the sense that I was *dreaming*—to me, the tiger was real and I was going to be ripped apart. A barrage of lights, images, and the most intense primary colors I had ever seen flashed all around me. I woke up in my study.

After we became extremely proficient in our *dreaming together*, I had the certainty then that we had managed to secure our detachment, and we were no longer in a hurry. The outcome of our efforts was not what moved us to act. It was rather an ulterior compulsion that gave us the impetus to act impeccably without thought of reward. Our subsequent sessions were like the first except for the speed and ease with which we entered into the second state of *dreaming, dynamic vigil*.

Our proficiency in *dreaming together* was such that we successfully repeated it every night. Without any such intention on our part, our *dreaming together* focused itself randomly on three areas: on the sand dunes, on the habitat of the saber-toothed tiger, and most important, on forgotten past events.

When the scenes that confronted us had to do with forgotten events in which la Gorda and I had played an important role, she had no difficulty in interlocking her arm with mine. That act gave me an irrational sense of security. La Gorda explained that it fulfilled a need to dispel the utter aloneness that the second attention produces. She said that to interlock the arms promoted a mood of objectivity, and as a result, we could watch the activity that took place in every scene. At times we were compelled to be part of the activity. At other times we were thoroughly objective and watched the scene as if we were in a movie theater.

When we visited the sand dunes or the habitat of the tiger, we were unable to interlock arms. In those instances our activity was never the same twice. Our actions were never premeditated, but seemed to be spontaneous reactions to novel situations.

According to la Gorda, most of our *dreaming together* grouped itself into three categories. The first and by far the largest was a reenactment of events we had lived together. The second was a review that both of us did of events I alone had "lived"—the land of the saber-toothed tiger was in this category. The third was an actual visit to a realm that existed as we saw it at the moment of our visit. She contended that those yellow mounds are present here and now, and that that is the way they look and stand always to the warrior who journeys into them.

I wanted to argue a point with her. She and I had had mysterious interactions with people we had forgotten, for reasons inconceivable to us, but whom we had nonetheless known in fact. The saber-toothed tiger, on the other hand, was a creature of my *dreaming*. I could not conceive both of them to be in the same category.

Before I had time to voice my thoughts, I got her answer. It was as if she were actually inside my mind, reading it like a text.

"They are in the same class," she said, and laughed nervously. "We can't explain why we have forgotten, or how it is that we are remembering now. We can't explain anything. The saber-toothed tiger is there, somewhere. We'll never know where. But why should we worry about a made-up inconsistency? To say that one is a fact and the other a *dream* has no meaning whatever to the other self."

La Gorda and I used *dreaming together* as a means of reaching an unimagined world of hidden memories. *Dreaming together* enabled us to recollect events that we were incapable of retrieving with our everyday-life memory. When we rehashed those events in our waking hours it triggered yet more detailed recollections. In this fashion we disinterred, so to speak, masses of memories that had been buried in us. It took us almost two years of prodigious effort and concentration to arrive at a modicum of understanding of what had happened to us.

Don Juan had told us that human beings are divided in two. The right side, which he called the *tonal*, encompasses everything the intellect can conceive of. The left side, called the *nagual*, is a realm of indescribable features: a realm impossible to contain in words. The left side is perhaps comprehended, if comprehension is what takes place, with the total body; thus its resistance to conceptualization.

Don Juan had also told us that all the faculties, possibilities, and accomplishments of sorcery, from the simplest to the most astounding, are in the human body itself.

Taking as a base the concepts that we are divided in two and that everything is in the body itself, la Gorda proposed an explanation of our memories. She believed that during the years of our association with the Nagual Juan Matus, our time was divided between states of normal awareness, on the right side, the *tonal*, where the first attention prevails, and states of heightened awareness, on the left side, the *nagual*, or the site of the second attention.

La Gorda thought that the Nagual Juan Matus's efforts were to lead us to the other self by means of the self-control of the second attention through *dreaming*. He put us in direct touch with the second attention, however, through bodily manipulation. La Gorda remembered that he used to force her to go from one side to the other by pushing or massaging her back. She said that sometimes he would even give her a sound blow over or around her right shoulder blade. The result was her entrance into an extraordinary state of clarity. To la Gorda, it seemed that everything in that state went faster, yet nothing in the world had been changed.

It was weeks after la Gorda told me this that I remembered the same had been the case with me. At any given time don Juan might give me a blow on my back. I always felt the blow on my spine, high between my shoulder blades. An extraordinary clarity would follow. The world was the same but sharper. Everything stood by itself. It may have been that my reasoning faculties were numbed by don Juan's blow, thus allowing me to perceive without their intervention.

I would stay clear indefinitely or until don Juan would give me another blow on the same spot to make me revert back to a normal state of awareness. He never pushed or massaged me. It was always a direct sound blow—not like the blow of a fist, but rather a smack that took my breath away for an instant. I would have to gasp and take long, fast gulps of air until I could breathe normally again.

La Gorda reported the same effect: all the air would be forced out of her lungs by the Nagual's blow and she would have to breathe extra hard to fill them up again. La Gorda believed that breath was the all-important factor. In her opinion, the gulps of air that she had to take after being struck were what made the difference, yet she could not explain in what way breathing would affect her perception and awareness. She also said that she was never hit back into normal awareness; she reverted back to it by her own means, though without knowing how.

Her remarks seemed relevant to me. As a child, and even as an adult, I had occasionally had the wind knocked out of me when I took a fall on my back. But the effect of don Juan's blow, though it left me breathless, was not like that at all. There was no pain involved; instead it brought on a sensation impossible to describe. The closest I can come is to say that it created a feeling like dryness in me. The blows to my back seemed to dry out my lungs and fog up everything else. Then, as la Gorda had observed, everything that had become hazy after the Nagual's blow became crystal clear as I breathed, as if breath were the catalyst, the all-important factor.

The same thing would happen to me on the way back to the awareness of everyday life. The air would be knocked out of me, the world I was watching would become foggy, and then it would clear as I filled up my lungs.

Another feature of those states of heightened awareness was the incomparable richness of personal interaction, a richness that our bodies understood as a sensation of speeding. Our back-and-forth movement between the right and the left sides made it easier for us to realize that on the right side too much energy and time is consumed in the actions and interactions of our daily life. On the left side, on the other hand, there is an inherent need for economy and speed.

La Gorda could not describe what this speed really was, and neither could I. The best I could do would be to say that on the left side I could grasp the meaning of things with precision and directness. Every facet of activity was free of preliminaries or introductions. I acted and rested; I went forth and retreated without any of the thought processes that are usual to me. This was what la Gorda and I understood as speeding.

La Gorda and I discerned at one moment that the richness of our perception on the left side was a post-facto realization. Our interaction appeared to be rich in the light of our capacity to remember it. We became cognizant then that in these states of heightened awareness we had perceived everything in one clump, one bulky mass of inextricable detail. We called this ability to perceive everything at once *intensity*. For years we had found it impossible to examine the separate constituent parts of those chunks of experience; we had been unable to synthesize those parts into a sequence that would make sense to the intellect. Since we were incapable of those syntheses, we could not remember. Our incapacity to remember was in reality an incapacity to put the memory of our perception on a linear basis. We could not lay our experiences flat, so to speak, and arrange them in a sequential order. The experiences were available to us, but at the same time they were impossible to retrieve, for they were blocked by a wall of *intensity*.

The task of remembering, then, was properly the task of joining our left and right sides, of reconciling those two distinct forms of perception into a unified whole. It was the task of consolidating the totality of oneself by rearranging *intensity* into a linear sequence.

It occurred to us that the activities we remembered taking part in might not have taken long to perform, in terms of time measured by the clock. By reason of our capacity to perceive in terms of *intensity*, we may have had only a subliminal sensation of lengthy passages of time. La Gorda felt that if we could rearrange *intensity* into a linear sequence, we would honestly believe that we had lived a thousand years.

The pragmatic step that don Juan took to aid our task of remembering was to make us interact with certain people while we were in a state of heightened awareness. He was very careful not to let us see those people when we were in a state of normal awareness. In this way he created the appropriate conditions for remembering.

Upon completing our remembering, la Gorda and I entered into a bizarre state. We had detailed knowledge of social interactions which we had shared with don Juan and his companions. These were not memories in the sense that I would remember an episode from my childhood; they were more than vivid moment-to-moment recollections of events. We reconstructed conversations that seemed to be reverberating in our ears, as if we were listening to them. Both of us felt that it was superfluous to try to speculate about what was happening to us. What we remembered, from the point of view of our experiential selves, was taking place now. Such was the character of our remembering.

At last la Gorda and I were able to answer the questions that had driven us so hard. We remembered who the Nagual woman was, where she fit among us, what her role had been. We deduced, more than remembered, that we had spent equal amounts of time with don Juan and don Genaro in normal states of awareness, and with don Juan and his other companions in states of heightened awareness. We recaptured every nuance of those interactions, which had been veiled by *intensity*.

Upon a thoughtful review of what we had found, we realized that we had bridged the two sides of ourselves in a minimal fashion. We turned then to other topics, new questions that had come to take precedence over the old ones. There were three subjects, three questions, that summarized all of our concerns. Who was don Juan and who were his companions? What had they really done to us? And where had all of them gone?

Part Three

THE EAGLE'S GIFT

9

The Rule of the Nagual

Don Juan had been extremely sparing with information about his background and personal life. His reticence was, fundamentally, a didactic device; as far as he was concerned, his time began when he became a warrior; anything that had happened to him before was of very little consequence.

All la Gorda and I knew about his early life was that he was born in Arizona of Yaqui and Yuma Indian parentage. When he was still an infant his parents took him to live with the Yaquis in northern Mexico. At ten years of age he was caught in the tide of the Yaqui wars. His mother was killed then, and his father was apprehended by the Mexican army. Both don Juan and his father were sent to a relocation center in the farthest southern state of Yucatan. He grew up there.

Whatever happened to him during that period was never disclosed to us. Don Juan believed there was no need to tell us about it. I felt otherwise. The importance that I gave to that segment of his life arose from my conviction that the distinctive features and the emphasis of his leadership grew out of that personal inventory of experience.

But that inventory, important as it might have been, was not what gave him the paramount significance he had in our eyes, and in the eyes of his other companions. His total preeminence rested on the fortuitous act of becoming involved with the "rule."

Being involved with the rule may be described as living a myth. Don Juan lived a myth, a myth that caught him and made him the Nagual.

Don Juan said that when the rule caught him he was an aggressive, unruly man living in exile, as thousands of other Yaqui Indians from northern Mexico lived at that time. He worked in the tobacco plantations of southern Mexico. One day after work, in a nearly fatal encounter with a fellow worker over matters of money, he was shot in the chest. When he regained consciousness an old Indian was leaning over him, poking the small wound in his chest with his fingers. The bullet had not penetrated the chest cavity but was lodged in the muscle against a rib. Don Juan fainted two or three times from shock, loss of blood, and in his own words, from fear of dying. The old Indian removed the bullet, and since don Juan had no place to stay, he took him to his own house and nursed him for over a month.

The old Indian was kind but severe. One day when don Juan was fairly strong, almost recovered, the old man gave him a sound blow on his back and forced him into a state of heightened awareness. Then, without any further preliminaries, he revealed to don Juan the portion of the rule which pertained to the Nagual and his role.

Don Juan did exactly the same thing with me, and with la Gorda; he made us shift levels of awareness and told us the rule of the Nagual in the following way:

The power that governs the destiny of all living beings is called the Eagle, not because it is an eagle or has anything to do with an eagle, but because it appears to the seer as an immeasurable jet-black eagle, standing erect as an eagle stands, its height reaching to infinity.

As the seer gazes on the blackness that the Eagle is, four blazes of light reveal what the Eagle is like. The first blaze, which is like a bolt of lightning, helps the seer make out the contours of the Eagle's body. There are patches of whiteness that look like an eagle's feathers and talons. A second blaze of lightning reveals the flapping, wind-creating blackness that looks like an eagle's wings. With the third blaze of lightning the seer beholds a piercing, inhuman eye. And the fourth and last blaze discloses what the Eagle is doing.

The Eagle is devouring the awareness of all the creatures that, alive on earth a moment before and now dead, have floated to the Eagle's beak, like a ceaseless swarm of fireflies, to meet their owner, their reason for having had life. The Eagle disentangles these tiny flames, lays them flat, as a tanner stretches out a hide, and then consumes them; for awareness is the Eagle's food.

The Eagle, that power that governs the destinies of all living things, reflects equally and at once all those living things. There is no way, therefore, for man to pray to the Eagle, to ask favors, to hope for grace. The human part of the Eagle is too insignificant to move the whole.

It is only from the Eagle's actions that a seer can tell what it wants. The Eagle, although it is not moved by the circumstances of any living thing, has granted a gift to each of those beings. In its own way and right, any one of them, if it so desires, has the power to keep the flame of awareness, the power to disobey the summons to die and be consumed. Every living thing has been granted the power, if it so desires, to seek an opening to freedom and to go through it. It is evident to the seer who sees the opening, and to the creatures that go through it, that the Eagle has granted that gift in order to perpetuate awareness.

For the purpose of guiding living things to that opening, the Eagle created the Nagual. The Nagual is a double being to whom the rule has been revealed. Whether it be in the form of a human being, an animal, a plant, or anything else that lives, the Nagual by virtue of its doubleness is drawn to seek that hidden passageway.

The Nagual comes in pairs, male and female. A double man and a double woman become the Nagual only after the rule has been told to each of them, and each of them has understood it and accepted it in full.

To the eye of the seer, a Nagual man or Nagual woman appears as a luminous egg with four compartments. Unlike the average human being, who has two sides only, a left and a right, the Nagual has a left side divided into two long sections, and a right side equally divided in two.

The Eagle created the first Nagual man and Nagual woman as seers and immediately put them in the world to see. It provided them with four female warriors who were stalkers, three male warriors, and one male courier, whom they were to nourish, enhance, and lead to freedom.

The female warriors are called the four directions, the four corners of a square, the four moods, the four winds, the four different female personalities that exist in the human race.

The first is the east. She is called order. She is optimistic, lighthearted, smooth, persistent like a steady breeze.

The second is the north. She is called strength. She is resourceful, blunt, direct, tenacious like a hard wind.

The third is the west. She is called feeling. She is introspective, remorseful, cunning, sly, like a cold gust of wind.

The fourth is the south. She is called growth. She is nurturing, loud, shy, warm, like a hot wind.

The three male warriors and the courier are representative of the four types of male activity and temperament.

The first type is the knowledgeable man, the scholar; a noble, dependable, serene man, fully dedicated to accomplishing his task, whatever it may be.

The second type is the man of action, highly volatile, a great humorous fickle companion.

The third type is the organizer behind the scenes, the mysterious, unknowable man. Nothing can be said about him because he allows nothing about himself to slip out.

The courier is the fourth type. He is the assistant, a taciturn, somber man who does very well if properly directed but who cannot stand on his own.

In order to make things easier, the Eagle showed the Nagual man and Nagual woman that each of these types among men and women of the earth has specific features in its luminous body.

The scholar has a sort of shallow dent, a bright depression at his solar plexus. In some men it appears as a pool of intense luminosity, sometimes smooth and shiny like a mirror without a reflection.

The man of action has some fibers emanating from the area of the will. The number of fibers varies from one to five, their size ranging from a mere string to a thick, whiplike tentacle up to eight feet long. Some have as many as three of these fibers developed into tentacles.

The man behind the scenes is recognized not by a feature but by his ability to create, quite involuntarily, a burst of power that effectively blocks the attention of seers. When in the presence of this type of man, seers find themselves immersed in extraneous detail rather than seeing.

The assistant has no obvious configuration. To seers he appears as a clear glow in a flawless shell of luminosity.

In the female realm, the east is recognized by the almost imperceptible blotches in her luminosity, something like small areas of discoloration.

The north has an overall radiation; she exudes a reddish glow, almost like heat.

The west has a tenuous film enveloping her, a film which makes her appear darker than the others.

The south has an intermittent glow; she shines for a moment and then gets dull, only to shine again.

The Nagual man and the Nagual woman have two different movements in their luminous bodies. Their right sides wave, while their left sides whirl.

In terms of personality, the Nagual man is supportive, steady, unchangeable. The Nagual woman is a being at war and yet relaxed, ever aware but without strain. Both of them reflect the four types of their sex, as four ways of behaving.

The first command that the Eagle gave the Nagual man and Nagual woman was to find, on their own, another set of four female warriors, four directions, who were the exact replicas of the stalkers but who were dreamers.

Dreamers appear to a seer as having an apron of hairlike fibers at their midsections. Stalkers have a similar apronlike feature, but instead of fibers the apron consists of countless small, round protuberances.

The eight female warriors are divided into two bands, which are called the right and left planets. The right planet is made up of four stalkers, the left of four dreamers. The warriors of each planet were taught by the Eagle the rule of their specific task: stalkers were taught stalking; dreamers were taught dreaming.

The two female warriors of each direction live together. They are so alike that they mirror each other, and only through impeccability can they find solace and challenge in each other's reflection.

The only time when the four dreamers or four stalkers get together is when they have to accomplish a strenuous task; but only under special circumstances should the four of them join hands, for their touch fuses them into one being and should be used only in cases of dire need, or at the moment of leaving this world.

The two female warriors of each direction are attached to one of the males, in any combination that is necessary. Thus they make a set of four households, which are capable of incorporating as many warriors as needed.

The male warriors and the courier can also form an independent unit of four men, or each can function as a solitary being, as dictated by necessity.

Next the Nagual and his party were commanded to find three more couriers. These could be all males or all females or a mixed set, but the male couriers had to be of the fourth type of man, the assistant, and the females had to be from the south.

In order to make sure that the first Nagual man would lead his party to freedom and not deviate from that path or become corrupted, the Eagle took the Nagual woman to the other world to serve as a beacon, guiding the party to the opening.

The Nagual and his warriors were then commanded to forget.

They were plunged into darkness and were given new tasks: the task of remembering themselves, and the task of remembering the Eagle. The command to forget was so great that everyone was separated. They did not remember who they were. The Eagle intended that if they were capable of remembering themselves again, they would find the totality of themselves. Only then would they have the strength and forebearance necessary to seek and face their definitive journey.

Their last task, after they had regained the totality of themselves, was to get a new pair of double beings and transform them into a new Nagual man and a new Nagual woman by virtue of revealing the rule to them. And just as the first Nagual man and Nagual woman had been provided with a minimal party, they had to supply the new pair of Naguals with four female warriors who were stalkers, three male warriors, and one male courier.

When the first Nagual and his party were ready to go through the passageway, the first Nagual woman was waiting to guide them. They were ordered then to take the new Nagual woman with them to the other world to serve as a beacon for her people, leaving the new Nagual man in the world to repeat the cycle.

While in the world, the minimal number under a Nagual's leadership is sixteen: eight female warriors, four male warriors, counting the Nagual, and four couriers. At the moment of leaving the world, when the new Nagual woman is with them, the Nagual's number is seventeen. If his personal power permits him to have more warriors, then more must be added in multiples of four.

I had confronted don Juan with the question of how the rule became known to man. He explained that the rule was endless and covered every facet of a warrior's behavior. The interpretation and the accumulation of the rule is the work of seers whose only task throughout the ages has been to *see* the Eagle, to observe its ceaseless flux. From their observations, the seers have concluded that, providing the luminous shell that comprises one's humanness has been broken, it is possible to find in the Eagle the faint reflection of man. The Eagle's irrevocable dictums can then be apprehended by seers, properly interpreted by them, and accumulated in the form of a governing body.

Don Juan explained that the rule was not a tale, and that to cross over to freedom did not mean eternal life as eternity is commonly understood—that is, as living forever. What the rule stated was that one could keep the awareness which is ordinarily relinquished at the moment of dying. Don Juan could not explain what it meant to keep that awareness, or perhaps he could not even conceive of it. His benefactor had told him that at the moment of crossing, one enters into the third attention, and the body in its entirety is kindled with knowledge. Every cell at once becomes aware of itself, and also aware of the totality of the body.

His benefactor had also told him that this kind of awareness is meaningless to our compartmentalized minds. Therefore the crux of the warrior's struggle was not so much to realize that the crossing over stated in the rule meant crossing to the third attention, but rather to conceive that there exists such an awareness at all.

Don Juan said that in the beginning the rule was to him something strictly in the realm of words. He could not imagine how it could lapse into the domain of the actual world and its ways. Under the effective guidance of his benefactor, however, and after a great deal of work, he finally succeeded in grasping the true nature of the rule, and totally accepted it as a set of pragmatic directives rather than a myth. From then on, he had no problem in dealing with the reality of the third attention. The only obstacle in his way arose from his being so thoroughly convinced that the rule was a map that he believed he had to look for a literal opening in the world, a passageway. Somehow he had become needlessly stuck at the first level of a warrior's development.

Don Juan's own work as a leader and teacher, as a result, was directed at helping the apprentices, and especially me, to avoid repeating his mistake. Whqt he succeeded in doing with us was to lead us through the three stages of a warrior's development without overemphasizing any of them. First he guided us to take the rule as a map; then he guided us to the understanding that one can attain a paramount awareness, because there is such a thing; and finally he guided us to an actual passageway into that other concealed world of awareness.

In order to lead us through the first stage, the acceptance of the rule as a map, don Juan took the section which pertains to the Nagual and his role and showed us that it corresponds to unequivocal facts. He accomplished this by allowing us to have, while we were in stages of heightened awareness, an unrestricted interaction with the members of his group, who were the living personifications of the eight types of people described by the rule. As we interacted with them, more complex and inclusive aspects of the rule were revealed to us, until we were capable of realizing that we were caught in the network of something which at first we had conceptualized as a myth, but which in essence was a map.

Don Juan told us that in this respect his case had been identical to ours. His benefactor helped him go through that first stage by allowing him the same type of interaction. To that effect he made him shift back and forth from the right side to the left side awareness, just as don Juan had done to us. On the left side, he introduced him to the members of his own group, the eight female and three male warriors, and the four couriers, who were, as is mandatory, the strictest examples of the types described by the rule. The impact of knowing them and dealing with them was staggering to don Juan. Not only did it force him to regard the rule as a factual guide, but it made him realize the magnitude of our unknown possibilities.

He said that by the time all the members of his own group had been gathered, he was so deeply committed to the warrior's way that he took for granted the fact that, without any overt effort on anybody's part, they had turned out to be perfect replicas of the warriors of his benefactor's party. The similarity of their personal likes, dislikes, affiliations, and so forth, was not a result of imitation; don Juan said that they belonged, as the rule had stated, to specific blocks of people who had the same input and output. The only differences among members of the same block were in the pitch of their voices, the sound of their laughter.

In trying to explain to me the effects that the interaction with his benefactor's warriors had had on him, don Juan touched on the subject of the very meaningful difference between his benefactor and himself in how they interpreted the rule, and also in how they led and taught other warriors to accept it as a map. He said that there are two types of interpretations—universal and individual. Universal interpretations take the statements that make up the body of the rule at face value. An example would be to say that the Eagle does not care about man's actions and yet it has provided man with a passageway to freedom.

An individual interpretation, on the other hand, is a current conclusion arrived at by seers using universal interpretations as premises. An example would be to say that because of the Eagle's lack of concern I would have to make sure that my chances to reach freedom are enhanced, perhaps by my own dedication.

According to don Juan, he and his benefactor were quite different in the methods they used to lead their wards. Don Juan said that his benefactor's mode was severity; he led with an iron hand, and following his conviction that with the Eagle free handouts are out of the question, he never did anything for anyone in a direct way. Instead, he actively helped everyone to help themselves. He considered that the Eagle's gift of freedom is not a bestowal but a chance to have a chance.

Don Juan, although he appreciated the merits of his benefactor's method, disagreed with it. Later on, when he was on his own, he himself *saw* that it wasted precious time. For him it was more expedient to present everyone with a given situation and force them to accept it, rather than wait until they were ready to face it on their own. That was his method with me and the other apprentices.

The instance in which that difference in leadership had the greatest bearing for don Juan was during the mandatory interaction that he had with his benefactor's warriors. The command of the rule was that his benefactor had to find for don Juan first a Nagual woman and then a group of four women and four men to make up his warrior's party. His benefactor *saw* that don Juan did not yet have enough personal power to assume the responsibility of a Nagual woman, and so he reversed the sequence and asked the females of his own group to find don Juan the four women first, and then the four men.

Don Juan confessed that he was enthralled with the idea of such a reversal. He had understood that those women were for his use, and in his mind that meant sexual use. His downfall, however, was to reveal his expectations to his benefactor, who immediately put don Juan in contact with the men and women of his own party and left him alone to interact with them.

For don Juan, to meet those warriors was a true ordeal, not only because they were deliberately difficult with him, but because the nature of that encounter is meant to be a breakthrough.

Don Juan said that interaction in the left-side awareness cannot take place unless all the participants share that state. This was why he would not let us enter into the left-side awareness except to carry on our interaction with his warriors. That was the procedure his benefactor had followed with him.

Don Juan gave me a brief account of what had taken place during his first meeting with the members of his benefactor's group. His idea was that I could use his experience perhaps as a sample of what to expect. He said that his benefactor's world had a magnificent regularity. The members of his party were Indian warriors from all over Mexico. At the time he met them they lived in a remote mountainous area in southern Mexico.

Upon reaching their house, don Juan was confronted with two identical women, the biggest Indian women he had ever seen. They were sulky and mean, but had very pleasing features. When he tried to go between them, they caught him between their enormous bellies, grabbed his arms, and started beating him up. They threw him to the ground and sat on him, nearly crushing his rib cage. They kept him immobilized for over twelve hours while they conducted on-the-spot negotiations with his benefactor, who had to talk nonstop throughout the night, until they finally let don Juan get up around midmorning. He said that what scared him the most was the determination that showed in the eyes of those women. He thought he was done for, that they were going to sit on him until he died, as they had said they would.

Normally there should have been a waiting period of a few weeks before meeting the next set of warriors, but due to the fact that his benefactor was planning to leave him in their midst, don Juan was immediately taken to meet the others. He met everyone in one day and all of them treated him like dirt. They argued that he was not the man for the job, that he was too coarse and way too stupid, young but already senile in his ways. His benefactor argued brilliantly in his defense; he told them that they could change those conditions, and that it should be an ultimate delight for them and for don Juan to take up that challenge.

Don Juan said that his first impression was right. For him there was only work and hardship from then on. The women *saw* that don Juan was unruly and could not be trusted to fulfill the complex and delicate task of leading four women. Since they were seers themselves, they made their own individual interpretation of the rule and decided that it would be more helpful for don Juan to have the four male warriors first and then the four females. Don Juan said that their *seeing* had been correct, because in order to deal with women warriors a

Nagual has to be in a state of consummate personal power, a state of serenity and control in which human feelings play a minimal part, a state which at the time was inconceivable for him.

His benefactor put him under the direct supervision of his two westerly women, the most fierce and uncompromising warriors of them all. Don Juan said that all westerly women, in accordance with the rule, are raving mad and have to be cared for. Under the duress of *dreaming* and *stalking* they lose their right sides, their minds. Their reason burns up easily due to the fact that their left-side awareness is extraordinarily keen. Once they lose their rational side, they are peerless *dreamers* and *stalkers*, since they no longer have any rational ballast to hold them back.

Don Juan said that those women cured him of his lust. For six months he spent most of his time in a harness suspended from the ceiling of their rural kitchen, like a ham that was being smoked, until he was thoroughly purified from thoughts of gain and personal gratification.

Don Juan explained that a leather harness is a superb device for curing certain maladies that are not physical. The idea is that the higher a person is suspended and the longer that person is kept from touching the ground, dangling in midair, the better the possibilities of a true cleansing effect.

While he was being cleansed by the westerly warriors, the other women were involved in the process of finding the men and the women for his party. It took years to accomplish this. Don Juan, meantime, was forced to interact with all his benefactor's warriors by himself. The presence of those warriors and his contact with them was so overwhelming to don Juan that he believed he would never get out from under them. The result was his total and literal adherence to the body of the rule. Don Juan said that he spent irreplaceable time pondering the existence of an actual passageway into the other world. He viewed such a concern as a pitfall to be avoided at all costs. To protect me from it, he allowed the required interaction with the members of his group to be carried on while I was protected by the presence of la Gorda or any of the other apprentices.

In my case, meeting don Juan's warriors was the end result of a long process. There was never any mention of them in casual conversations with don Juan. I knew of their existence solely by inference from the rule, which he was revealing to me in installments. Later on, he admitted that they existed, and that eventually I would have to meet them. He prepared me for the encounter by giving me general instructions and pointers.

He warned me about a common error, that of overestimating the left-side awareness, of becoming dazzled by its clarity and power. He said that to be in the left-side awareness does not mean that one is immediately liberated from one's folly—it only means an extended capacity for perceiving, a greater facility to understand and learn, and above all, a greater ability to forget.

As the time approached for me to meet don Juan's own warriors, he gave me a scanty description of his benefactor's party, again as a guideline for my own use. He said that to an onlooker, his benefactor's world may have appeared at certain times as consisting of four households. The first was formed by the southerly women and the Nagual's courier; the second by the easterly women, the scholar, and a male courier; the third by the northerly women, the man of action, and another male courier; and the fourth by the westerly women, the man behind the scenes, and a third male courier.

At other times that world may have seemed to be composed of groups. There was a group of four thoroughly dissimilar older men, who were don Juan's benefactor and his three male warriors. Then a group of four men who were very similar to one another, who were the couriers. A group composed of two sets of apparently identical female twins who lived together and were the southerly and easterly women.

And two other sets of apparently sisters, who were the northerly and westerly women.

None of these women were relatives—they just looked alike because of the enormous amount of personal power that don Juan's benefactor had. Don Juan described the southerly women as being two mastodons, scary in appearance but very friendly and warm. The easterly women were very beautiful, fresh and funny, a true delight to the eyes and the ears. The northerly women were utterly womanly, vain, coquettish, concerned with their aging, but also terribly direct and impatient. The westerly women were mad at times, and at other times they were the epitome of severity and purpose. They were the ones who disturbed don Juan the most, because he could not reconcile the fact that they were so sober, kind, and helpful with the fact that at any given moment they could lose their composure and be raving mad.

The men, on the other hand, were in no way memorable to don Juan. He thought that there was nothing remarkable about them. They seemed to have been thoroughly absorbed by the shocking force of the women's determination and by his benefactor's overpowering personality.

Insofar as his own awakening was concerned, don Juan said that upon being thrust into his benefactor's world, he realized how easy and convenient it had been for him to go through life with no self-restraint. He understood that his mistake had been to believe that his goals were the only worthwhile ones a man could have. All his life he had been a pauper; his consuming ambition, therefore, was to have material possessions, to be *somebody*. He had been so preoccupied with his desire to get ahead and his despair at not being successful, that he had had no time for examining anything. He had gladly sided with his benefactor because he realized that he was being offered an opportunity to make something of himself. If nothing else, he thought he might learn to be a sorcerer. He conceived that immersion in his benefactor's world might have an effect on him analogous to the effect of the Spanish Conquest on the Indian culture. It destroyed everything, but it also forced a shattering self-examination.

My response to the preparations to meet don Juan's party of warriors was not, strangely enough, awe or fear, but a petty intellectual concern about two topics. The first was the proposition that there are only four types of men and four types of women in the world. I argued with don Juan that the range of individual variation in people is too great for such a simple scheme. He disagreed with me. He said that the rule was final, and that it did not allow for an indefinite number of types of people.

The second topic was the cultural context of don Juan's knowledge. He did not know that himself. He viewed it as the product of a sort of Pan-Indianism. His conjecture about its origin was that at one time, in the Indian world prior to the Conquest, the handling of the second attention became vitiated. It was developed without any hindrance over perhaps thousands of years, to the point that it lost its strength. The practitioners of that time may have had no need for controls, and thus without restraint, the second attention, instead of becoming stronger, became weaker by virtue of its increased intricacy. Then the Spanish invaders came and, with their superior technology, destroyed the Indian world. Don Juan said that his benefactor was convinced that only a handful of those warriors survived and were capable of reassembling their knowledge and redirecting their path. Whatever don Juan and his benefactor knew about the second attention was the restructured version, a new version which had built-in restraints because it had been forged under the harshest conditions of suppression.

10

The Nagual's Party of Warriors

When don Juan judged that the time was right for me to have my first encounter with his warriors, he made me shift levels of awareness. He then made it perfectly clear that he would have nothing to do with their way of meeting me. He warned me that if they decided to beat me, he could not stop them. They could do anything they wanted, except kill me. He stressed over and over again that the warriors of his party were a perfect replica of his benefactor's, except that some of the women were more fierce, and all the men were utterly unique and powerful. Therefore, my first encounter with them might resemble a head-on collision.

I was nervous and apprehensive on the one hand, but curious on the other. My mind was running wild with endless speculations, most of them about what the warriors would look like.

Don Juan said that he had the choice either of coaching me to memorize an elaborate ritual, as he had been made to do, or of making it the most casual encounter possible. He waited for an omen to point out which alternative to take. His benefactor had done something similar, only he had insisted don Juan learn the ritual before the omen presented itself. When don Juan revealed his sexual daydreams of sleeping with four women, his benefactor interpreted it as the omen, chucked the ritual, and ended up pleading like a hog dealer for don Juan's life.

In my case, don Juan wanted an omen before he taught me the ritual. That omen came when don Juan and I were driving through a border town in Arizona and a policeman stopped me. The policeman thought I was an illegal alien. Only after I had shown him my passport, which he suspected of being a forgery, and other documents, did he let me go. Don Juan had been in the'front seat next to me all the time, and the policeman had not given him a second glance. He had focused solely on me. Don Juan thought the incident was the omen he was waiting for. His interpretation of it was that it would be very dangerous for me to call attention to myself, and he concluded that my world had to be one of utter simplicity and candor—elaborate ritual and pomp were out of character for me. He conceded, however, that a minimal observance of ritualistic patterns was in order when I made my acquaintance with his warriors. I had to begin by approaching them from the south, because that is the direction that power follows in its ceaseless flux. Life force flows to us from the south, and leaves us flowing toward the north. He said that the only opening to a Nagual's world was through the south, and that the gate was made by two female warriors, who would have to greet me and would let me go through if they so decided.

He took me to a town in central Mexico, to a house in the countryside. As we approached it on foot from a southerly direction, I saw two massive Indian women standing four feet apart, facing each other. They were about thirty or forty feet away from the main door of the house, in an area where the dirt was hard-packed. The two women were extraordinarily muscular and stern. Both had long, jet-black hair held together in a single thick braid. They looked like sisters. They were about the same height and weight—I figured that they must have been around five feet four, and weighed 150 pounds. One of them was extremely dark, almost black, the other much lighter. They were dressed like typical Indian women from central Mexico—long, full dresses and shawls, homemade sandals.

Don Juan made me stop three feet from them. He turned to the woman on our left and made me face her. He said that her name was Cecilia and that she was a *dreamer*. He then turned abruptly, without giving me time to say anything, and made me face the darker woman, to our right. He said that her name was Delia and that she was a *stalker*. The women nodded at me. They did not smile or move to shake hands with me, or make any gesture of welcome.

Don Juan walked between them as if they were two columns marking a gate. He took a couple of steps and turned as if waiting for the women to invite me to go through. The women stared at me calmly for a moment. Then Cecilia asked me to come in, as if I were at the threshold of an actual door.

Don Juan led the way to the house. At the front door we found a man. He was very slender. At first sight he looked extremely young, but on closer examination he appeared to be in his late fifties. He gave me the impression of being an old child: small, wiry, with penetrating dark eyes. He was like an elfish apparition, a shadow. Don Juan introduced him to me as Emilito, and said that he was his courier and all-around helper, who would welcome me on his behalf.

It seemed to me that Emilito was indeed the most appropriate being to welcome anyone. His smile was radiant; his small teeth were perfectly even. He shook hands with me, or rather he crossed his forearms and clasped both my hands. He seemed to be exuding enjoyment; anyone would have sworn that he was ecstatic in meeting me. His voice was very soft and his eyes sparkled.

We walked into a large room. There was another woman there. Don Juan said that her name was Teresa and that she was Cecilia's and Delia's courier. She was perhaps in her early thirties, and she definitely looked like Cecilia's daughter. She was very quiet but very friendly. We followed don Juan to the back of the house, where there was a roofed porch. It was a warm day. We sat there around a table, and after a frugal dinner we talked until after midnight.

Emilito was the host. He charmed and delighted everyone with his exotic stories. The women opened up. They were a great audience for him. To hear the women's laughter was an exquisite pleasure. They were tremendously muscular, bold, and physical. At one point, when Emilito said that Cecilia and Delia were like two mothers to him, and Teresa like a daughter, they picked him up and tossed him in the air like a child.

Of the two women, Delia seemed the more rational, down-to-earth. Cecilia was perhaps more aloof, but appeared to have greater inner strength. She gave me the impression of being more intolerant, or more impatient; she seemed to get annoyed with some of Emilito's stories. Nonetheless, she was definitely on the edge of her chair when he would tell what he called his "tales of eternity." He would preface every story with the phrase, "Do you, dear friends, know that. . . ?" The story that impressed me most was about some creatures that he said existed in the universe, who were the closest thing to human beings without being human; creatures who were obsessed with movement and capable of detecting the slightest fluctuation inside themselves or around them. These creatures were so sensitive to motion that it was a curse to them. It gave them such pain that their ultimate ambition was to find quietude.

Emilito would intersperse his tales of eternity with the most outrageous dirty jokes. Because of his incredible gifts as a raconteur, I understood every one of his stories as a metaphor, a parable, with which he was teaching us something.

Don Juan said that Emilito was merely reporting about things he had witnessed in his journeys through eternity. The role of a courier was to travel ahead of the Nagual, like a scout in a military operation. Emilito went to the limits of the second attention, and whatever he witnessed he passed on to the others.

My second encounter with don Juan's warriors was just as contrived as the first. One day don Juan made me shift levels of awareness and told me that I had a second appointment. He made me drive to Zacatecas in northern Mexico. We arrived there very early in the morning. Don Juan said that that was only a stopover, and that we had until the next day to relax before we embarked on my second formal meeting to make the acquaintance of the eastern women and the scholar warrior of his party. He explained then an intricate and delicate point of choice. He said that we had met the south and the courier in the midafternoon, because he had made an individual interpretation of the rule and had picked that hour to represent the night. The south was really the night—a warm, friendly, cozy night—and properly we should have gone to meet the two southerly women after midnight. However, that would have been inauspicious for me because my general direction was toward the light, toward optimism, an optimism that works itself harmoniously into the mystery of darkness. He said that that was precisely what we had done that day; we had enjoyed each other's company and talked until it was pitch-black. I had wondered why they did not light their lanterns.

Don Juan said that the east, on the other hand, was the morning, the light, and that we would meet the easterly women the next day at midmorning.

Before breakfast we went to the plaza and sat down on a bench. Don Juan told me that he wanted me to remain there and wait for him while he ran some errands. He left and shortly after he had gone, a woman came and sat down on the other end of the bench. I did not pay any attention to her and started reading a newspaper. A moment later another woman joined her. I wanted to move to another bench, but I remembered that don Juan had specifically said that I should sit there. I turned my back to the women and had even forgotten that they were there, since they were so quiet, when a man greeted them and stood facing me. I became aware from their conversation that the women had been waiting for him. The man apologized for being late. He obviously wanted to sit down. I slid over to make room for him. He thanked me profusely and apologized for inconveniencing me. He said that they were absolutely lost in the city because they were rural people, and that once they had been to Mexico City and had nearly died in the traffic. He asked me if I lived in Zacatecas. I said no and was going to end our conversation right there but there was something very winning about his smile. He was an old man, remarkably fit for his age. He was not an Indian. He seemed to be a gentleman farmer from a small rural town. He was wearing a suit and had a straw hat on. His features were very delicate. His skin was almost transparent. He had a high-bridged nose, a small mouth, and a perfectly groomed white beard. He looked extraordinarily healthy and yet he seemed frail. He was of medium height and well built, but at the same time gave the impression of being slender, almost effete.

He stood up and introduced himself to me. He told me that his name was Vicente Medrano, and that he had come to the city on business only for the day. He then pointed to the two women and said that they were his sisters. The women stood up and faced us. They were very slim and darker than their brother. They were also much younger. One of them could have been his daughter. I noticed that their skin was not like his; theirs was dry. The two women were very good-looking. Like the man, they had fine features, and their eyes were clear and peaceful. They were about five feet four. They were wearing beautifully tailored dresses, but with their shawls, low heeled shoes, and dark cotton stockings they looked like well-to-do farm women. The older one appeared to be in her fifties, the younger in her forties.

The man introduced them to me. The older woman was named Carmela and the younger one Hermelinda. I stood up and briefly shook hands with them. I asked them if they had any children. That question was usually a sure conversation opener for me. The women laughed and in unison ran their hands down their stomachs to show me how lean they were. The man calmly explained that his sisters were spinsters, and that he himself was an old bachelor. He confided to me, in a half-joking tone, that unfortunately his sisters were too mannish, they lacked the femininity that makes a woman desirable, and so they had been unable to find husbands.

I said that they were better off, considering the subservient role of women in our society. The women disagreed with me; they said that they would not have minded at all being servants if they had only found men who wanted to be their masters. The younger one said that the real problem was that their father had failed to teach them to behave like women. The man commented with a sigh that their father was so domineering that he had also prevented him from marrying by deliberately neglecting to teach him how to be a macho. All three of them sighed and looked gloomy. I wanted to laugh.

After a long silence we sat down again and the man said that if I stayed a while longer on that bench I would have a chance to meet their father, who was still very spirited for his advanced age. He added in a shy tone that their father was going to take them to eat breakfast, because they themselves never carried any money. Their father handled the purse strings.

I was aghast. Those old people who looked so strong were in reality like weak, dependent children. I said goodbye to them and got up to leave. The man and his sisters insisted that I stay. They assured me that their father would love it if

I would join them for breakfast. I did not want to meet their father and yet I was curious. I told them that I myself was waiting for someone. At that, the women began to chuckle and then broke into a roaring laughter. The man also abandoned himself to uncontained laughter. I felt stupid. I wanted to get out of there. At that moment don Juan showed up and I became aware of their maneuver. I did not think it was amusing.

All of us stood up. They were still laughing as don Juan told me that those women were the east, that Carmela was the *stalker* and Hermelinda the *dreamer*, and that Vicente was the warrior scholar and his oldest companion.

As we were leaving the plaza, another man joined us, a tall, dark Indian, perhaps in his forties. He was wearing Levi's and a cowboy hat. He seemed terribly strong and sullen. Don Juan introduced him to me as Juan Tuma, Vicente's courier and research assistant.

We walked to a restaurant a few blocks away. The women held me between them. Carmela said that she hoped I was not offended by their joke, that they had had the choice of just introducing themselves to me or kidding me. What made them decide to kid me was my thoroughly snobbish attitude in turning my back to them and wanting to move to another bench. Hermelinda added that one has to be utterly humble and carry nothing to defend, not even one's person; that one's person should be protected, but not defended. In snubbing them, I was not protecting but merely defending myself.

I felt quarrelsome. I was frankly put out by their masquerade. I began to argue, but before I had made my point don Juan came to my side. He told the two women that they should overlook my belligerence, that it takes a very long time to clean out the garbage that a luminous being picks up in the world.

The owner of the restaurant where we went knew Vicente and had prepared a sumptuous breakfast for us. All of them were in great spirits, but I was unable to let go of my brooding. Then, at don Juan's request, Juan Tuma began to talk about his journeys. He was a factual man. I became mesmerized by his dry accounts of things beyond my comprehension. To me the most fascinating was his description of some beams of light or energy that allegedly crisscross the earth. He said that these beams do not fluctuate as everything else in the universe does, but are fixed into a pattern. This pattern coincides with hundreds of points in the luminous body. Hermelinda had understood that all the points were in our physical body, but Juan Tuma explained that, since the luminous body is quite big, some of the points are as much as three feet away from the physical body. In a sense they are outside of us, and yet they are not; they are on the periphery of our luminosity and thus still belong to the total body. The most important of those points is located a foot away from the stomach, 40 degrees to the right of an imaginary line shooting straight forward. Juan Tuma told us that that was a center of assembling for the second attention, and that it is possible to manipulate it by gently stroking the air with the palms of the hands. Listening to Juan Tuma, I forgot my anger.

My next encounter with don Juan's world was with the west. He gave me ample warning that the first contact with the west was a most important event, because it would decide, in one way or another, what I should subsequently do. He also alerted me to the fact that it was going to be a trying event, especially for me, as I was so stiff and felt so self-important. He said that the west is naturally approached at dusk, a time of day which is difficult just in itself, and that his warriors of the west were very powerful, bold, and downright maddening. At the same time, I was also going to meet the male warrior who was the man behind the scenes. Don Juan admonished me to exercise the utmost caution and patience; not only were the women raving mad, but they and the man were the most powerful warriors he had ever known. They were, in his opinion, the ultimate authorities of the second attention. Don Juan did not elaborate any further.

One day, as though on the spur of the moment, he suddenly decided that it was time to start on our trip to meet the westerly women. We drove to a city in northern Mexico. Just at dusk, don Juan directed me to stop in front of a big unlit house on the outskirts of town. We got out of the car and walked to the main door. Don Juan knocked several times. No one answered. I had the feeling that we had come at the wrong time. The house seemed empty.

Don Juan kept on knocking until he apparently got tired. He signaled me to knock. He told me to keep on doing it without stopping because the people who lived in there were hard of hearing. I asked him if it would be better to return later or the next day. He told me to keep on banging on the door.

After a seemingly endless wait, the door began to open slowly. A weird-looking woman stuck her head out and asked me if my intention was to break down the door or to anger the neighbors and their dogs.

Don Juan stepped forward to say something. The woman stepped out and forcefully brushed him aside. She began to shake her finger at me, yelling that I was behaving as if I owned the world, as if there were no one else besides myself. I protested that I was merely doing what don Juan had told me to do. The woman asked if I had been told to break the door down. Don Juan tried to intervene but was again brushed away.

The woman looked as if she had just gotten out of bed. She was a mess. Our knocking had probably awakened her and she must have put on a dress from her basket of dirty clothes. She was barefoot; her hair was graying and terribly unkempt. She had red, beady eyes. She was a homely woman, but somehow very impressive: rather tall, about five feet eight, dark and enormously muscular; her bare arms were knotted with hard muscles. I noticed that she had beautifully shaped calves.

She looked me up and down, towering over me, and shouted that she had not heard my apologies. Don Juan whispered to me that I should apologize loud and clear.

Once I had done that, the woman smiled and turned to don Juan and hugged him as if he were a child. She grumbled that he should not have made me knock because my touch on the door was too shifty and disturbing. She held don Juan's arm and led him inside, helping him over the high threshold. She called him "dearest little old man." Don Juan laughed. I was appalled to see him acting as if he were delighted at the absurdities of that scary woman. Once she had helped the "dearest little old man" into the house, she turned to me and made a gesture with her hand to shoo me away, as if I were a dog. She laughed at my surprise; her teeth were big and uneven, and filthy. Then she seemed to change her mind and told me to come in.

Don Juan was heading to a door that I could barely see at the end of a dark hall. The woman scolded him for not knowing where he was going. She took us through another dark hall. The house seemed to be enormous, and there was not a single light in it. The woman opened a door to a very large room, almost empty except for two old armchairs in the center, under the weakest light bulb I had ever seen. It was an old-fashioned long bulb.

Another woman was sitting in one of the armchairs. The first woman sat down on a small straw mat on the floor and rested her back against the other chair. Then she put her thighs against her breasts, exposing herself completely. She was not wearing underpants. I stared at her dumbfounded.

In an ugly gruff tone, the woman asked me why I was staring at her vagina. I did not know what to say except to deny it. She stood up and seemed about to hit me. She demanded that I tell her that I had gaped at her because I had never seen a vagina in my life. I felt guilty. I was thoroughly embarrassed and also annoyed at having been caught in such a situation.

The woman asked don Juan what kind of Nagual I was if I had never seen a vagina. She began repeating this over and over, yelling it at the top of her voice. She ran around the room and stopped by the chair where the other woman was sitting. She shook her by the shoulders and, pointing at me, said that I was a man who had never seen a vagina in his whole life. She laughed and taunted me.

I was mortified. I felt that don Juan should have done something to save me from that humiliation. I remembered that he had told me these women were quite mad. He had understated it; this woman was ready for an institution. I looked at don Juan for support and advice. He looked away. He seemed to be equally at a loss, although I thought I caught a malicious smile, which he quickly hid by turning his head.

The woman lay down on her back and pulled up her skirt, and commanded me to look to my heart's content instead of sneaking glances. My face must have been red, judging by the heat in my head and neck. I was so annoyed that I almost lost control. I felt like bashing her head in.

The woman who was sitting in the chair suddenly stood up and grabbed the other one by the hair and made her stand up in one single motion, seemingly with no effort at all. She stared at me through half-closed eyes, bringing her face no more than two or three inches from mine. She smelled surprisingly fresh.

In a high-pitched voice, she said that we should get down to business. Both of the women stood close to me under the light bulb. They did not look alike. The second woman was older, or looked older, and her face was covered by a thick coat of cosmetic powder that gave her a clownish appearance. Her hair was neatly arranged in a chignon. She seemed calm except for a continuous tremor in her lower lip and chin.

Both women were equally tall and strong-looking; they

towered menacingly over me and stared at me for a long time. Don Juan did not do anything to break their fixation. The older woman nodded her head, and don Juan told me that her name was Zuleica and that she was a *dreamer*. The woman who had opened the door was named Zoila, and she was a *stalker*.

Zuleica turned to me and, in a parrotlike voice, asked me if it was true that I had never seen a vagina. Don Juan could not hold his composure any longer and began to laugh. With a gesture, I signaled him that I did not know what to say. He whispered in my ear that it would be better for me to say that I had not; otherwise I should be prepared to describe a vagina, because that was what Zuleica would demand that I do next.

I answered accordingly, and Zuleica said that she felt sorry for me. Then she ordered Zoila to show me her vagina. Zoila lay down on her back under the light bulb and opened her legs.

Don Juan was laughing and coughing. I begged him to get me out of that madhouse. He whispered in my ear again that I had better take a good look and appear attentive and interested, because if I did not we would have to stay there until kingdom come.

After my careful and attentive examination, Zuleica said that from then on I could brag that I was a connoisseur, and that if I ever stumbled upon a woman without pants, I would not be so coarse and obscene as to let my eyes pop out of their sockets, because now I had seen a vagina.

Zuleica very quietly led us to the patio. She whispered that there was someone out there waiting to meet me. The patio was pitch black. I could hardly make out the silhouettes of the others. Then I saw the dark outline of a man standing a few feet away from me. My body experienced an involuntary jolt.

Don Juan spoke to the man in a very low voice, saying that he had brought me to meet him. He told the man my name. After a moment's silence, don Juan said to me that the man's name was Silvio Manuel, and that he was the warrior of dark-

ness and the actual leader of the whole warrior's party. Then
Silvio Manuel spoke to me. I thought that he must have had a
speech disorder—his voice was muffled and the words came
out of him like spurts of soft coughing.

He ordered me to come closer. As I tried to approach him,
he receded, just as if he were floating. He led me into an even
darker recess of a hall, walking, it seemed, noiselessly backwards. He muttered something I could not understand. I
wanted to speak; my throat itched and was parched. He repeated something two or three times until it dawned on me
that he was ordering me to undress. There was something
overpowering about his voice and the darkness around him. I
was incapable of disobeying. I took off my clothes and stood
stark naked, shivering with fear and cold.

It was so dark that I could not see if don Juan and the two
women were around. I heard a soft prolonged hissing from a
source a few feet away from me; then I felt a cool breeze. I
realized that Silvio Manuel was exhaling his breath all over
my body.

He then asked me to sit on my clothes and look at a bright
point which I could easily distinguish in the darkness, a point
that seemed to give out a faint amber light. I stared at it for
what seemed hours, until I suddenly realized that the point of
brightness was Silvio Manuel's left eye. I could then make out
the contour of his whole face and his body. The hall was not
as dark as it had seemed. Silvio Manuel advanced to me and
helped me up. To see in the dark with such clarity enthralled
me. I did not even mind that I was naked or that, as I then
saw, the two women were watching me. Apparently they
could also see in the dark; they were staring at me. I wanted
to put on my pants, but Zoila snatched them out of my hands.

The two women and Silvio Manuel stared at me for a long
time. Then don Juan came out of nowhere, handed me my
shoes, and Zoila led us through a corridor to an open patio
with trees. I made out the dark silhouette of a woman standing
in the middle of the patio. Don Juan spoke to her and she

mumbled something in reply. He told me that she was a southerly woman, that her name was Marta, and that she was a courier to the two westerly women. Marta said that she could bet I had never been introduced to a woman while I was naked; that the normal procedure is to get acquainted and then undress. She laughed out loud. Her laughter was so pleasing, so clear and youthful, that it sent chills through me; it reverberated through the whole house, enhanced by the darkness and the silence there. I looked to don Juan for support. He was gone and so was Silvio Manuel. I was alone with the three women. I became very nervous and asked Marta if she knew where don Juan had gone. At that precise moment, someone grabbed the skin of my armpits. I yelled with pain. I knew that it was Silvio Manuel. He lifted me up as if I weighed nothing and shook my shoes off me. Then he stood me in a shallow tub of ice-cold water that came up to my knees.

I remained in the tub for a long time while all of them scrutinized me. Then Silvio Manuel lifted me up again and set me down next to my shoes, which someone had neatly placed next to the tub.

Don Juan again came out of nowhere and handed me my clothes. He whispered that I should put them on and stay only long enough to be polite. Marta gave me a towel to dry myself. I looked around for the other two women and Silvio Manuel, but they were nowhere in sight.

Marta, don Juan, and I stood in the darkness talking for a long time. She seemed to be speaking mainly to don Juan, but I believed that I was her real audience. I waited for a clue from don Juan to leave, but he appeared to be enjoying Marta's agile conversation. She told him that Zoila and Zuleica had been at the peak of their madness that day. Then she added for my benefit that they were extremely rational most of the time.

As if she were revealing a secret, Marta told us that the reason Zoila's hair looked so unkempt was because at least one third of it was Zuleica's hair. What had happened was that the two of them had had a moment of intense camaraderie and were helping one another to groom their hair. Zuleica braided Zoila's hair as she had done hundreds of times, except that, being out of control, she had braided portions of her own hair in with Zoila's. Marta said that when they got up from their chairs they went into a commotion. She ran to their rescue, but by the time she entered the room, Zuleica had taken over, and since she was more lucid than Zoila that day, she had decided to cut the portion of Zoila's hair that was braided to hers. She got confused in the melee that ensued and cut her own hair instead.

Don Juan was laughing as if it were the funniest thing ever. I heard soft coughlike bursts of laughter coming from the darkness on the far side of the patio.

Marta added that she had to improvise a chignon until Zuleica's hair grew out.

I laughed along with don Juan. I liked Marta. The two other women were abhorrent to me; they gave me a sensation of nausea. Marta, on the other hand, seemed a paragon of calm and silent purpose. I could not see her features, but I imagined her to be very beautiful. The sound of her voice was haunting.

She very politely asked don Juan if I would accept something to eat. He replied that I did not feel comfortable with Zuleica and Zoila, and that I would probably get sick to my stomach. Marta assured me that the two women were gone and took my arm and led us through the darkest hall yet into a well-lit kitchen. The contrast was too great for my eyes. I stood in the doorway trying to get used to the light.

The kitchen had a very high ceiling and was fairly modern and adequate. We sat in a sort of dinette area. Marta was young and very strong; she had a plump, voluptuous figure, a round face, and a small nose and mouth. Her jet-black hair was braided and coiled around her head.

I thought that she must have been as curious to examine me

as I had been to see her. We sat and ate and talked for hours. I was fascinated by her. She was an uneducated woman but she held me spellbound with her talk. She gave us detailed accounts of the preposterous things that Zoila and Zuleica did when they were mad.

As we drove away, don Juan expressed his admiration for Marta. He said that she was perhaps the finest example he knew of how determination can affect a human being. With no background or preparation at all, except for her unbending intent, Marta had successfully tackled the most arduous task imaginable, that of taking care of Zoila, Zuleica, and Silvio Manuel.

I asked don Juan why Silvio Manuel had refused to let me look at him in the light. He replied that Silvio Manuel was in his element in darkness, and that I was going to have countless opportunities to see him. For our first meeting, nonetheless, it was mandatory that he maintain himself within the boundaries of his power, the darkness of the night. Silvio Manuel and the two women lived together because they were a team of formidable *sorcerers*.

Don Juan advised me that I should not make hasty judgments about the westerly women. I had met them at a moment when they were out of control, but their lack of control pertained only to surface behavior. They had an inner core which was unalterable; thus, even at the time of their worst madness they were capable of laughing at their own aberration, as if it were a performance staged by someone else.

Silvio Manuel's case was different. He was in no way deranged; in fact, it was his profound sobriety that enabled him to deal so effectively with those two women, because he and they were opposite extremes. Don Juan said that Silvio Manuel had been born that way and everyone around him acknowledged his difference. Even his benefactor, who was stern and unsparing with everybody, lavished a great deal of attention on Silvio Manuel. It took don Juan years to understand the reason for this preference. Due to something inexplicable in his nature, once Silvio Manuel had entered into the left-side awareness, he never came out of it. His proclivity to remain in a state of heightened awareness, coupled with the superb leadership of his benefactor, allowed him to arrive before anyone else not only at the conclusion that the rule is a map and there is in fact another kind of awareness but also to the actual passageway into that other world of awareness. Don Juan said that Silvio Manuel, in a most impeccable manner, balanced his excessive gains by putting them at the service of their common purpose. He became the silent force behind don Juan.

My last introductory encounter with don Juan's warriors was with the north. Don Juan took me to the city of Guadalajara to fulfill that meeting. He said that our appointment was only a short distance from the center of town and had to be at noon, because the north was the midday. We left the hotel around 11 A.M. and took an easy stroll through the downtown area.

I was walking along without watching where I was going, worried about the meeting, and I collided head-on with a lady who was rushing out of a store. She was carrying packages, which scattered all over the ground. I apologized and began to help her pick them up. Don Juan urged me to hurry because we were going to be late. The lady seemed to be stunned. I held her arm. She was a very slender, tall woman, perhaps in her sixties, very elegantly dressed. She seemed to be a lady of social standing. She was exquisitely polite and assumed the blame, saying that she had been distracted looking for her manservant. She asked me if I would help her locate him in the crowd. I turned to don Juan; he said that the least I could do after nearly killing her was to help her.

I took her packages and we walked back into the store. A short distance away I spotted a forlorn-looking Indian who seemed thoroughly out of place there. The lady called him and he came to her side like a lost puppy. He looked as if he was about to lick her hand.

Don Juan was waiting for us outside the store. He explained to the lady that we were in a hurry and then told her my name. The lady smiled graciously and initiated a handshake. I thought that in her youth she must have been ravishing, because she was still beautiful and alluring.

Don Juan turned to me and abruptly said that her name was Nelida, that she was of the north, and that she was a *dreamer*. Then he made me face the manservant and said that his name was Genaro Flores, and that he was the man of action, the warrior of deeds in the party. My surprise was total. All three of them had a belly laugh; the greater my dismay, the more they seemed to enjoy it.

Don Genaro gave the packages away to a group of children, telling them that his employer, the kind lady who was talking, had bought those things as a present for them; it was her good deed for the day. Then we strolled in silence for half a block. I was tongue-tied. Suddenly Nelida pointed to a store and asked us to wait just an instant because she had to pick up a box of nylons that they were holding for her there. She peered at me, smiling, her eyes shining, and told me that, all kidding aside, sorcery or no sorcery, she had to wear nylons and lace panties. Don Juan and don Genaro laughed like two idiots. I stared at Nelida because I could not do anything else. There was something about her that was utterly earthly and yet she was almost ethereal.

She kiddingly told don Juan to hold on to me because I was about to pass out. Then she politely asked don Genaro to run in and get her order from a specific clerk. As he started in, Nelida seemed to change her mind and called him back, but he apparently did not hear her and disappeared inside the store. She excused herself and ran after him.

Don Juan pressed my back to get me out of my turmoil. He said that I would meet the other northerly woman, whose name was Florinda, by herself at another time, because she was to be my link into another cycle, another mood. He described Florinda as a carbon copy of Nelida, or vice versa.

I remarked that Nelida was so sophisticated and stylish that I could imagine seeing her in a fashion magazine. The fact that she was beautiful and so fair, perhaps of French or northern Italian extraction, had surprised me. Although Vicente was not an Indian either, his rural appearance made him less of an anomaly. I asked don Juan why there were non-Indians in his world. He said that power is what selects the warriors of a Nagual's party, and that it is impossible to know its designs.

We waited in front of the store for perhaps half an hour. Don Juan seemed to get impatient and asked me to go inside and tell them to hurry. I walked into the store. It was not a big place, there was no back door, and yet they were nowhere in sight. I asked the clerks, but they could not help me.

I confronted don Juan and demanded to know what had happened. He said that they had either disappeared into thin air, or had sneaked out while he was cracking my back.

I raged at him that most of his people were tricksters. He laughed until tears were rolling down his cheeks. He said that I was the ideal dupe. My self-importance made me a most enjoyable subject. He was laughing so hard at my annoyance that he had to lean against a wall.

La Gorda gave me an account of her first meeting with the members of don Juan's party. Her version differed only in content; the form was the same. The warriors were perhaps a bit more violent with her, but she had understood this as their attempt to shake her out of her slumber, and also as a natural reaction to what she considered her ugly personality.

As we reviewed don Juan's world, we realized that it was a replica of his benefactor's world. It could be seen as consisting either of groups or households. There was a group of four independent pairs of apparent sisters who worked and lived together; another group of three men who were don Juan's age and were very close to him; a team of two somewhat younger men, the couriers Emilito and Juan Tuma; and finally a team of two younger, southerly women who seemed to be related to each other, Marta and Teresa. At other times it could be seen as consisting of four separate households, located quite far from one another in different areas of Mexico. One was made up of the two westerly women, Zuleica and Zoila, Silvio Manuel, and the courier Marta. The next was composed of the southerly women, Cecilia and Delia, don Juan's courier, Emilito, and the courier Teresa. Another household was formed by the easterly women, Carmela and Hermelinda, Vicente, and the courier Juan Tuma; and the last, of the northerly women, Nelida and Florinda, and don Genaro.

According to don Juan, his world did not have the harmony and balance of his benefactor's. The only two women who thoroughly balanced one another, and who looked like identical twins were the northerly warriors, Nelida and Florinda. Nelida once told me in casual conversation, they were so alike that they even had the same blood type.

For me one of the most pleasant surprises of our interaction was the transformation of Zuleica and Zoila, who had been so abhorrent. They turned out to be, as don Juan had said, the most sober and dutiful warriors imaginable. I could not believe my eyes when I saw them again. Their mad spell had passed and they now looked like two well-dressed Mexican ladies, tall, dark, and muscular, with brilliant dark eyes like pieces of shiny black obsidian. They laughed and joked with me about what had happened the night of our first meeting, as if someone else and not they had been involved in it. I could easily understand don Juan's turmoil with the westerly warriors of his benefactor's party. It was impossible for me to accept that Zuleica and Zoila could ever turn into such obnoxious, nauseating creatures as I had first encountered. I was to witness their metamorphoses many times, yet I was never again able to judge them as harshly as I had on our first encounter. More than anything else, their outrages made me feel sad.

But the biggest surprise to me was Silvio Manuel. In the darkness of our first meeting I had imagined him to be an imposing man, an overpowering giant. In fact, he was tiny, but not small-boned tiny. His body was like the body of a jockey—small, yet perfectly proportioned. He looked to me as if he might be a gymnast. His physical control was so remarkable that he could puff himself up like a toad, to nearly twice his size, by contracting all the muscles of his body. He used to give astounding demonstrations of how he could dislodge his joints and put them back together again without any overt signs of pain. Looking at Silvio Manuel, I always experienced a deep unfamiliar feeling of fright. To me he seemed like a visitor from another time. He was pale-dark, like a bronze statue. His features were sharp; his aquiline nose, full lips, and widely separated, slanted eyes made him look like a stylized figure on a Mayan fresco. He was friendly and warm during the daytime, but as soon as the twilight set in, he would become unfathomable. His voice would change. He would sit in a dark corner and let the darkness swallow him. All that was visible of him was his left eye, which remained open and acquired a strange shine, reminiscent of the eyes of a feline.

A secondary issue that came up in the course of our interaction with don Juan's warriors was the subject of *controlled folly*. Don Juan gave me a succinct explanation once when he was discussing the two categories into which all the women warriors are mandatorily divided, the *dreamers* and the *stalkers*. He said that all the members of his party did *dreaming* and *stalking* as part of their daily lives, but that the women who made up the planet of the *dreamers* and the planet of the *stalkers* were the foremost authorities on their respective activities.

The *stalkers* are the ones who take the brunt of the daily world. They are the business managers, the ones who deal with people. Everything that has to do with the world of

ordinary affairs goes through them. The *stalkers* are the practitioners of *controlled folly*, just as the *dreamers* are the practitioners of *dreaming*. In other words, *controlled folly* is the basis
for *stalking*, as dreams are the basis for *dreaming*. Don Juan
said that, generally speaking, a warrior's greatest accomplishment in the second attention is *dreaming*, and in the first attention his greatest accomplishment is *stalking*.

I had misunderstood what don Juan's warriors were doing
to me in our first meetings. I took their actions as instances of
trickery—and that would still be my impression today had it
not been for the idea of *controlled folly*. Don Juan said that their
actions with me had been masterful lessons in *stalking*. He told
me that the art of *stalking* was what his benefactor had taught
him before anything else. In order to survive among his benefactor's warriors he had had to learn that art quickly. In my
case, he said, since I did not have to contend by myself with
his warriors, I had to learn *dreaming* first. When the time was
right, Florinda would step out to guide me into the complexi-
ties of *stalking*. No one else could deliberately talk to me about
it; they could only give me direct demonstrations, as they had
already done in our first meetings.

Don Juan explained to me at great length that Florinda was
one of the foremost practitioners of *stalking* because she had
been trained in every intricacy of it by his benefactor and his
four female warriors who were *stalkers*. Florinda was the first
female warrior to come into don Juan's world, and because of
that, she was to be my personal guide—not only in the art of
stalking, but also in the mystery of the third attention, if I ever
got there. Don Juan did not elaborate on this. He said it
would have to wait until I was ready, first to learn *stalking*,
and then to enter into the third attention.

Don Juan said that his benefactor had taken extra time and
care with him and his warriors in everything that pertained to
their mastering the art of *stalking*. He used complex ploys to
create an appropriate context for a counterpoint between the
dictums of the rule and the behavior of the warriors in the

daily world as they interacted with people. He believed that that was the way to convince them that, in the absence of self-importance, a warrior's only way of dealing with the social milieu is in terms of *controlled folly*.

In the course of working out his ploys, don Juan's benefactor would pit the actions of people and the actions of the warriors against the commands of the rule, and would then sit back and let the natural drama unfold itself. The folly of the people would take the lead for a while and drag the warriors into it, as seems to be the natural course, only to be vanquished in the end by the more encompassing designs of the rule.

Don Juan told us that at first he resented his benefactor's control over the players. He even told him that to his face. His benefactor was not fazed. He argued that his control was merely an illusion created by the Eagle. He was only an impeccable warrior, and his actions were a humble attempt to mirror the Eagle.

Don Juan said that the force with which his benefactor carried out his designs originated from his knowledge that the Eagle is real and final, and that what people do is utter folly. The two together gave rise to *controlled folly*, which don Juan's benefactor described as the only bridge between the folly of people and the finality of the Eagle's dictums.

11

The Nagual Woman

Don Juan said that when he was put in the care of the westerly women to be cleansed, he was also put under the guidance of the northerly woman who was comparable to Florinda, the number-one *stalker*, who taught him the principles of that art. She and his benefactor gave him the actual means to secure the three male warriors, the one courier, and the four female *stalkers* who were to make up his party.

The eight female seers of his benefactor's group had searched for the distinctive configurations of luminosity and had had no difficulty whatever in finding the appropriate types of male and female warriors for don Juan's party. His benefactor, however, did not permit those seers to do anything to gather the warriors they had found. It was left to don Juan to apply the principles of *stalking* and secure them.

The first warrior to appear was Vicente. Don Juan did not have enough of a command of *stalking* to be able to draft him. His benefactor and the northerly *stalker* had to do most of the work. Then came Silvio Manuel, later don Genaro, and finally Emilito, the courier.

Florinda was the first female warrior. She was followed by Zoila, then Delia, and then Carmela. Don Juan said that his benefactor had insisted relentlessly that they deal with the world exclusively in terms of *controlled folly*. The end result was a stupendous team of practitioners, who thought up and executed the most intricate schemes.

When they had all acquired a degree of proficiency in the art of *stalking*, their benefactor thought it was time for him to find the Nagual woman for them. True to his policy of helping everyone to help themselves, he waited to bring her into their world, not only until all of them were expert *stalkers*, but until don Juan had learned to *see*. Although don Juan regretted immensely the time wasted in waiting, he conceded that their joint effort in securing her created a stronger tie among all of them. It revitalized their commitment to seek their freedom.

His benefactor began to unfold his strategy for drawing in the Nagual woman by all of a sudden becoming a devout Catholic. He demanded that don Juan, being the heir to his knowledge, behave like a son and go to church with him. He dragged him to mass nearly every day. Don Juan said that his benefactor, who was very charming and glib, would introduce him to everyone in church as his son, a bone-setter.

Don Juan, by his own account an uncivilized pagan at that time, was mortified to find himself in social situations where he had to talk and give an account of himself. He put his mind at ease with the idea that his benefactor had an ulterior motive for everything he was doing. He attempted to deduce from observing him what his reasons might be. His benefactor's actions were consistent and seemed aboveboard. As an exemplary Catholic, he gained the trust of scores of people, especially the parish priest, who held him in high esteem, considering him a friend and confidant. Don Juan could not figure out what he was up to. The thought crossed his mind that his benefactor might have sincerely taken up Catholicism, or gone mad. He had not yet understood that a warrior never loses his mind under any circumstances.

Don Juan's qualms about going to church vanished when his benefactor began introducing him to the daughters of people he was acquainted with. He enjoyed that, although he felt ill at ease. Don Juan thought that his benefactor was helping him to exercise his tongue. He was neither glib nor charming, and his benefactor had said that a Nagual, perforce, has to be both.

One Sunday during mass, after nearly a year of almost daily attendance, don Juan found out the real reason for their going to church. He was kneeling next to a girl named Olinda, the daughter of one of his benefactor's acquaintances. He turned to exchange a glance with her, as had become their custom after months of daily contact. Their eyes met, and suddenly don Juan *saw* her as a luminous being—and then he *saw* her doubleness. Olinda was a double woman. His benefactor had known it all along, and had taken the most difficult path in order to put don Juan in touch with her. Don Juan confessed to us that the moment was overwhelming to him.

His benefactor knew that don Juan had *seen*. His mission to put the double beings together had been completed successfully and impeccably. He stood up and his eyes swept every corner of that church, then he walked out without a backward glance. There was nothing more for him to do there.

Don Juan said that when his benefactor walked out in the middle of mass, all heads turned. Don Juan wanted to follow him, but Olinda boldly clasped his hand and held him back. He knew then that the power of *seeing* had not been his alone. Something had gone through both of them and they were transfixed. Don Juan realized all of a sudden that not only had the mass ended, but that they were already outside the church. His benefactor was trying to calm Olinda's mother, who was incensed and shamed by their unexpected and inadmissible display of affection.

Don Juan was at a loss as to what to do next. He knew that it was up to him to figure out a plan. He had the resources, but the importance of the event made him lose confidence in his ability. He forsook his training as a *stalker* and became lost in the intellectual dilemma of whether or not to treat Olinda as *controlled folly*.

His benefactor told him that he could not help him. His duty had been only to put them together, and that was where his responsibility ended. It was up to don Juan to take the necessary steps to secure her. He suggested that don Juan even consider marrying her, if that was what was needed. Only after she came to him of her own accord could he help don Juan by directly intervening with her as a Nagual.

Don Juan tried a formal courtship. He was not well received by her parents, who could not conceive of someone from a different social class as a suitor for their daughter. Olinda was not an Indian; her family were middle-class urban dwellers, owners of a small business. The father had other plans for his daughter. He threatened to send her away if don Juan persisted in his intention to marry her.

Don Juan said that double beings, especially women, are extraordinarily conservative, even timid. Olinda was no exception. After their initial exhilaration in church, she was overtaken by caution, and then by fear. Her own reactions scared her.

As a strategic maneuver, his benefactor made don Juan retreat, to make it appear as if he were acquiescing to his father, who had not approved of the girl—which was the assumption of everyone who had witnessed the incident in church. People gossiped that their display had displeased his father so intensely that his father, who was such a devout Catholic, had never returned to church.

His benefactor told don Juan that a warrior is never under siege. To be under siege implies that one has personal possessions that could be blockaded. A warrior has nothing in the world except his impeccability, and impeccability cannot be threatened. Nonetheless, in a battle for one's life, such as the one don Juan was waging to secure the Nagual woman, a warrior should strategically use every means available.

Accordingly, don Juan resolved to use any portion of his *stalker's* knowledge that he had to, to get the girl. To that end, he engaged Silvio Manuel to use his sorcerer's arts, which even at that early stage were formidable, to abduct the girl. Silvio Manuel and Genaro, who was a true daredevil, stole into the girl's house disguised as old washerwomen. It was midday and everyone in the house was busy preparing food for a large group of relatives and friends who were coming to dinner. They were having an informal going-away party for Olinda. Silvio Manuel was counting on the likelihood that people who saw two strange washerwomen coming in with bundles of clothes would assume that it had to do with Olinda's party and would not get suspicious. Don Juan had supplied Silvio Manuel and Genaro beforehand with all the information they needed concerning the routines of the members of the household. He told them that the washerwomen usually carried their bundles of washed clothes into the house and left them in a storage room to be ironed. Carrying a large bundle of clothes, Silvio Manuel and Genaro went directly into that room, knowing that Olinda would be there.

Don Juan said that Silvio Manuel went up to Olinda and used his mesmeric powers to make her faint. They put her inside a sack, wrapped the sack with her bed sheets, and walked out, leaving behind the bundle they had carried in. They bumped into her father at the door. He did not even glance at them.

Don Juan's benefactor was utterly put out with their maneuver. He ordered don Juan to take the girl back immediately to her house. It was imperative, he said, that the double woman come to the benefactor's house of her own free will, perhaps not with the idea of joining them but at least because they interested her.

Don Juan felt that everything was lost—the odds against getting her back into her house unnoticed were too great—but Silvio Manuel figured out a solution. He proposed that they should let the four women of don Juan's party take the girl to a deserted road, where don Juan would rescue her.

Silvio Manuel wanted the women to pretend that they were kidnapping her. At some point along the road someone would see them and come in pursuit. Their pursuer would overtake them and they would drop the sack, with a degree of force so as to be convincing. The pursuer would be, of course, don Juan, who would happen miraculously to be at just the right place at the right time.

Silvio Manuel demanded true-to-life action. He ordered the women to gag the girl, who by then would surely be awake and screaming inside the sack, and then to run for miles carrying the sack. He told them to hide from their pursuer. Finally, after a truly exhausting ordeal, they were to drop the sack in such a way that the girl could witness a most vicious fight between don Juan and the four women. Silvio Manuel told the women that this had to be utterly realistic. He armed them with sticks and instructed them to hit don Juan convincingly before they were driven away.

Of the women, Zoila was the one most easily carried away by hysteria; as soon as they began whacking don Juan she became possessed by her role and gave a chilling performance, striking don Juan so hard that flesh was torn from his back and shoulders. For a moment it seemed that the kidnappers were going to win. Silvio Manuel had to come out of his hiding place and, pretending to be a passerby, remind them that it was only a ploy and that it was time to run away.

Don Juan thus became Olinda's savior and protector. He told her that he could not take her back to her house himself because he had been injured, but he would send her back instead with his pious father.

She helped him walk to his benefactor's house. Don Juan said that he did not have to pretend injury; he was bleeding profusely and barely made it to the door. When Olinda told his benefactor what had happened his benefactor's desire to laugh was so excruciating he had to disguise it as weeping.

Don Juan had his wounds bandaged and then went to bed. Olinda began to explain to him why her father was opposed to him, but she did not finish. Don Juan's benefactor came into the room and told her that it was evident to him, from observing her walk, that the kidnappers had injured her back. He offered to align it for her before it became critical.

Olinda hesitated. Don Juan's benefactor reminded her that the kidnappers had not been playing—they had nearly killed his son, after all. That comment sufficed; she came to the benefactor's side and let him give her a sound blow on her shoulder blade. It made a cracking sound and Olinda entered into a state of heightened awareness. He disclosed the rule to her, and just like don Juan, she accepted it in full. There was no doubt, no hesitation.

The Nagual woman and don Juan found completeness and silence in each other's company. Don Juan said that the feeling they had for each other had nothing to do with affection or need; it was rather a shared physical sense that an ominous barrier had been broken within them, and they were one and the same being.

Don Juan and his Nagual woman, as the rule prescribed, worked together for years to find the set of four female *dreamers*, who turned out to be Nelida, Zuleica, Cecilia, and Hermelinda and the three couriers, Juan Tuma, Teresa, and Marta. Finding them was another occasion when the pragmatic nature of the rule was made clear to don Juan: All of them were exactly what the rule said they were going to be. Their advent introduced a new cycle for everyone, don Juan's benefactor and his party included. For don Juan and his warriors it meant the cycle of *dreaming*, and for his benefactor and his party it meant a period of unequalled impeccability in their acts.

His benefactor explained to don Juan that when he was young and was first introduced to the idea of the rule as the means to freedom, he had been elated, transfixed with joy. Freedom to him was a reality around the corner. When he came to understand the nature of the rule as a map, his hopes and optimism were redoubled. Later on, sobriety took hold of his life; the older he got, the less chance he saw for his success and the success of his party. Finally he became convinced that

THE EAGLE'S GIFT

no matter what they did, the odds were too great against their
tenuous human awareness ever flying free. He made peace
with himself and his fate, and surrendered to failure. He told
the Eagle from his inner self that he was glad and proud to
have nourished his awareness. The Eagle was welcome to it.

Don Juan told us that the same mood was shared by all the
members of his benefactor's party. The freedom proposed in
the rule was something they considered unattainable. They
had caught glimpses of the annihilating force that the Eagle is,
and felt that they did not stand a chance against it. All of them
had agreed, nevertheless, that they would live their lives impeccably for no other reason than to be impeccable.

Don Juan said that his benefactor and his party, in spite of
their feelings of inadequacy, or perhaps because of those feelings, did find their freedom. They did enter into the third
attention—not as a group, however, but one by one. The fact
that they found the passageway was the final corroboration of
the truth contained in the rule. The last one to leave the world
of everyday-life awareness was his benefactor. He complied
with the rule and took don Juan's Nagual woman with him.
As the two of them dissolved into total awareness, don Juan
and all his warriors were made to explode from within—he
could find no other way of describing the feeling entailed in
being forced to forget all they had witnessed of their benefactor's world.

The one who never forgot was Silvio Manuel. It was he
who engaged don Juan in the backbreaking effort of bringing
back together the members of their group, all of whom had
been scattered. He then plunged them into the task of finding
the totality of themselves. It took them years to accomplish
both tasks.

Don Juan had extensively discussed the topic of forgetting,
but only in connection with their great difficulty in getting
together again and starting over without their benefactor. He
never told us exactly what it entailed to forget or to gain the
totality of oneself. In that respect he was true to his benefac-

tor's teachings, only helping us to help ourselves.

To this effect, he trained la Gorda and me to *see together* and was able to show us that, although human beings appear to a seer as luminous eggs, the egglike shape is an external cocoon, a shell of luminosity that houses a most intriguing, haunting, mesmeric core made up of concentric circles of yellowish luminosity, the color of a candle's flame. During our final session, he had us *see* people milling around a church. It was late afternoon, almost dark, yet the creatures inside their rigid, luminous cocoons radiated enough light to render everything around them crystal clear. The sight was wondrous.

Don Juan explained that the egg-shaped shells which seemed so bright to us were indeed dull. The luminosity emanated from the brilliant core; the shell in fact dulled its radiance. Don Juan revealed to us that the shell must be broken in order to liberate that being. It must be broken from the inside at the right time, just as creatures that hatch out of eggs break their shells. If they fail to do so, they suffocate and die. As with creatures that hatch out of eggs, there is no way for a warrior to break the shell of his luminosity until the time is right.

Don Juan told us that losing the human form was the only means of breaking that shell, the only means of liberating that haunting luminous core, the core of awareness which is the Eagle's food. To break the shell means remembering the other self, and arriving at the totality of oneself.

Don Juan and his warriors did arrive at the totality of themselves, and turned then to their last task, which was to find a new pair of double beings. Don Juan said that they thought it was going to be a simple matter—everything else had been relatively easy for them. They had no idea that the apparent effortlessness of their accomplishments as warriors was a consequence of their benefactor's mastery and personal power.

Their quest for a new pair of double beings was fruitless. In all their searching, they never came across a double woman. They found several double men, but they were all well-situated, busy, prolific, and so satisfied with their lives that it would have been useless to approach them. They did not need to find purpose in life. They thought they had already found it.

Don Juan said that one day he realized that he and his group were getting old, and there seemed to be no hope of ever accomplishing their task. That was the first time they felt the sting of despair and impotence.

Silvio Manuel insisted that they should resign themselves and live impeccably without hope of finding their freedom. It seemed plausible to don Juan that this might indeed be the key to everything. In this respect he found himself following in his benefactor's footsteps. He came to accept that an unconquerable pessimism overtakes a warrior at a certain point on his path. A sense of defeat, or perhaps more accurately, a sense of unworthiness, comes upon him almost unawares. Don Juan said that, before, he used to laugh at his benefactor's doubts and could not bring himself to believe that he worried in earnest. In spite of the protests and warnings of Silvio Manuel, don Juan had thought it was all a giant ploy designed to teach them something.

Since he could not believe that his benefactor's doubts were real, neither could he believe that his benefactor's resolution to live impeccably without hope of freedom was genuine. When he finally grasped that his benefactor, in all seriousness, had resigned himself to fail, it also dawned on him that a warrior's resolution to live impeccably in spite of everything cannot be approached as a strategy to ensure success. Don Juan and his party proved this truth for themselves when they realized for a fact that the odds against them were astonishing. Don Juan said that at such moments a lifelong training takes over, and the warrior enters into a state of unsurpassed humility; when the true poverty of his human resources becomes undeniable, the warrior has no recourse but to step back and lower his head.

Don Juan marveled that this realization seems to have no

effect on the female warriors of a party; the disarray seems to leave them unfazed. He told us that he had noted this in his benefactor's party: the females were never as worried and morose about their fate as were the males. They seemed simply to acquiesce in the judgment of don Juan's benefactor and follow him without showing signs of emotional wear and tear. If the women were ruffled at some level, they were indifferent to it. To be busy was all that counted for them. It was as if only the males had bid for freedom and felt the impact of a counter-bidding.

In his own group, don Juan observed the same contrast. The women readily agreed with him when he said that his resources were inadequate. He could only conclude that the women, although they never mentioned it, had never believed they had any resources to begin with. There was consequently no way they could feel disappointed or despondent at finding out they were impotent: They had known it all along.

Don Juan told us that the reason the Eagle demanded twice as many female warriors as males was precisely because females have an inherent balance which is lacking in males. At the crucial moment, it is the men who get hysterical and commit suicide if they judge that everything is lost. A woman may kill herself due to lack of direction and purpose, but not because of the failure of a system to which she happens to belong.

After don Juan and his party of warriors had given up hope —or rather, as don Juan put it, after he and the male warriors had reached rock bottom and the women had found suitable ways to humor them—don Juan finally stumbled upon a double man he could approach. I was that double man. He said that since no one in his right mind is going to volunteer for such a preposterous project as a struggle for freedom, he had to follow his benefactor's teachings and, in true *stalker's* style, reel me in as he had reeled in the members of his own party. He needed to have me alone at a place where he could apply physical pressure to my body, and it was necessary that I go there of my own accord. He lured me into his house with great ease—as he said, securing the double man is never a great problem. The difficulty is to find one who is available.

That first visit to his house was, from the point of view of my daily awareness, an uneventful session. Don Juan was charming and joked with me. He guided the conversation to the fatigue the body experiences after long drives, a subject that seemed thoroughly inconsequential to me, as a student of anthropology. Then he made the casual comment that my back appeared to be out of alignment, and without another word put a hand on my chest and straightened me up and gave me a sound rap on the back. He caught me so unprepared that I blacked out. When I opened my eyes again I felt as if he had broken my spine, but I knew that I was different. I was someone else and not the me I knew. From then on, whenever I saw him he would make me shift from my right-side awareness to my left, and then he would reveal the rule to me.

Almost immediately after finding me, don Juan encountered a double woman. He did not put me in touch with her through a scheme, as his benefactor had done with him, but devised a ploy, as effective and elaborate as any of his benefactor's, by which he himself enticed and secured the double woman. He assumed this burden because he believed that it was the benefactor's duty to secure both double beings immediately upon finding them, and then to put them together as partners in an inconceivable enterprise.

He told me that one day, when he was living in Arizona, he had gone to a government office to fill out an application. The lady at the desk told him to take it to an employee in the adjacent section, and without looking, she pointed to her left. Don Juan followed the direction of her outstretched arm and *saw* a double woman sitting at a desk. When he took his application to her he realized that she was just a young girl. She told him that she had nothing to do with applications. Nevertheless, out of sympathy for a poor old Indian, she took the time to help him process it.

Some legal documents were needed, documents which don Juan had in his pocket, but he pretended total ignorance and helplessness. He made it seem that the bureaucratic organization was an enigma to him. It was not difficult at all to portray total mindlessness, don Juan said; all he had to do was revert to what had once been his normal state of awareness. It was to his purpose to prolong his interaction with the girl for as long as he could. His mentor had told him, and he himself had verified it in his search, that double women are quite rare. His mentor had also warned him that they have inner resources that make them highly volatile. Don Juan was afraid that if he did not play his cards expertly she would leave. He played on her sympathy to gain time. He created further delay by pretending that the legal documents were lost. Nearly every day he would bring in a different one to her. She would read it and regretfully tell him that it was not the right one. The girl was so moved by his sorry condition that she even volunteered to pay for a lawyer to draw him up an affidavit in lieu of the papers.

After three months of this, don Juan thought it was time to produce the documents. By then she had gotten used to him and almost expected to see him every day. Don Juan came one last time to express his thanks and say goodbye. He told her that he would have liked to bring her a gift to show his appreciation, but he did not have money even to eat. She was moved by his candor and took him to lunch. As they were eating he mused that a gift does not necessarily have to be an object that one buys. It could be something that is only for the eyes of the beholder. Something to remember rather than to possess.

She was intrigued by his words. Don Juan reminded her that she had expressed compassion for the Indians and their condition as paupers. He asked her if she would like to see the Indians in a different light—not as paupers but as artists. He told her that he knew an old man who was the last of his line of power dancers. He assured her that the man would dance for her at his request; and furthermore, he promised her that never in her life had she seen anything like it nor would she ever again. It was something that only Indians witnessed.

She was delighted at the idea. She picked him up after her work, and they headed for the hills where he told her the Indian lived. Don Juan took her to his own house. He made her stop the car quite a distance away, and they began to walk the rest of the way. Before they reached the house he stopped and drew a line with his foot in the sandy, dried dirt. He told her that the line was a boundary and coaxed her to step across.

The Nagual woman herself told me that up to that point she had been very intrigued with the possibility of witnessing a genuine Indian dancer, but when the old Indian drew a line on the dirt and called it a boundary, she began to hesitate. Then she became outright alarmed when he told her that the boundary was for her alone, and that once she stepped over it there was no way of returning.

The Indian apparently saw her consternation and tried to put her at ease. He politely patted her on the arm and gave her his guarantee that no harm would come to her while he was around. The boundary could be explained, he told her, as a form of symbolic payment to the dancer, for he did not want money. Ritual was in lieu of money, and ritual required that she step over the boundary of her own accord.

The old Indian gleefully stepped over the line and told her that to him all of it was sheer Indian nonsense, but that the dancer, who was watching them from inside the house, had to be humored if she wanted to see him dance.

The Nagual woman said that she suddenly became so afraid that she could not move to cross the line. The old Indian made an effort to persuade her, saying that stepping over that boundary was beneficial to the entire body. Crossing it had not only made him feel younger, it had actually *made* him younger, such power did that boundary have. To demonstrate his point, he crossed back again and immediately his shoulders slouched, the corners of his mouth drooped, his eyes lost their shine. The Nagual woman could not deny the differences the crossings had made.

Don Juan recrossed the line a third time. He breathed deeply, expanding his chest, his movements brisk and bold. The Nagual woman said that the thought crossed her mind that he might even make sexual advances. Her car was too far away to make a run for it. The only thing she could do was to tell herself that it was stupid to fear that old Indian.

Then the old man made another appeal to her reason and to her sense of humor. In a conspiratorial tone, as if he were revealing a secret with some reluctance, he told her that he was just pretending to be young to please the dancer, and that if she did not help him by crossing the line, he was going to faint at any moment from the stress of walking without slouching. He walked back and forth across the line to show her the immense strain involved in his pantomime.

The Nagual woman said that his pleading eyes revealed the pain his old body was going through to mimic youth. She crossed the line to help him and be done with it; she wanted to go home.

The moment she crossed the line, don Juan took a prodigious jump and glided over the roof of the house. The Nagual woman said that he flew like a huge boomerang. When he landed next to her she fell on her back. Her fright was beyond anything she had ever experienced, but so was her excitement at having witnessed such a marvel. She did not even ask how he had accomplished such a magnificent feat. She wanted to run back to her car and head for home.

The old man helped her up and apologized for having tricked her. In fact, he said, he himself was the dancer and his flight over the house had been his dance. He asked her if she had paid attention to the direction of his flight. The Nagual woman circled her hand counterclockwise. He patted her head paternally and told her that it was very auspicious that she had been attentive. Then he said that she may have injured her back in her fall, and that he could not just let her go without making sure she was all right. Boldly, he straightened her shoulders and lifted her chin and the back of her head, as if he were directing her to extend her spine. He then gave her a sound smack between her shoulder blades, literally knocking all the air out of her lungs. For a moment she was unable to breathe and she fainted.

When she regained consciousness, she was inside his house. Her nose was bleeding, her ears were buzzing, her breathing was accelerated, she could not focus her eyes. He instructed her to take deep breaths to a count of eight. The more she breathed, the clearer everything became. At one point, she told me, the whole room became incandescent; everything glowed with an amber light. She became stupefied and could not breathe deeply any more. The amber light by then was so thick it resembled fog. Then the fog turned into amber cobwebs. It finally dissipated, but the world remained uniformly amber for a while longer.

Don Juan began to talk to her then. He took her outside the house and showed her that the world was divided into two halves. The left side was clear but the right side was veiled in amber fog. He told her that it is monstrous to think that the world is understandable or that we ourselves are understandable. He said that what she was perceiving was an enigma, a mystery that one could only accept in humbleness and awe.

He then revealed the rule to her. Her clarity of mind was so intense that she understood everything he said. The rule seemed to her appropriate and self-evident.

He explained to her that the two sides of a human being are totally separate and that it takes great discipline and determination to break that seal and go from one side to the other. A double being has a great advantage: the condition of being double permits relatively easy movement between the compartments on the right side. The great disadvantage of double beings is that by virtue of having two compartments they are sedentary, conservative, afraid of change.

Don Juan said to her that his intention had been to make

her shift from her extreme right compartment to her more lucid, sharper left-right side, but instead, through some inexplicable quirk, his blow had sent her all across her doubleness, from her everyday extreme-right side to her extreme-left side. He tried four times to make her revert back to a normal state of awareness, but to no avail. His blows helped her, however, to turn her perception of the wall of fog on and off at will. Although he had not intended it, don Juan had been right in saying that the line was a one-way boundary for her. Once she crossed it, just like Silvio Manuel, she never returned.

When don Juan put the Nagual woman and me face to face, neither of us had known of the other's existence, yet we instantly felt that we were familiar with one another. Don Juan knew from his own experience that the solace double beings feel in each other's company is indescribable, and far too brief. He told us that we had been put together by forces incomprehensible to our reason, and that the only thing we did not have was time. Every minute might be the last; therefore, it had to be lived with the spirit.

Once don Juan had put us together, all that was left for him and his warriors to do was find four female *stalkers*, three male warriors, and one male courier to make up our party. To that end, don Juan found Lydia, Josefina, la Gorda, Rosa, Benigno, Nestor, Pablito, and the courier Eligio. Each one of them was a replica in an undeveloped form of the members of don Juan's own party.

12

The Not-Doings of Silvio Manuel

Don Juan and his warriors sat back to allow the Nagual woman and myself room to enact the rule—that is, to nourish, enhance, and lead the eight warriors to freedom. Everything seemed perfect, yet something was wrong. The first set of female warriors don Juan had found were *dreamers* when they should have been *stalkers*. He did not know how to explain this anomaly. He could only conclude that power had put those women in his path in a manner that made it impossible to refuse them.

There was another striking anomaly that was even more baffling to don Juan and his party; three of the women and the three male warriors were incapable of entering into a state of heightened awareness, despite don Juan's titanic efforts. They were groggy, out of focus, and could not break the seal, the membrane that separates their two sides. They were nicknamed the drunkards, because they staggered around without muscular coordination. The courier Eligio and la Gorda were the only ones with an extraordinary degree of awareness, especially Eligio, who was par with any of don Juan's own people.

The three girls clustered together and made an unshakable unit. So did the three men. Groups of three when the rule prescribes four were something ominous. The number three is a symbol of dynamics, change, movement, and above all, a symbol of revitalization.

The rule was no longer serving as a map. And yet it was not conceivable that an error was involved. Don Juan and his warriors argued that power does not make mistakes. They pondered the question in their *dreaming* and *seeing*. They wondered whether they had perhaps been too hasty, and simply had not *seen* that the three women and the three men were inept.

Don Juan confided to me that he saw two relevant questions. One was the pragmatic problem of our presence among them. The other was the question of the rule's validity. Their benefactor had guided them to the certainty that the rule encompassed everything a warrior might be concerned with. He had not prepared them for the eventuality that the rule might prove to be inapplicable.

La Gorda said that the women of don Juan's party never had any problems with me; it was only the males who were at a loss. To the men, it was incomprehensible and unacceptable that the rule was incongruous in my case. The women, however, were confident that sooner or later the reason for my being there was going to be made clear. I had observed how the women kept themselves detached from the emotional turmoil, seeming to be completely unconcerned with the outcome. They seemed to know without any reasonable doubt that my case had to be somehow included in the rule. After all, I had definitely helped them by accepting my role. Thanks to the Nagual woman and myself, don Juan and his party had completed their cycle and were almost free.

The answer came to them at last through Silvio Manuel. His *seeing* revealed that the three little sisters and the Genaros were not inept; it was rather that I was not the right Nagual for them. I was incapable of leading them because I had an unsuspected configuration that did not match the pattern laid down by the rule, a configuration which don Juan as a seer had overlooked. My luminous body gave the appearance of having four compartments when in reality it had only three. There was another rule for what they called a "three-pronged Nagual." I belonged to that other rule. Silvio Manuel said that I was like a bird hatched by the warmth and care of birds of a different species. All of them were still bound to help me, as I myself was bound to do anything for them, but I did not belong with them.

Don Juan assumed responsibility for me because he had brought me into their midst, but my presence among them forced them all to exert themselves to the maximum, searching for two things: an explanation of what I was doing among them, and a solution to the problem of what to do about it.

Silvio Manuel very quickly hit upon a way to dislodge me from their midst. He took over the task of directing the project, but since he did not have the patience or energy to deal with me personally, he commissioned don Juan to do so as his surrogate. Silvio Manuel's goal was to prepare me for a moment when a courier bearing the rule pertinent to a three-pronged Nagual would make himself or herself available to me. He said that it was not his role to reveal that portion of the rule. I had to wait, just as all the others had to wait, for the right time.

There was still another serious problem that added more confusion. It had to do with la Gorda, and in the long run with me. La Gorda had been accepted into my party as a southerly woman. Don Juan and the rest of his seers had attested to it. She seemed to be in the same category with Cecilia, Delia, and the two female couriers. The similarities were undeniable. Then la Gorda lost all her superfluous weight and slimmed down to half her size. The change was so radical and profound that she became something else.

She had gone unnoticed for a long time simply because all the other warriors were too preoccupied with my difficulties to pay any attention to her. Her change was so drastic, however, that they were forced to focus on her, and what they *saw* was that she was not a southerly woman at all. The bulkiness of her body had misled their previous *seeing*. They remembered then that from the first moment she came into their midst, la Gorda could not really get along with Cecilia, Delia, and the other southerly women. She was, on the other hand, utterly charmed and at ease with Nelida and Florinda, because in fact she had always been like them. That meant that there were two northerly *dreamers* in my party, la Gorda and Rosa—a blatant discrepancy with the rule.

Don Juan and his warriors were more than baffled. They understood everything that was happening as an omen, an indication that things had taken an unforeseeable turn. Since they could not accept the idea of human error overriding the rule, they assumed that they had been made to err by a superior command, for a reason which was difficult to discern but real.

They pondered the question of what to do next, but before any of them came up with an answer, a true southerly woman, doña Soledad, came into the picture with such a force that it was impossible for them to refuse her. She was congruous with the rule. She was a *stalker*.

Her presence distracted us for a time. For a while it seemed as if she were going to pull us off to another plateau. She created vigorous movement. Florinda took her under her wing to instruct her in the art of *stalking*. But whatever good it did, it was not enough to remedy a strange loss of energy that I felt, a listlessness that seemed to be increasing.

Then one day Silvio Manuel said that in his *dreaming* he had received a master plan. He was exhilarated and went off to discuss its details with don Juan and the other warriors. The Nagual woman was included in their discussions, but I was not. This made me suspect that they did not want me to find out what Silvio Manuel had discovered about me.

I confronted every one of them with my suspicions. They all laughed at me, except for the Nagual woman, who told me that I was right. Silvio Manuel's *dreaming* had revealed the reason for my presence among them, but I would have to surrender to my fate, which was not to know the nature of my task until I was ready for it.

There was such finality in her tone that I could only accept without question everything she said. I think that if don Juan or Silvio Manuel had told me the same thing, I would not have acquiesced so easily. She also said that she disagreed with don Juan and the others—she thought I should be informed of the general purpose of their actions, if only to avoid unnecessary friction and rebelliousness.

Silvio Manuel intended to prepare me for my task by taking me directly into the second attention. He planned a series of bold actions that would galvanize my awareness.

In the presence of all the others he told me that he was taking over my guidance, and that he was shifting me to his area of power, the night. The explanation he gave was that a number of *not-doings* had presented themselves to him in *dreaming*. They were designed for a team composed of la Gorda and myself as the doers, and the Nagual woman as the overseer.

Silvio Manuel was awed by the Nagual woman and had only words of admiration for her. He said that she was in a class by herself. She could perform on a par with him or any of the other warriors of his party. She did not have experience, but she could manipulate her attention in any way she needed. He confessed that her prowess was as great a mystery to him as was my presence among them, and that her sense of purpose and her conviction were so keen that I was no match for her. In fact, he asked la Gorda to give me special support, so I could withstand the Nagual woman's contact.

For our first *not-doing*, Silvio Manuel constructed a wooden crate big enough to house la Gorda and me, if we sat back-to-back with our knees up. The crate had a lid made of lattice-work to let in a flow of air. La Gorda and I were to climb inside it and sit in total darkness and total silence, without falling asleep. He began by letting us enter the box for short periods; then he increased the time as we got used to the procedure, until we could spend the entire night inside it without moving or dozing off.

The Nagual woman stayed with us to make sure that we would not change levels of awareness due to fatigue. Silvio Manuel said that our natural tendency under unusual conditions of stress is to shift from the heightened state of awareness to our normal one, and vice versa.

The general effect of the *not-doing* every time we performed it was to give us an unequalled sense of rest, which was a complete puzzle to me, since we never fell asleep during our nightlong vigils. I attributed the sense of rest to the fact that we were in a state of heightened awareness, but Silvio Manuel said that the one had nothing to do with the other, that the sense of rest was the result of sitting with our knees up.

The second *not-doing* consisted of making us lie on the ground like curled-up dogs, almost in the fetal position, resting on our left sides, our foreheads on our folded arms. Silvio Manuel insisted that we keep our eyes closed as long as possible, opening them only when he told us to shift positions and lie on our right sides. He told us that the purpose of this *not-doing* was to allow our sense of hearing to separate from our sight. As before, he gradually increased the length of time until we could spend the entire night in auditory vigil.

Silvio Manuel was then ready to move us to another area of activity. He explained that in the first two *not-doings* we had broken a certain perceptual barrier while we were stuck to the ground. By way of analogy, he compared human beings to trees. We are like mobile trees. We are somehow rooted to the ground; our roots are transportable, but that does not free us from the ground. He said that in order to establish balance we had to perform the third *not-doing* while dangling in the air. If we succeeded in channeling our *intent* while we were suspended from a tree inside a leather harness, we would make a triangle with our *intent*, a triangle whose base was on the ground and its vertex in the air. Silvio Manuel thought that we had gathered our attention with the first two *not-doings* to the point that we could perform the third perfectly from the beginning.

One night he suspended la Gorda and me in two separate harnesses like strap chairs. We sat in them and he lifted us with a pulley to the highest large branches of a tall tree. He wanted us to pay attention to the awareness of the tree, which he said would give us signals, since we were its guests. He made the Nagual woman stay on the ground and call our names from time to time during the entire night.

While we were suspended from the tree, in the innumerable times we performed this *not-doing*, we experienced a glorious flood of physical sensations, like mild charges of electrical impulses. During the first three or four attempts, it was as if the tree were protesting our intrusion; then after that the impulses became signals of peace and balance. Silvio Manuel told us that the awareness of a tree draws its nourishment from the depths of the earth, while the awareness of mobile creatures draws it from the surface. There is no sense of strife in a tree, whereas moving beings are filled to the brim with it.

His contention was that perception suffers a profound jolt when we are placed in states of quietude in darkness. Our hearing takes the lead then, and the signals from all the living and existing entities around us can be detected—not with our hearing only, but with a combination of the auditory and visual senses, in that order. He said that in darkness, especially while one is suspended, the eyes become subsidiary to the ears.

He was absolutely right, as la Gorda and I discovered. Through the exercise of the third *not-doing*, Silvio Manuel gave a new dimension to our perception of the world around us.

He then told la Gorda and me that the next set of three *not-doings* would be intrinsically different and more complex. These had to do with learning to handle the other world. It was mandatory to maximize their effect by moving our time of action to the evening or predawn twilight. He told us that the first *not-doing* of the second set had two stages. In stage one we had to bring ourselves to our keenest state of heightened awareness so as to detect the wall of fog. Once that was done, stage two consisted of making that wall stop rotating in order to venture into the world between the parallel lines.

He warned us that what he was aiming at was to place us directly into the second attention, without any intellectual preparation. He wanted us to learn its intricacies without rationally understanding what we were doing. His contention was that a magical deer or a magical coyote handles the second attention without having any intellect. Through the forced practice of journeying behind the wall of fog, we were going to undergo, sooner or later, a permanent alteration in our total being, an alteration that would make us accept that the world between the parallel lines is real, because it is part of the total world, as our luminous body is part of our total being.

Silvio Manuel also said that he was using la Gorda and me to probe into the possibility that we could someday help the other apprentices by ushering them into the other world, in which case they could accompany the Nagual Juan Matus and his party in their definitive journey. He reasoned that since the Nagual woman had to leave this world with the Nagual Juan Matus and his warriors, the apprentices had to follow her because she was their only leader in the absence of a Nagual man. He assured us that she was counting on us, that this was the reason she was supervising our work.

Silvio Manuel had la Gorda and me sit down on the ground in the area in back of his house, where we had performed all the *not-doings*. We did not need don Juan's aid to enter into our keenest state of awareness. Almost immediately I *saw* the wall of fog. La Gorda did too; yet no matter how we tried, we could not stop its rotation. Every time I moved my head, the wall moved with it.

The Nagual woman was able to stop it and go through it

by herself, but for all her efforts she could not take the two of us with her. Finally don Juan and Silvio Manuel had to stop the wall for us and physically push us through it. The sensation I had upon entering into that wall of fog was that my body was being twisted like the braids of a rope.

On the other side there was the horrible desolate plain with small round sand dunes. There were very low yellow clouds around us, but no sky or horizon; banks of pale yellow vapor impaired visibility. It was very difficult to walk. The pressure seemed much greater than what my body was used to. La Gorda and I walked aimlessly, but the Nagual woman seemed to know where she was going. The further we went away from the wall, the darker it got and the more difficult it was to move. La Gorda and I could no longer walk erect. We had to crawl. I lost my strength and so did la Gorda; the Nagual woman had to drag us back to the wall and out of there.

We repeated our journey innumerable times. At first we were aided by don Juan and Silvio Manuel in stopping the wall of fog, but then la Gorda and I became almost as proficient as the Nagual woman. We learned to stop the rotation of that wall. It happened quite naturally to us. In my case, on one occasion I realized that my *intent* was the key, a special aspect of my *intent* because it was not my volition as I know it. It was an intense desire that was focused on the midpoint of my body. It was a peculiar nervousness that made me shudder and then it turned into a force that did not really stop the wall, but made some part of my body turn involuntarily ninety degrees to the right. The result was that for an instant I had two points of view. I was looking at the world divided in two by the wall of fog and at the same time I was staring directly at a bank of yellowish vapor. The latter view gained predominance and something pulled me into the fog and beyond it.

Another thing that we learned was to regard that place as real; our journeys acquired for us the factuality of an excursion into the mountains, or a sea voyage in a sailboat. The deserted plain with sand-dune-like mounds was as real to us as any part of the world.

La Gorda and I had the rational feeling that the three of us spent an eternity in the world between the parallel lines, yet we were unable to remember what exactly transpired there. We could only remember the terrifying moments when we would have to leave it to return to the world of everyday life. It was always a moment of tremendous anguish and insecurity.

Don Juan and all his warriors followed our endeavors with great curiosity, but the one who was strangely absent from all our activities was Eligio. Although he was himself a peerless warrior, comparable to the warriors of don Juan's own party, he never took part in our struggle, nor did he help us in any way.

La Gorda said that Eligio had succeeded in attaching himself to Emilito and thus directly to the Nagual Juan Matus. He was never part of our problem, because he could go into the second attention at the drop of a hat. To him, journeying into the confines of the second attention was as easy as snapping his fingers.

La Gorda reminded me of the day when Eligio's unusual talents allowed him to find out that I was not their man, long before anyone else had even an inkling of the truth.

I was sitting on the back porch of Vicente's house in northern Mexico when Emilito and Eligio suddenly showed up. Everyone took for granted that Emilito had to disappear for long periods of time; when he would show up again, everyone also took for granted that he had returned from a voyage. No one asked him any questions. He would report his findings first to don Juan and then to whoever wanted to hear them.

On that day it was as if Emilito and Eligio had just come into the house through the back door. Emilito was ebullient as ever. Eligio was his usual quiet somber self. I had always thought, when both of them were together, that Emilito's exquisite personality overwhelmed Eligio and made him even more sullen.

Emilito went inside looking for don Juan and Eligio opened up to me. He smiled and came to my side. He put his arm around my shoulders and placing his mouth to my ear whispered that he had broken the seal of the parallel lines and he could go into something he said Emilito had called glory.

Eligio went on to explain certain things about glory which I was unable to comprehend. It was as if my mind could only focus on the periphery of that event. After explaining it to me, Eligio took me by the hand and made me stand in the middle of the patio, looking at the sky with my chin slightly turned up. He was to my right, standing with me in the same position. He told me to let go and fall backwards pulled by the heaviness of the very top of my head. Something grabbed me from behind and pulled me down. There was an abyss behind me. I fell into it. And then suddenly I was on the desolate plain with dune-like mounds.

Eligio urged me to follow him. He told me that the edge of glory was over the hills. I walked with him until I could not move any longer. He ran ahead of me with no effort at all, as if he were made of air. He stood on top of a large mound and pointed beyond. He ran back to me and begged me to crawl up that hill, which he told me was the edge of glory. It was perhaps only a hundred feet away from me, but I could not move another inch.

He tried to drag me up the hill; he could not budge me. My weight seemed to have increased a hundred-fold. Eligio finally had to summon don Juan and his party. Cecilia lifted me up on her shoulders and carried me out.

La Gorda added that Emilito had put Eligio up to it. Emilito was proceeding according to the rule. My courier had journeyed into glory. It was mandatory that he show it to me.

I could recollect the eagerness in Eligio's face and the fervor with which he urged me to make one last effort to witness glory. I could also recollect his sadness and disappointment when I failed. He never spoke to me again.

La Gorda and I had been so involved in our journeys behind the wall of fog that we had forgotten that we were due for the next *not-doing* of the series with Silvio Manuel. He told us that it could be devastating, and that it consisted of crossing the parallel lines with the three little sisters and the three Genaros, directly into the entrance to the world of total awareness. He did not include doña Soledad because his *not-doings* were only for *dreamers* and she was a *stalker*.

Silvio Manuel added that he expected us to become familiar with the third attention by placing ourselves at the foot of the Eagle over and over. He prepared us for the jolt; he explained that a warrior's journeys into the desolate sand dunes is a preparatory step for the real crossing of boundaries. To venture behind the wall of fog while one is in a state of heightened awareness or while one is doing *dreaming* entails only a very small portion of our total awareness, while to cross bodily into the other world entails engaging our total being.

Silvio Manuel had conceived the idea of using the bridge as the symbol of a true crossing. He reasoned that the bridge was adjacent to a power spot; and power spots are cracks, passageways into the other world. He thought that it was possible that la Gorda and I had acquired enough strength to withstand a glimpse of the Eagle.

He announced that it was my personal duty to round up the three women and the three men and help them get into their keenest states of awareness. It was the least I could do for them, since I had perhaps been instrumental in destroying their chances for freedom.

He moved our time of action to the hour just before dawn, or the morning twilight. I dutifully attempted to make them shift awareness, as don Juan did to me. Since I had no idea how to manipulate their bodies or what I really had to do with them I ended up beating them on the back. After several grueling attempts on my part, don Juan finally intervened. He got them as ready as they could possibly be and handed them over to me to herd like cattle onto the bridge. My task was to take them one by one across that bridge. The power spot was on the south side, a very auspicious omen. Silvio Manuel planned to cross first, wait for me to deliver them to him and then usher us as a group into the unknown.

Silvio Manuel walked across, followed by Eligio, who did not even glance at me. I held the six apprentices in a tight group on the north side of the bridge. They were terrified; they got loose from my grip and began to run in different directions. I caught the three women one by one and succeeded in delivering them to Silvio Manuel. He held them at the entrance of the crack between the worlds. The three men were too fast for me. I was too tired to run after them.

I looked at don Juan across the bridge for guidance. He and the rest of his party and the Nagual woman were clustered together looking at me; they had coaxed me with gestures to run after the women or the men, laughing at my fumbling attempts. Don Juan made a gesture with his head to disregard the three men and to cross over to Silvio Manuel with la Gorda.

We crossed. Silvio Manuel and Eligio seemed to be holding the sides of a vertical slit the size of a man. The women ran and hid behind la Gorda. Silvio Manuel urged all of us to step inside the opening. I obeyed him. The women did not. Beyond that entrance there was nothing. Yet it was filled to the brim with something that was nothing. My eyes were open; all my senses were alert. I strained myself trying to see in front of me. But there was nothing in front of me. Or if there was something there, I could not grasp it. My senses did not have the compartmentalization I have learned to regard as meaningful. Everything came to me at once, or rather nothingness came to me to a degree I had never experienced before or after. I felt that my body was being torn apart. A force from within myself was pushing outward. I was bursting, and not in a figurative way. Suddenly I felt a human hand snatching me out of there before I disintegrated.

The Nagual woman had crossed over and saved me. Eligio had not been able to move because he was holding the opening, and Silvio Manuel had the four women by their hair, two in each hand, ready to hurl them in.

I assume that the whole event must have taken at least a quarter of an hour to unfold, but at the time it never occurred to me to worry about people around the bridge. Time seemed to have been somehow suspended. Just as it had been suspended when we returned to the bridge on our way to Mexico City.

Silvio Manuel said that although the attempt had seemed to be a failure, it was a total success. The four women did see the aperture and through it into the other world; and what I experienced in there was a true sense of death.

"There is nothing gorgeous or peaceful about death," he said. "Because the real terror begins upon dying. With that incalculable force you felt in there, the Eagle will squeeze out of you every flicker of awareness you have ever had."

Silvio Manuel prepared la Gorda and me for another attempt. He explained that power spots were actual holes in a sort of canopy that prevents the world from losing its shape. A power spot could be utilized as long as one has gathered enough strength in the second attention. He told us that the key to withstanding the Eagle's presence was the potency of one's *intent*. Without *intent* there was nothing. He said to me that, since I was the only one who had stepped into the other world, what had nearly killed me was my incapacity to change my *intent*. He was confident, however, that with forced practice all of us would get to elongate our *intent*. He could not explain, however, what *intent* was. He joked that only the Nagual Juan Matus could explain it—but that he was not around.

Unfortunately our next attempt did not take place, for I

became deplenished of energy. It was a swift and devastating loss of vitality. I was suddenly so weak that I passed out in Silvio Manuel's house.

I asked la Gorda whether she knew what happened next; I myself had no idea. La Gorda said that Silvio Manuel told everyone that the Eagle had dislodged me from their group, and that finally I was ready for them to prepare me to carry out the designs of my fate. His plan was to take me to the world between the parallel lines while I was unconscious, and let that world draw out all the remaining and useless energy from my body. His idea was sound in the judgment of all his companions because the rule says that one could only enter in there with awareness. To enter without it brings death, since without consciousness the life force is exhausted by the physical pressure of that world.

La Gorda added that they did not take her with me. But the Nagual Juan Matus had told her that once I was empty of vital energy, practically dead, all of them took turns in blowing new energy into my body. In that world, anybody who has life force can give it to others by blowing on them. They put their breath in all the spots where there is a storage point. Silvio Manuel blew first, then the Nagual woman. The remaining part of me was made up of all the members of the Nagual Juan Matus' party.

After they had blown their energy into me, the Nagual woman brought me out of the fog to Silvio Manuel's house. She laid me on the ground with my head toward the southeast. La Gorda said that I looked as if I were dead. She and the Genaros and the three little sisters were there. The Nagual woman explained to them that I was ill, but that I was going to come back someday to help them find their freedom, because I would not be free myself until I did that. Silvio Manuel then gave me his breath and brought me back to life. That was why she and the little sisters remembered that he was my master. He carried me to my bed and let me sleep, as if nothing had happened. After I woke up I left and did not return. And then she forgot because no one ever pushed her into the left side again. She went to live in the town where I later found her with the others. The Nagual Juan Matus and Genaro had set up two different households. Genaro took care of the men; the Nagual Juan Matus looked after the women.

I had gone to sleep feeling depressed, feeble. When I woke up I was in perfect control of myself, ebullient, filled with extraordinary and unfamiliar energy. My well-being was marred only by don Juan's telling me that I had to leave la Gorda and strive alone to perfect my attention, until one day when I would be able to return to help her. He also told me not to fret or get discouraged, for the carrier of the rule would eventually make himself or herself known to me in order to reveal my true task.

Afterward I did not see don Juan for a very long time. When I came back he kept on making me shift from the right to the left side awareness for two purposes; first, so I could continue my relationship with his warriors and the Nagual woman, and second, so he could put me under the direct supervision of Zuleica, with whom I had a steady interaction throughout the remaining years of my association with don Juan.

He told me that the reason he had to entrust me to Zuleica was because according to Silvio Manuel's master plan there were to be two kinds of instruction for me, one for the right side and one for the left. The right side instruction pertained to the state of normal consciousness and had to do with leading me to the rational conviction that there is another type of awareness concealed in human beings. Don Juan was in charge of this instruction. The left side instruction had been assigned to Zuleica; it was related to the state of heightened awareness and had to do exclusively with the handling of the second attention. Thus every time I went to Mexico I would spend half of my time with Zuleica, and the other half with don Juan.

13

The Intricacies of Dreaming

Don Juan began the task of ushering me into the second attention by telling me that I had already had a great deal of experience in entering into it. Silvio Manuel had taken me to the very entrance. The flaw had been that I had not been given the appropriate rationales. Male warriors must be given serious reasons before they safely venture into the unknown. Female warriors are not subject to this and can go without any hesitation, providing that they have total confidence in whoever is leading them.

He told me that I had to start by learning first the intricacies of *dreaming*. He then put me under Zuleica's supervision. He admonished me to be impeccable and practice meticulously whatever I learned, and above all, to be careful and deliberate in my actions so as not to exhaust my life force in vain. He said that the prerequisite for entrance into any of the three stages of attention is the possession of life force, because without it warriors cannot have direction and purpose. He explained that upon dying our awareness also enters into the third attention; but only for an instant, as a purging action, just before the Eagle devours it.

La Gorda said that the Nagual Juan Matus made every one of the apprentices learn *dreaming*. She thought that all of them were given this task at the same time I was. Their instruction was also divided into right and left. She said that the Nagual and Genaro provided the instruction for the state of normal awareness. When they judged that the apprentices were ready, the Nagual made them shift into a state of heightened awareness and left them with their respective counterparts. Vicente taught Nestor, Silvio Manuel taught Benigno, Genaro taught Pablito. Lydia was taught by Hermelinda, and Rosa by Nelida. La Gorda added that Josefina and she were put under the care of Zuleica in order to learn together the finer points of *dreaming*, so they would be able to come to my aid someday.

Moreover, la Gorda deduced on her own that the men were also taken to Florinda to be taught *stalking*. The proof of this was their drastic change of behavior. She claimed that she knew, before she remembered anything, that she had been taught the principles of *stalking* but in a very superficial manner; she had not been made to practice, while the men were given practical knowledge and tasks. Their behavioral change was the proof. They became lighthearted and jovial. They enjoyed their lives, while she and the other women, because of their *dreaming* became progressively more somber and morose.

La Gorda believed that the men were unable to remember their instruction when I asked them to reveal their *stalking* knowledge to me, because they practiced it without knowing what they were doing. Their training was revealed, however, in their dealings with people. They were consummate artists in bending people to their wishes. Through their *stalking* practice the men had even learned *controlled folly*. For example, they carried on as if Soledad were Pablito's mother. To any onlooker, it would seem that they were mother and son pitted against each other, when in reality they were acting out a part. They convinced everybody. Sometimes Pablito would give such a performance that he would even convince himself.

La Gorda confessed that all of them were more than baffled

by my behavior. They did not know whether I was insane or myself a master of *controlled folly*. I gave all the outward indications that I believed their masquerade. Soledad told them not to be fooled, because I was indeed insane. I appeared to be in control but I was so completely aberrated that I could not behave like a Nagual. She engaged every one of the women in delivering a deadly blow to me. She told them that I had requested it myself at one time when I had been in control of my faculties.

La Gorda said that it took her several years, under Zuleica's guidance, to learn *dreaming*. When the Nagual Juan Matus had judged that she was proficient, he finally took her to her true counterpart, Nelida. It was Nelida who showed her how to behave in the world. She groomed her not only to be at ease in Western clothes, but to have good taste. Thus when she put on her city clothes in Oaxaca and amazed me with her charm and poise, she was already experienced in that transformation.

Zuleica was very effective as my guide into the second attention. She insisted that our interaction take place only at night, and in total darkness. For me, Zuleica was only a voice in the dark, a voice that started every contact we had by telling me to focus my attention on her words and nothing else. Her voice was the woman's voice that la Gorda thought she had heard in *dreaming*.

Zuleica told me that if *dreaming* is going to be done indoors, it is best to do it in total darkness, while lying down or sitting up on a narrow bed, or better yet, while sitting inside a coffin-like crib. She thought that outdoors, *dreaming* should be done in the protection of a cave, in the sandy areas of water holes, or sitting against a rock in the mountains; never on the flat floor of a valley, or next to rivers, or lakes, or the sea, because flat areas as well as water were antithetical to the second attention.

Every one of my sessions with her was imbued with mysterious overtones. She explained that the surest way to make a direct hit on the second attention is through ritual acts, monotonous chanting, intricate repetitious movements.

Her teachings were not about the preliminaries of *dreaming*, which had already been taught to me by don Juan. Her assumption was that whoever came to her already knew how to do *dreaming*, so she dealt exclusively with esoteric points of the left side awareness.

Zuleica's instructions began one day when don Juan took me to her house. We got there late in the afternoon. The place seemed to be deserted, although the front door opened as we approached. I expected Zoila or Marta to show up but no one was at the entrance. I felt that whoever had opened the door for us had also moved out of our way very quickly. Don Juan took me inside to the patio and made me sit on a crate that had a cushion and had been turned into a bench. The seat on the crate was bumpy and hard and very uncomfortable. I ran my hand underneath the thin cushion and found sharp-edged rocks. Don Juan said that my situation was unconventional because I had to learn the fine points of *dreaming* in a hurry. Sitting on a hard surface was a prop to keep my body from feeling it was in a normal sitting situation. Just a few minutes before arriving at the house, don Juan had made me change levels of awareness. He said that Zuleica's instruction had to be conducted in that state in order for me to have the speed that I needed. He admonished me to abandon myself and trust Zuleica implicitly. He then commanded me to focus my gaze with all the concentration I was capable of and memorize every detail of the patio that was within my field of vision. He insisted that I had to memorize the detail as much as the feeling of sitting there. He repeated his instructions to make sure that I had understood. Then he left.

It quickly got very dark and I started to fret, sitting there. I had not had enough time to concentrate on the detail of the patio. I heard a rustling sound just behind me and then Zuleica's voice jolted me. In a forceful whisper she told me to get up and follow her. I automatically obeyed her. I could not see her face, she was only a dark shape walking two steps ahead of me. She led me to an alcove in the darkest hall in her house. Although my eyes were used to the darkness I was still unable to see a thing. I stumbled on something and she commanded me to sit down inside a narrow crib and support my lower back with something I thought was a hard cushion.

I next felt that she had backed up a few steps behind me, a thing which baffled me completely, for I thought that my back was only a few inches from the wall. Speaking from behind me, she ordered me in a soft voice to focus my attention on her words and let them guide me. She told me to keep my eyes open and fixed on a point right in front of me, at my eye level; and that this point was going to turn from darkness to a bright and pleasing orange-red.

Zuleica spoke very softly with an even intonation. I heard every word she said. The darkness around me seemed to have effectively cut off any distracting external stimuli. I heard Zuleica's words in a vacuum, and then I realized that the silence in that hall was matched by the silence inside me.

Zuleica explained that a *dreamer* must start from a point of color; intense light or unmitigated darkness are useless to a *dreamer* in the initial onslaught. Colors such as purple or light green or rich yellow are, on the other hand, stupendous starting points. She preferred, however, orange-red, because through experience it had proven to be the one that gave her the greatest sensation of rest. She assured me that once I had succeeded in entering into the orange-red color I would have rallied my second attention permanently, providing that I could be aware of the sequence of physical events.

It took me several sessions with Zuleica's voice to realize with my body what she wanted me to do. The advantage of being in a state of heightened awareness was that I could follow my transition from a state of vigil to a state of *dreaming*. Under normal conditions that transition is blurred, but under those special circumstances I actually felt in the course of one session how my second attention took over the controls. The first step was an unusual difficulty in breathing. It was not a difficulty in inhaling or exhaling; I was not short of breath—rather, my breathing changed rhythm all of a sudden. My diaphragm began to contract and it forced my midsection to move in and out with great speed. The result was the fastest short breaths I had ever taken. I breathed in the lower part of my lungs and felt a great pressure in my intestines. I tried unsuccessfully to break the spasms of my diaphragm. The harder I tried, the more painful it got.

Zuleica ordered me to let my body do whatever was necessary and to forget about directing or controlling it. I wanted to obey her, but I did not know how. The spasms, which must have lasted ten to fifteen minutes, subsided as suddenly as they had appeared and were followed by another strange, shocking sensation. I felt it first as a most peculiar itch, a physical feeling which was not pleasing or displeasing; it was something like a nervous tremor. It became very intense, to the point of forcing me to focus my attention on it in order to determine where in my body it was happening. I was stunned by the realization that it was not taking place anywhere in my physical body, but outside of it, and yet I still felt it.

I disregarded Zuleica's order to enter into a patch of coloration that was forming right at my eye level, and gave myself fully to the exploration of that strange sensation outside me. Zuleica must have *seen* what I was going through; she suddenly began to explain that the second attention belongs to the luminous body, as the first attention belongs to the physical body. The point where, she said, the second attention assembles itself was situated right where Juan Tuma had described it the first time we met—approximately one and one-half feet in front of the midpoint between the stomach and the belly button and four inches to the right.

Zuleica ordered me to massage that place, to manipulate it by moving the fingers of both my hands right on that point as if I were playing a harp. She assured me that sooner or later I would end up feeling my fingers going through something as thick as water, and that finally I would feel my luminous shell.

As I kept on moving my fingers the air got progressively thicker until I felt a mass of sorts. An undefined physical pleasure spread all over me. I thought that I was touching a nerve in my body and felt silly at the absurdity of it. I stopped.

Zuleica warned me that if I did not move my fingers she was going to bop me on the head. The longer I kept up the wavering motion, the closer I felt the itching. It finally got as near as five or six inches from my body. It was as if something in me had shrunk. I actually thought I could feel a dent. I then had another eerie sensation. I was falling asleep and yet I was conscious. There was a buzzing in my ears, which reminded me of the sound of a bullroarer; next I felt a force rolling me over on my left side without waking me up. I was rolled very tightly, like a cigar, and was tucked into the itching depression. My awareness remained suspended there, incapable of waking up, but so tightly rolled on itself that I could not fall asleep either.

I heard Zuleica's voice telling me to look around. I could not open my eyes, but my tactile sense told me that I was in a ditch, lying on my back. I felt comfortable, secure. There was such a tightness to my body, such a compactness, that I did not ever want to get up. Zuleica's voice ordered me to stand up and open my eyes. I could not do it. She said that I had to will my movements, that it was no longer a matter of contracting my muscles to get up.

I thought that she was annoyed at my slowness. I realized then that I was fully conscious, perhaps more conscious than I had ever been in my entire life. I could think rationally and yet I seemed to be sound asleep. The thought occurred to me that Zuleica had put me in a state of deep hypnosis. It bothered me for an instant, then it did not matter. I abandoned myself to the feeling of being suspended, floating free.

I could not hear anything else she said. It was either that

she had stopped talking to me or that I had shut off the sound of her voice. I did not want to leave that haven. I had never been so peaceful and complete. I lay there unwilling to get up or to change anything. I could feel the rhythm of my breathing. Suddenly I woke up.

In my next session with Zuleica she told me that I had succeeded in making a dent in my luminosity all by myself, and that making a dent meant bringing a distant point in my luminous shell closer to my physical body, therefore closer to control. She asserted repeatedly that from the moment the body learns to make that dent, it is easier to enter into *dreaming*. I agreed with her. I had acquired a strange impulse, a sensation that my body had instantly learned to reproduce. It was a mixture of feeling at ease, secure, dormant, suspended without tactile sense and at the same time fully awake, aware of everything.

La Gorda said that the Nagual Juan Matus had struggled for years to create that dent in her, in all three little sisters, and in the Genaros as well, so as to give them the permanent ability to focus their second attention. He had told her that ordinarily the dent is created on the spur of the moment by the *dreamer* when it is needed, then the luminous shell changes back to its original shape. But in the apprentices' case, because they did not have a Nagual leader, the depression was created from the outside and was a permanent feature of their luminous bodies, a great help but also a hindrance. It made all of them vulnerable and moody.

I remembered then that once I had *seen* and kicked a depression in the luminous shells of Lydia and Rosa. I thought that the dent was at the height of the upper portion of the outside of their right thigh, or perhaps just at the crest of their hipbone. La Gorda explained that I had kicked them in the dent of their second attention and that I had nearly killed them.

La Gorda said that she and Josefina lived in Zuleica's house for several months. The Nagual Juan Matus had delivered them to her one day after making them shift levels of awareness. He did not tell them what they were going to do there nor what to expect, he simply left them by themselves in the hall of her house and walked away. They sat there until it got dark. Zuleica then came to them. They never saw her, they only heard her voice as if she were talking to them from a point on the wall.

Zuleica was very demanding from the moment she took over. She made them undress on the spot and ordered both of them to crawl inside thick fluffy cotton bags, some poncho-like garments that were lying on the floor. They covered them from neck to toes. She ordered them next to sit back to back on a mat in the same alcove where I myself used to sit. She told them that their task was to gaze at the darkness until it began to acquire a hue. After many sessions they indeed began to see colors in the darkness, at which time Zuleica made them sit side by side and gaze at the same spot.

La Gorda said that Josefina learned very fast, and that one night she dramatically entered into the patch of orange-red by swishing physically out of the poncho. La Gorda thought that either Josefina had reached out for the blotch of color or it had reached out for her. The result was that in one instant Josefina was gone from inside the poncho. Zuleica separated them from then on, and la Gorda started her slow, solitary learning.

La Gorda's account made me remember that Zuleica had also made me crawl inside a fluffy garment. In fact, the commands she used to order me to crawl inside revealed to me the rationale for its use. She directed me to feel its fluffiness with my naked skin, especially with the skin of my calves. She repeated over and over that human beings have a superb center of perception on the outside of the calves, and that if the skin in that area could be made to relax or be soothed, the scope of our perception would be enhanced in ways that would be impossible to fathom rationally. The garment was very soft and warm, and it induced an extraordinary sensation of pleasurable relaxation in my legs. The nerves in my calves became highly stimulated.

La Gorda reported the same sensation of physical pleasure. She went as far as to say that it was the power of that poncho that guided her to find the patch of orange-red color. She was so impressed with the garment that she made herself one, copying the original, but its effect was not the same, although it still provided her solace and well-being. She said that she and Josefina ended up spending all of their available time inside the ponchos that she had sewn for both of them.

Lydia and Rosa had also been placed inside the garment, but they were never particularly fond of it. Neither was I.

La Gorda explained Josefina's and her own attachment as a direct consequence of having been led to finding their *dreaming color* while they were inside the garment. She said that the reason for my indifference to it was the fact that I did not enter into the area of coloration at all—rather the hue had come to me. She was right. Something else besides Zuleica's voice dictated the outcome of that preparatory phase. By all indications Zuleica was leading me through the same steps she had led la Gorda and Josefina. I had stared at the darkness throughout many sessions and was ready to visualize the spot of coloration. In fact, I witnessed its entire metamorphosis from plain darkness to a precisely outlined blotch of intense brightness, and then I was swayed by the external itch, on which I focused my attention, until I ended up entering into a state of *restful vigil*. It was then that I first became immersed in an orange-red coloration.

After I had learned to remain suspended between sleep and vigil, Zuleica seemed to relax her pace. I even believed that she was not in any hurry to get me out of that state. She let me stay in it without interfering, and never asked me about it, perhaps because her voice was only for commands and not for asking questions. We never really talked, at least not the way I talked with don Juan.

While I was in the state of *restful vigil*, I realized one time that it was useless for me to remain there, that no matter how pleasant it was, its limitations were blatant. I sensed then a tremor in my body and I opened my eyes, or rather my eyes became open by themselves. Zuleica was staring at me. I experienced a moment of bafflement. I thought I had woken up, and to be faced with Zuleica in the flesh was something I had not expected. I had gotten used to hearing only her voice. It also surprised me that it was no longer night. I looked around. We were not in Zuleica's house. Then the realization struck me that I was *dreaming* and I woke up.

Zuleica started then on another facet of her teachings. She taught me how to move. She began her instruction by commanding me to place my awareness on the midpoint of my body. In my case the midpoint is below the lower edge of my belly button. She told me to sweep the floor with it, that is, make a rocking motion with my belly as if a broom were attached to it. Throughout countless sessions I attempted to accomplish what her voice was urging me to do. She did not allow me to go into a state of *restful vigil*. It was her intention to guide me to elicit the perception of sweeping the floor with my midsection while I remained in a waking state. She said that to be on the left side awareness was enough of an advantage to do well in the exercise.

One day, for no reason I could think of, I succeeded in having a vague feeling in the area of my stomach. It was not something defined, and when I focused my attention on it I realized that it was a prickling sensation inside the cavity of my body, not quite in my stomach area but above it. The closer I examined it, the more details I noticed. The vagueness of the sensation soon turned into a certainty. There was a strange connection of nervousness or a prickling sensation between my solar plexus and my right calf.

As the sensation became more acute I involuntarily brought my right thigh up to my chest. Thus the two points were as close to each other as my anatomy permitted. I shivered for a moment with an unusual nervousness and then I clearly felt that I was sweeping the floor with my midsection; it was a tactile sensation that happened over and over every time I rocked my body in my sitting position.

In my next session Zuleica allowed me to enter into a state of *restful vigil*. But this time that state was not quite as it had been before. There seemed to be a sort of control in me that curtailed my enjoying it freely, as I had done in the past—a control that also made me focus on the steps I had taken to get into it. First I noticed the itch on the point of the second attention in my luminous shell. I massaged that point by moving my fingers on it as if I were playing a harp and the point sunk towards my stomach. I felt it almost on my skin. I experienced a prickling sensation on the outside of my right calf. It was a mixture of pleasure and pain. The sensation radiated to my whole leg and then to my lower back. I felt that my buttocks were shaking. My entire body was transfixed by a nervous ripple. I thought that my body had been caught upside down in a net. My forehead and my toes seemed to be touching. I was like a closed U-shape. Then I felt as if I were being folded in two and rolled inside a sheet. My nervous spasms were what made the sheet roll into itself, with me in the center. When the rolling ended I could not sense my body any more. I was only an amorphous awareness, a nervous spasm wrapped in itself. That awareness came to rest inside a ditch, inside a depression of itself.

I understood then the impossibility of describing what takes place in *dreaming*. Zuleica said that the right and left side awareness are wrapped up together. Both of them come to rest in one single bundle in the dent, the depressed center of the second attention. To do *dreaming* one needs to manipulate both the luminous body and the physical body. First, the center of assembling for the second attention has to be made accessible by being pushed in from the outside by someone else, or sucked in from within by the *dreamer*. Second, in order to dislodge the first attention, the centers of the physical body located in the midsection and the calves, especially the right one, have to be stimulated and placed as close to one another as possible until they seem to join. Then the sensation of being bundled takes place and automatically the second attention takes over.

Zuleica's explanation, given in commands, was the most cogent way of describing what takes place, for none of the sensory experiences involved in *dreaming* are part of our normal inventory of sensory data. All of them were baffling to me. The sensation of an itch, a tingling outside myself, was localized and because of that the turmoil of my body upon feeling it was minimal. The sensation of being rolled on myself, on the other hand, was by far the most disquieting. It included a range of sensations that left my body in a state of shock. I was convinced that at one point my toes were touching my forehead, which is a position I am not able to attain. And yet I knew beyond the shadow of a doubt that I was inside a net, hanging upside down in a pear shape with my toes right against my forehead. On a physical plane I was sitting down and my thighs were against my chest.

Zuleica also said that the feeling of being rolled up like a cigar and placed inside the dent of the second attention was the result of merging my right and left awareness into one in which the order of predominance has been switched and the left has gained supremacy. She challenged me to be attentive enough to catch the reversal motion, the two attentions again becoming what they normally are with the right holding the reins.

I never caught the feelings involved, but her challenge obsessed me to the point that I became trapped in deadly vacillations in my effort to watch everything. She had to withdraw her challenge by ordering me to stop my scrutinies, for I had other things to do.

Zuleica said that first of all I had to perfect my command of moving at will. She began her instruction by directing me time and time again to open my eyes while I was in a state of *restful vigil*. It took a great deal of effort for me to do it. One time my eyes opened suddenly and I saw Zuleica looming over me. I was lying down but I could not determine where. The light was extremely bright, as if I were just underneath a powerful electric bulb, but the light was not shining directly on my eyes. I could see Zuleica without any effort.

She ordered me to stand up by willing my movement. She said that I had to push myself up with my midsection, that I had three thick tentacles there which I could use as crutches to lift up my whole body.

I tried every conceivable way to get up. I failed. I had a sensation of despair and physical anguish reminiscent of nightmares I used to have as a child in which I was unable to wake up and yet I was fully awake desperately trying to scream.

Zuleica finally spoke to me. She said that I had to follow a certain sequence, and that it was wasteful and downright dumb of me to fret and get agitated as if I were dealing with the world of everyday life. Fretting was proper only in the first attention; the second attention was calmness itself. She wanted me to repeat the sensation I had had of sweeping the floor with my midsection. I thought that in order to repeat it I would have to be sitting. Without any deliberation on my part I sat up and adopted the position I had used when my body first elicited that sensation. Something in me rocked, and suddenly I was standing. I could not figure out what I had done to move. I thought that if I started all over again I could catch the sequence. As soon as I had that thought I found myself lying down again. Upon standing up once more I realized that there was no procedure involved, that in order to move I had to intend my moving at a very deep level. In other words, I had to be utterly convinced that I wanted to move, or perhaps it would be more accurate to say that I had to be convinced that I needed to move.

Once I had understood that principle, Zuleica made me practice every conceivable aspect of volitional movement. The more I practiced, the clearer it became for me that *dreaming* was in fact a rational state. Zuleica explained it. She said that in *dreaming*, the right side, the rational awareness, is wrapped up inside the left side awareness in order to give the *dreamer* a sense of sobriety and rationality; but that the influence of rationality has to be minimal and used only as an inhibiting mechanism to protect the *dreamer* from excesses and bizarre undertakings.

The next step was learning to direct my *dreaming body*. Don Juan had proposed, from the first time I met Zuleica, the task of gazing at the patio as I sat on the crate. I religiously engaged myself, sometimes for hours, in gazing at it. I was always alone in Zuleica's house. It seemed that on the days when I went there everyone was gone or was hiding. The silence and the solitude worked in my favor and I succeeded in memorizing the details of that patio.

Zuleica presented to me, accordingly, the task of opening my eyes from a state of *restful vigil* to see the patio. It took many sessions to accomplish it. At first I would open my eyes and I would see her, and she, with a jerk of her body, would make me bounce back like a ball into the state of *restful vigil*. On one of those bounces I felt an intense tremor; something that was located in my feet rattled its way up to my chest and I coughed it up; the scene of the patio at night came out of me just as if it had emerged out of my bronchial tubes. It was something like the roar of an animal.

I heard Zuleica's voice coming to me as a faint murmur. I could not understand what she was saying. I vaguely noticed that I was sitting on the crate. I wanted to get up but I felt that I was not solid. It was as if a wind were blowing me away. Then I heard Zuleica's voice very clearly telling me not to move. I tried to remain motionless but some force pulled me and I woke up in the alcove in the hall. Silvio Manuel was facing me.

After every session of *dreaming* in Zuleica's house, don Juan would be waiting for me in the pitch-black hall. He would take me out of the house and make me shift levels of awareness. This time Silvio Manuel was there. Without saying a word to me, he put me inside a harness and hoisted me up against the beams of the roof. He kept me there until midday, at which time don Juan came and let me down. He explained that to be kept without touching the ground for a period of time tunes the body, and that it is essential to do this before embarking on a dangerous journey such as the one I was about to undertake.

It took many more sessions of *dreaming* for me to learn at last to open my eyes to see either Zuleica or to see the dark patio. I realized then that she herself had been *dreaming* all along. She had never been in person behind me in the alcove in the hall. I had been right the first night when I thought that my back was against the wall. Zuleica was merely a voice from *dreaming*.

During one of the *dreaming* sessions, when I opened my eyes deliberately to see Zuleica, I was shocked to find la Gorda as well as Josefina looming over me together with Zuleica. The final facet of her teaching began then. Zuleica taught the three of us to journey with her. She said that our first attention was hooked to the emanations of the earth, while our second attention was hooked to the emanations of the universe. What she meant by that was that a *dreamer* by definition is outside the boundaries of the concerns of everyday life. As a traveler in *dreaming* then, Zuleica's last task with la Gorda, Josefina, and me was to tune our second attention to follow her around in her voyages into the unknown.

In successive sessions Zuleica's voice told me that her "obsession" was going to lead me to a rendezvous, that in matters of the second attention the *dreamer*'s obsession serves as a guide, and that hers was focused on an actual place beyond this earth. From there she was going to call me and I had to use her voice as a line to pull myself.

Nothing happened for two sessions; Zuleica's voice would become more and more faint as she spoke, and I worried that I was incapable of following her. She had not told me what to do. I also experienced an unusual heaviness. I could not break a binding force around me that prevented me from getting out of the state of *restful vigil*.

During the third session I suddenly opened my eyes without even trying to. Zuleica, la Gorda and Josefina were staring at me. I was standing with them. I immediately realized that we were in some place completely unknown to me. The most obvious feature was a brilliant indirect light. The whole scene was inundated by a white, powerful, neonlike light. Zuleica was smiling as if inviting us to look around. La Gorda and Josefina seemed to be as cautious as I was. They gave me and Zuleica furtive glances. Zuleica signaled us to move around. We were outdoors, standing in the middle of a glaring circle. The ground seemed to be hard, dark rock, yet it reflected a great deal of the blinding white light, which came from above. The strange thing was that although I knew that the light was too intense for my eyes, I was not at all hurt when I looked up and spotted its source. It was the sun. I was staring directly at the sun, which, perhaps due to the fact that I was *dreaming*, was intensely white.

La Gorda and Josefina were also staring at the sun, apparently without any injurious effect. Suddenly I felt frightened. The light was alien to me. It was a merciless light; it seemed to attack us, creating a wind that I could feel. I could not sense any heat, however. I believed it to be malignant. In unison, la Gorda, Josefina and I huddled together like frightened children around Zuleica. She held us, and then the white, glaring light began to diminish by degrees until it had completely vanished. In its place there was a mild, very soothing, yellowish light.

I became aware then that we were not in this world. The ground was the color of wet terra-cotta. There were no mountains, but where we were standing was not flat land either. The ground was cracked and parched. It looked like a rough dry sea of terra-cotta. I could see it all around me, just as if I were in the middle of the ocean. I looked up; the sky had lost its maddening glare. It was dark, but not blue. A bright, incandescent star was near the horizon. It dawned on me at that instant that we were in a world with two suns, two stars. One was enormous and had gone over the horizon, the other was smaller or perhaps more distant.

I wanted to ask questions, to walk around and look for things. Zuleica signaled us to relax, to wait patiently. But something seemed to be pulling us. Suddenly la Gorda and Josefina were gone. And I woke up.

From that time on I never went back to Zuleica's house. Don Juan would make me shift levels of awareness in his own house or wherever we were, and I would enter into *dreaming*. Zuleica, la Gorda and Josefina were always waiting for me. We went back to the same unearthly scene over and over, until we were thoroughly familiar with it. Whenever we could do it we would skip the time of glare, the daytime, and go there at night, just in time to witness the rise over the horizon of a colossal celestial body: something of such magnitude that when it erupted over the jagged line of the horizon it covered at least half of the one hundred and eighty degree range in front of us. The celestial body was beautiful, and its ascent over the horizon was so breathtaking that I could have stayed there for an eternity, just to witness that sight.

The celestial body took up nearly the entire firmament when it reached the zenith. Invariably we would lie on our backs in order to gaze at it. It had consistent configurations, which Zuleica taught us to recognize. I realized that it was not a star. Its light was reflected; it must have been an opaque body because the reflected light was mellow in relation to its monumental size. There were enormous, unchanging brown spots on its saffron-yellow surface.

Zuleica took us systematically on voyages that were beyond words. La Gorda said that Zuleica took Josefina even farther and deeper into the unknown, because Josefina was, just like Zuleica herself, quite a bit crazy; neither of them had that core of rationality that supplies a *dreamer* with sobriety—thus they had no barriers and no interest in finding out rational causes or reasons for anything.

The only thing that Zuleica told me about our journeys that sounded like an explanation was that the *dreamers'* power to focus on their second attention made them into living slingshots. The stronger and the more impeccable the *dreamers* were, the farther they could project their second attention into the unknown and the longer their *dreaming* projection would last.

Don Juan said that my journeys with Zuleica were no illusion, and that everything I had done with her was a step toward the control of the second attention; in other words, Zuleica was teaching me the perceptual bias of that other realm. He could not explain, however, the exact nature of those journeys. Or perhaps he did not want to commit himself. He said that if he attempted to explain the perceptual bias of the second attention in terms of the perceptual bias of the first, he would only trap himself hopelessly in words. He wanted me to draw my own conclusion, and the more I thought about the whole matter, the clearer it became to me that his reluctance was functional.

Under Zuleica's guidance during her instruction for the second attention, I made factual visitations to mysteries that were certainly beyond the scope of my reason, but obviously within the possibilities of my total awareness. I learned to voyage into something incomprehensible and ended up, like Emilito and Juan Tuma, having my own tales of eternity.

14

Florinda

La Gorda and I were in total agreement that by the time Zuleica had taught us the intricacies of *dreaming* we had accepted the undeniable fact that the rule is a map, that there is another awareness concealed in us, and that it is possible to enter into that awareness. Don Juan had accomplished what the rule prescribed.

The rule determined that his next movement was to introduce me to Florinda, the only one of his warriors whom I had not met. Don Juan told me that I had to go to her house by myself, because whatever transpired between Florinda and myself was of no concern to others. He said that Florinda was to be my personal guide exactly as if I were a Nagual like him. He had had that kind of relationship with the warrior of his benefactor's party who was comparable to Florinda.

Don Juan left me one day at the door of Nelida's house. He told me to walk in, that Florinda was waiting for me inside.

"It's an honor to make your acquaintance," I said to the woman who was facing me in the hall.

"I'm Florinda," she said.

We looked at each other in silence. I was awestruck. My state of awareness was as keen as it had ever been. Never again have I experienced a comparable sensation.

"That's a beautiful name," I managed to say, but I meant more than that.

The soft and long enunciation of the Spanish vowels made the name fluid and sonorous; especially the i after the r. The name was not rare; I simply had never met anyone, until that day, who was the essence of that name. The woman in front of me fit into it as if it had been made for her, or perhaps as if she herself had made her person fit into it.

Physically she looked exactly like Nelida, except that she seemed more self-confident, more powerful. She was rather tall and slender. She had the olive skin of Mediterranean people. Spanish, or perhaps French. She was old and yet she was not feeble or even aged. Her body seemed to be supple and lean. Long legs, angular features, small mouth, a beautifully chiseled nose, dark eyes and braided white hair. No jowls, no sagging skin on her face and neck. She was old as if she had been made up to look old.

Remembering, in retrospect, my first meeting with her, I am reminded of something thoroughly unrelated but apropos. I saw once in a weekly newspaper a reprint of a twenty-year-old photograph of a then-young Hollywood actress who had been made up to look twenty years older in order to play the role of an aging woman. Next to it, the paper had printed a current picture of the same actress as she looked after twenty real years of hard living. Florinda, in my subjective judgment, was like the first picture of the movie actress, a young girl made up to look old.

"What do we have here?" she said pinching me. "You don't look like much. Soft. Indulging to the core no doubt."

Her bluntness reminded me of don Juan's; so did the inner life of her eyes. It had occurred to me, looking back at my life with don Juan, that his eyes were always in repose. One could see no agitation in them. It was not that don Juan's eyes were beautiful to look at. I have seen gorgeous eyes, but never have I found them to say anything. Florinda's eyes, like don Juan's, gave me the feeling that they had witnessed all there is to witness; they were calm, but not bland. The excitement had been driven inward and had turned into something I could only describe as inner life.

Florinda took me through the living room and out to a roofed patio. We sat on some comfortable sofalike chairs. Her eyes seemed to look for something in my face.

"Do you know who I am and what I'm supposed to do for you?" she asked.

I said that all I knew about her and her relation to me was what don Juan had sketched out. In the course of explaining my position I called her doña Florinda.

"Don't call me doña Florinda," she said with a childish gesture of annoyance and embarrassment. "I'm not that old yet, or even that respectable."

I asked her how she expected me to address her.

"Just Florinda will do," she said. "Insofar as to who I am, I can tell you right off that I am a woman warrior who knows the secrets of *stalking*. And insofar as what I am supposed to do for you, I can tell you that I am going to teach you the first seven principles of *stalking*, the first three principles of the rule for *stalkers*, and the first three maneuvers of *stalking*."

She added that the normal thing was for every warrior to forget what transpires when the interaction is on the left side, and that it would take years for me to come to grips with whatever she was going to teach me. She said that her instruction was merely the beginning, and that some day she would finish teaching me, but under different circumstances.

I asked her if she minded my asking her questions.

"Do as you please," she said. "All I need from you is your commitment to practice. After all, you know in one way or another whatever we're going to discuss. Your shortcomings are that you have no self-confidence and are unwilling to claim your knowledge as power. The Nagual, being a man, mesmerized you. You cannot act on your own. Only a woman can liberate you from that.

"I will begin by telling you the story of my life, and in doing so, things will become clear to you. I will have to tell it to you in bits, so you will have to come here quite often."

Her apparent willingness to tell me about her life struck me as being at odds with the reticence of everyone else to reveal anything personal about themselves. After years with them I had accepted their ways so unquestioningly that her voluntary intent to reveal her personal life was freakish to me. Her statement put me immediately on guard.

"I beg your pardon," I said. "Did you say that you are going to reveal your personal life to me?"

"Why not?" she asked.

I answered her with a long explanation of what don Juan had told me about the encumbering force of personal history, and the need that a warrior has to erase it. I wrapped it up by telling her that he had prohibited me from ever talking about my life.

She laughed in a high falsetto voice. She seemed to be delighted.

"That applies only to men," she said. "The *not-doing* of your personal life is to tell endless stories, but not a single one about your real self. You see, being a man means that you have a solid history behind you. You have family, friends, acquaintances, and every one of them has a definite idea of you. Being a man means that you're accountable. You cannot disappear that easily. In order to erase yourself, you needed a lot of work.

"My case is different. I'm a woman and that gives me a splendid advantage. I'm not accountable. Don't you know that women are not accountable?"

"I don't know what you mean by accountable," I said.

"I mean that a woman can easily disappear," she replied. "A woman can, if nothing else, get married. A woman belongs to the husband. In a family with lots of children, the daughters are discarded very early. No one counts on them and chances are that some will vanish without leaving a trace. Their disappearance is easily accepted.

"A son, on the other hand, is something one banks on. It's not that easy for a son to slip off and vanish. And even if he does, he will leave traces behind him. A son feels guilty for disappearing. A daughter does not.

"When the Nagual trained you to keep your mouth shut about your personal life, he intended to help you to overcome your feeling of having done wrong to your family and friends who were counting on you one way or another.

"After a lifetime struggle the male warrior ends up, of course, erasing himself, but that struggle takes its toll on the man. He becomes secretive, forever on guard against himself. A woman doesn't have to contend with that hardship. A woman is already prepared to disintegrate into thin air. In fact, it's expected of her.

"Being a woman, I'm not compelled to secrecy. I don't give a fig about it. Secrecy is the price you men have to pay for being important to society. The struggle is only for the men, because they resent erasing themselves and would find curious ways to pop up somewhere, somehow. Take yourself for instance; you go around giving lectures."

Florinda made me nervous in a very peculiar way. I felt strangely restless in her presence. I would admit without hesitation that don Juan and Silvio Manuel also made me feel nervous and apprehensive, but it was a different feeling. I was actually afraid of them, especially Silvio Manuel. He terrified me and yet I had learned to live with my terror. Florinda did not frighten me. My nervousness was rather the result of being annoyed, threatened by her savoir faire.

She did not stare at me the way don Juan or Silvio Manuel used to. They would always fix their eyes on me until I moved my face away in a gesture of submission. Florinda only glanced at me. Her eyes moved continually from thing to thing. She seemed to examine not only my eyes, but every inch of my face and body. As she talked, she would shift in quick glances from my face to my hands, or to her feet, or to the roof.

"I make you ill at ease, don't I?" she asked.

Her question caught me thoroughly off guard. I laughed. Her tone was not threatening at all.

"You do," I said.

"Oh, it's perfectly understandable," she went on. "You are used to being a man. A woman for you is something made for your benefit. A woman is stupid to you. And the fact that you're a man and the Nagual makes things even more difficult."

I felt obligated to defend myself. I thought that she was a very opinionated lady and I wanted to tell her so. I started off in great form but petered out almost immediately upon hearing her laughter. It was a joyous, youthful laughter. Don Juan and don Genaro used to laugh at me all the time and their laughter was also youthful, but Florinda's had a different vibration. There was no hurry in her laughter, no pressure.

"I think we'd better go inside," she said. "There shouldn't be any distractions. The Nagual Juan Matus has already taken you around, showing you the world; that was important for what he had to tell you. I have other things to talk about, which require another setting."

We sat on a leather couch in a den off the patio. I felt more at ease indoors. She went right into the story of her life.

She said that she had been born in a fairly large Mexican city to a well-to-do family. As she was an only child, her parents spoiled her from the moment she was born. Without a trace of false modesty Florinda admitted that she had always been aware of being beautiful. She said that beauty is a demon that breeds and proliferates when admired. She assured me that she could say without the shadow of a doubt that that demon is the hardest one to overcome, and that if I would look around to find those who are beautiful I would find the most wretched beings imaginable.

I did not want to argue with her, yet I had the most intense desire to tell her that she was somehow dogmatic. She must have caught my feelings; she winked at me.

"They are wretched, you'd better believe it," she continued. "Try them. Be unwilling to go along with their idea that they are beautiful, and because of it, important. You'll see what I mean."

She said that she could hardly give her parents or herself full blame for her conceit. Everyone around her had conspired from her infancy on to make her feel important and unique.

"When I was fifteen," she went on, "I thought I was about the greatest thing that ever came to earth. Everybody said so, especially men."

She confessed that throughout her adolescent years she indulged in the attention and adulation of scores of admirers. At eighteen, she judiciously chose the best possible husband from the ranks of no less than eleven serious suitors. She married Celestino, a man of means, fifteen years her senior.

Florinda described her married life as heaven on earth. To the enormous circle of friends she already had she added Celestino's friends. The total effect was that of a perennial holiday.

Her bliss, however, lasted only six months, which went by almost unnoticed. It all came to a most abrupt and brutal end, when she contracted a mysterious and crippling disease. Her left foot, ankle and calf began to swell. The line of her beautiful leg was ruined; the swelling became so intense that the cutaneous tissues started to blister and burst. Her whole lower leg from the knee down became the site of scabs and a pestilent secretion. The skin became hard. The disease was diagnosed as elephantiasis. Doctors' attempts to cure her condition were clumsy and painful, and their final conclusion was that only in Europe were there medical centers advanced enough to possibly undertake a cure.

In a matter of three months Florinda's paradise had turned into hell on earth. Desperate and in true agony she wanted to die rather than go on. Her suffering was so pathetic that one day a servant girl, not being able to bear it any longer, confessed to her that she had been bribed by Celestino's former mistress to slip a certain concoction into her food—a poison manufactured by sorcerers. The servant girl, as an act of contrition, promised to take her to a curer, a woman reported to be the only person who could counteract such a poison.

Florinda chuckled, remembering her dilemma. She had been raised a devout Catholic. She did not believe in witchcraft or in Indian curers. But her pain was so intense and her condition so serious that she was willing to try anything. Celestino was deadly opposed. He wanted to turn the servant girl over to the authorities. Florinda interceded, not so much out of compassion, but out of the fear that she might not find the curer on her own.

Florinda suddenly stood up. She told me that I had to leave. She held my arm and walked me to the door as if I had been her oldest and dearest friend. She explained that I was exhausted, because to be in the left side awareness is a special and frail condition which has to be used sparingly. It certainly is not a state of power. The proof was that I had nearly died when Silvio Manuel had tried to rally my second attention by forcing me to enter boldly into it. She said that there is no way on earth that we can order anyone or ourselves to rally knowledge. It is rather a slow affair; the body, at the right time and under the proper circumstances of impeccability, rallies its knowledge without the intervention of desire.

We stood at the front door for a while exchanging pleasant remarks and trivialities. She suddenly said that the reason the Nagual Juan Matus had brought me to her that day was because he knew that his time on earth was coming to an end. The two forms of instruction that I had received, according to Silvio Manuel's master plan, had already been completed. All that was left pending was what she had to say to me. She stressed that hers was not instruction proper, but rather the establishing of my link to her.

The next time don Juan took me to see Florinda, just before he left me at the door he repeated what she had told me, that the time was approaching for him and his party to enter into the third attention. Before I could question him, he shoved me inside the house. His shove sent me not only into the house, but into my keenest state of awareness. I saw the wall of fog.

Florinda was standing in the hall, as if she had been waiting for don Juan to shove me in. She held my arm and quietly led me to the living room. We sat down. I wanted to start a conversation but I could not talk. She explained that a shove from an impeccable warrior, like the Nagual Juan Matus, can cause a shift into another area of awareness. She said that my mistake all along had been to believe that the procedures are important. The procedure of shoving a warrior into another state of consciousness is utilizable only if both participants, especially the one who shoves, are impeccable and imbued with personal power.

The fact that I was seeing the wall of fog made me feel utterly nervous, on a physical level. My body was shaking uncontrollably. Florinda said that my body was shaking because it had learned to crave for activity while it remained in that state of awareness, and that my body could also learn to focus its keenest attention on whatever was being said, rather than whatever was being done.

She told me then that to be placed on the left side consciousness was an expediency. By forcing me into a state of heightened awareness and allowing me to interact with his warriors only when I was in that state, the Nagual Juan Matus was making sure that I would have a ledge to stand on. Florinda said that his strategy was to cultivate a small part of the other self by deliberately filling it with memories of interaction. The memories are forgotten only to resurface someday in order to serve as a rational outpost from where to depart into the immeasurable vastness of the other self.

Because I was so nervous, she proposed to calm me down by proceeding with the story of her life, which, she clarified, was not really the story of her life as a woman in the world, but the story of how a crummy woman was helped to become a warrior.

She said that once she made up her mind to see the curer there was no way to stop her. She started off, carried on a stretcher by the servant girl and four men, on the two-day trip that changed the course of her life. There were no roads. It was mountainous and sometimes the men had to carry her on their backs.

They arrived at the curer's house at dusk. The place was well lit and there were lots of people in the house. Florinda said that a polite old man told her that the curer was away for the day treating a patient. The man seemed to be very well informed about the curer's activities and Florinda found it easy to talk to him. He was solicitous and he confided that he was a patient himself. He described his disease as an incurable condition that made him oblivious to the world. They chatted amicably until late. The old man was so helpful that he even gave Florinda his bed so she could rest and wait until the next day when the curer would return.

In the morning Florinda said that she was suddenly awakened by a sharp pain in her leg. A woman was moving her leg, pressing it with a piece of shiny wood.

"The curer was a very pretty woman," Florinda went on. "She took a look at my leg and shook her head. 'I know who has done this to you!' she said. 'He must have been handsomely paid, or he must have surmised that you are a useless human being. Which do you think it was?' "

Florinda laughed. She said that she thought the curer was either crazy or was being rude. She had no conception that anyone in the world could possibly believe that she was a useless human being. Even though she was in excruciating pain, she let the woman know, in so many words, that she was a rich and worthy person, and nobody's fool.

Florinda recalled that the curer changed her attitude on the spot. She seemed to have gotten scared. She respectfully addressed her as "Missy" and got up from her chair and ordered everyone out of the room. When they were alone the curer sat on Florinda's chest and pushed her head backward over the edge of the bed. Florinda said that she fought her. She thought that she was going to be killed. She tried to scream, to alert her servants, but the curer quickly covered her head with a blanket and plugged her nose. Florinda gasped for air and had to breathe through her open mouth. The more the curer pressed on Florinda's chest and the tighter she plugged her nose, the wider Florinda opened her mouth. When she realized what the curer was really doing, she had already drunk the foul liquid contents of a large bottle which the curer had put into her open mouth. Florinda commented that the curer had maneuvered her so well that she did not even choke in spite of the fact that her head was dangling over the side of the bed.

"I drank so much liquid that I was about to get sick," Florinda continued. "She made me sit up and looked right into my eyes without blinking. I wanted to put my finger down my throat and vomit. She slapped me until my lips bled. An Indian slapping me! Drawing blood from my lips! Neither my father nor my mother had ever laid a hand on me. My surprise was so great that I forgot the discomfort in my stomach.

"She called my men and told them to take me home. Then she leaned over and put her mouth to my ear so no one would hear, 'If you don't come back in nine days, you asshole,' she whispered, 'you'll swell up like a toad and wish to God you were dead.' "

Florinda said that the liquid had irritated her throat and vocal cords. She could not utter a word. This, however, was the least of her worries. When she arrived at her home Celestino was waiting in a state of frenzy. Being incapable of speaking, Florinda was in the position to observe him. She noticed that his anger had nothing to do with worrying about her health, but with concern about his standing as a man of wealth and social status. He could not bear to be seen by his influential friends as resorting to Indian curers. He was raging, shouting that he was going to take his complaint to the army headquarters, have the soldiers capture the woman curer and bring her to town to be thrashed and thrown in jail. These were not just empty threats; he actually pressed a military commander to send a patrol after the curer. The soldiers came back a few days later with the news that the woman had fled.

Florinda was put at ease by her maid, who assured her that the curer would be waiting for her if she cared to go back. Although the inflammation of her throat persisted to the point that she could not eat solid food and could barely swallow liquids, Florinda could hardly wait for the day when she was supposed to go back to see the curer. The medicine had eased the pain in her leg.

When she let Celestino know her intentions, he became furious enough to round up some help in order to put an end to the nonsense himself. He and three of his trusted men went on horseback ahead of her.

Florinda said that when she arrived at the curer's house, she expected to find her perhaps dead, but instead she found Celestino sitting alone. He had sent his men to three different places in the vicinity with orders to bring back the curer, by force if necessary. Florinda saw the same old man she had met the time before; he was trying to calm her husband down, assuring him that any one of his men would be back shortly with the woman.

As soon as Florinda was placed on a cot in the front porch, the curer stepped out of the house. She began to insult Celestino, calling him names, yelling obscenities at him until she got him so angry that he rushed to strike her. The old man held him back and begged him not to hit her. He implored on his knees, pointing out that she was an old woman. Celestino was unmoved. He said that he was going to horsewhip her regardless of her age. He advanced to grab her but was stopped cold. Six awesome-looking men came out from behind the bushes wielding their machetes. Florinda said that fear froze Celestino to the spot. He was ashen. The curer came to him and told him that either he would meekly let her whip him on the buttocks or her helpers would hack him to pieces. As proud a man as he was, he bent over meekly to be whipped. The curer had reduced him in a few moments to a helpless man. She laughed in his face. She knew that he was pinned down and she let him sink. He had walked into her trap, like the careless fool that he was, drunk with his own inflated ideas about his worth.

Florinda looked at me and smiled. She was quiet for a while.

"The first principle of the art of *stalking* is that warriors choose their battleground," she said. "A warrior never goes into battle without knowing what the surroundings are. The woman curer had shown me, through her battle with Celestino, the first principle of *stalking*.

"Then she came over to where I was lying down. I was crying. That was the only thing I could do. She seemed concerned. She tucked my blanket around my shoulders and smiled and winked at me.

" 'The deal is still on, asshole,' she said. 'Come back as soon as you can if you want to live. But don't bring your master with you, you little whore. Come only with those who are absolutely necessary.' "

Florinda fixed her eyes on me for a moment. From her silence I surmised that she wanted my comments.

"To discard everything that is unnecessary is the second principle of the art of *stalking*," she said without giving me time to say anything.

Her account had absorbed me so intensely that I had not noticed that the wall of fog had disappeared—or when. I simply realized that it was not there anymore. Florinda got up from her chair and led me to the door. We stood there for awhile, as we had done at the end of our first meeting.

Florinda said that Celestino's anger had also permitted the curer to point out, not to her reason, but to her body, the first three precepts of the rule for *stalkers*. Although her mind was focused entirely on herself, since nothing else existed for her outside her physical pain and the anguish of losing her beauty, still her body had acknowledged what had happened, and needed later on only a reminder in order to put everything in place.

"Warriors don't have the world to cushion them, so they must have the rule," she went on. "Yet the rule of *stalkers* applies to everyone.

"Celestino's arrogance was his undoing and the beginning of my instruction and liberation. His self-importance, which was also mine, forced us both to believe that we were above practically everybody. The curer brought us down to what we really are—nothing.

"The first precept of the rule is that everything that surrounds us is an unfathomable mystery.

"The second precept of the rule is that we must try to unravel these mysteries, but without ever hoping to accomplish this.

"The third, that a warrior, aware of the unfathomable mystery that surrounds him and aware of his duty to try to unravel it, takes his rightful place among mysteries and regards himself as one. Consequently, for a warrior there is no end to the mystery of being, whether being means being a pebble, or an ant, or oneself. That is a warrior's humbleness. One is equal to everything."

There was a long and forced silence. Florinda smiled, playing with the tip of her long braid. She said that I had had enough.

The third time I went to see Florinda, don Juan did not leave me at the door but walked in with me. All the members of his party were congregated in the house, and they greeted me as if I were returning home from a long trip. It was an exquisite event; it integrated Florinda with the rest of them in my feelings since that was the first time she had joined them while I was present.

The next time I went to Florinda's house, don Juan unexpectedly shoved me as he had done before. My shock was immense. Florinda was waiting for me in the hall. I had entered instantly into the state where the wall of fog is visible.

"I've told you how the principles of the art of *stalking* were shown to me," she said as soon as we sat down on the couch in her living room. "Now, you must do the same for me. How did the Nagual Juan Matus show them to you?"

I told her that I could not remember offhand. I had to think about it, and I could not think. My body was frightened.

"Don't complicate things," she said in a tone of command. "Aim at being simple. Apply all the concentration you have to decide whether or not to enter into battle, for any battle is a battle for one's life. This is the third principle of the art of *stalking*. A warrior must be willing and ready to make his last stand here and now. But not in a helter-skelter way."

I simply could not organize my thoughts. I stretched my legs and lay down on the couch. I took deep breaths to relax my midsection, which seemed to be tied in knots.

"Good," Florinda said. "I see that you're applying the

fourth principle of the art of *stalking*. Relax, abandon yourself, fear nothing. Only then will the powers that guide us open the road and aid us. Only then."

I struggled to remember how don Juan had shown me the principles of the art of *stalking*. For some inexplicable reason my mind refused to focus on my past experience. Don Juan was so vague a memory. I stood up and began to look around.

The room we were in was exquisitely arranged. The floor was made of large buff-colored tiles; excellent craftsmanship had been involved in laying it. I was about to examine the furniture. I moved toward a beautiful dark-brown table. Florinda jumped to my side and shook me vigorously.

"You've correctly applied the fifth principle of the art of *stalking*," she said. "Don't let yourself wander away."

"What is the fifth principle?" I asked.

"When faced with odds that cannot be dealt with, warriors retreat for a moment," she said. "They let their minds meander. They occupy their time with something else. Anything would do.

"You've done just that. But now that you've accomplished it, you must apply the sixth principle: Warriors compress time; even an instant counts. In a battle for your life, a second is an eternity; an eternity that may decide the outcome. Warriors aim at succeeding, therefore they compress time. Warriors don't waste an instant."

All of a sudden a bulk of memories erupted into my awareness. I excitedly told Florinda that I could certainly remember the first time don Juan had acquainted me with those principles. Florinda put her fingers to her lips in a gesture that demanded my silence. She said that she had only been interested in bringing me face to face with the principles but she did not want me to relate those experiences to her.

Florinda went on with her story. She said that as the curer was telling her to come back without Celestino, she had her drink a concoction that alleviated her pain almost instantly, and she also whispered in her ear that she, Florinda, had to make a momentous decision by herself, that she should put her mind at ease by doing something else, but that she should not waste a moment once she had reached her decision.

At home she stated her desire to go back. Celestino did not see any point in objecting because her conviction was unshakable.

"Almost immediately I went back to see the curer," Florinda continued. "This time we went on horseback. I took my most trusted servants with me, the girl who had given me the poison and a man to handle the horses. We had a rough time going over those mountains; the horses were very nervous because of the stench of my leg, but we somehow made it. Without knowing I had used the third principle of the art of *stalking*. I had put my life, or what was left of it, on the line. I was willing and ready to die. It wasn't such a great decision for me, I was dying anyway. It is a fact that when one is half dead, as in my case, not with great pain but with great discomfort, the tendency is to get so lazy and weak that no effort is possible.

"I stayed at the curer's house for six days. By the second day I felt better already. The swelling went down. The oozing from the leg had stopped. There was no more pain. I was just a little weak and wobbly in the knees when I tried to walk.

"During the sixth day the curer took me to her room. She was very careful with me and, showing me every consideration, made me sit on her bed and gave me coffee. She sat on the floor at my feet, facing me. I can remember her exact words. 'You are very, very sick and only I can cure you,' she said. 'If I don't, you'll die a death that is not to be believed. Since you're an imbecile, you'll last to the bitter end. On the other hand, I could cure you in one day but I won't. You will have to keep coming here until you have understood what I have to show you. Only then will I cure you completely; otherwise, being the imbecile you are, you will never come back.' "

Florinda said that the curer, with great patience, explained to her the very delicate points of her decision to help her. She did not understand a word of it. The explanation made her believe more than ever that the curer was a bit touched in the head.

When the curer realized she was not getting through to Florinda, she became more stern and made her repeat over and over, as if Florinda were a child, that without the curer's help her life was finished, and that the curer could choose to cancel the cure and leave her hopelessly to die. Finally the woman lost her patience when Florinda begged her to finish healing her and send her home to her family; she picked up a bottle containing the medicine and smashed it on the ground and told Florinda that she was through with her.

Florinda said that she cried then—the only real tears of her life. She told the curer that all she wanted was to be cured and that she was more than willing to pay for it. The woman said it was too late for monetary payment, that what she wanted from Florinda was her attention, not her money.

Florinda admitted to me that she had learned during the course of her life how to get anything she wanted. She knew how to be obstinate, and she raised the point that there must have been thousands of patients that had come to the curer, half dead just like herself, and that the curer took their money —why was her case different? The curer's reply, which was no explanation at all for Florinda, was that being a seer she had *seen* Florinda's luminous body and she and the curer were exactly alike. Florinda thought that the woman had to be mad not to realize that there was a world of difference between them. The curer was a rude Indian, uneducated and primitive, while Florinda was rich and beautiful and white.

Florinda asked the woman what she was planning to do to her. The curer told her that she had been commissioned to heal her and then teach her something of great importance. Florinda wanted to know who had commissioned her. The woman replied that it was the Eagle—a reply which convinced Florinda that the woman was absolutely crazy. And yet Florinda saw no alternative to complying with the woman's demands. She told her that she was willing to do anything.

The woman changed her belligerent attitude instantly. She gave Florinda some medicine to take home and told her to come back as soon as she could.

"As you yourself know," Florinda went on, "a teacher must trick the disciple. She tricked me with my cure. She was right. I was such an idiot that if she had cured me right away I would've gone back to my stupid life, as if nothing had ever happened to me. Don't we all do that?"

Florinda returned the following week. Upon arriving she was greeted by the old man she had met before. He talked to her as if they were the best of friends. He said that the curer had been away for several days and would not be back for several more, and that she had entrusted him with some medicine for her in case she showed up. He told Florinda in a very friendly but commanding tone that the curer's absence had left her with only two alternatives: she could either go back home, possibly in worse physical shape than before due to the strenuous trip, or she could follow the curer's carefully outlined instructions. He added that if she decided to stay and start her treatment right away, in three to four months she would be as good as new. There was, however, one stipulation: if she decided to stay, she had to remain in the curer's house for eight consecutive days and had, perforce, to send her servants home.

Florinda said that there was nothing to decide—that she had to stay. The old man immediately gave her the potion that the curer had apparently left for her. He sat up with her most of the night. He was reassuring, and his easy talk kindled Florinda's optimism and confidence.

Her two servants left the next morning after breakfast. Florinda was not at all afraid. She trusted the old man implicitly. He told her that he had to build a box for her treatment, in accordance with the curer's instructions. He made her sit on a low chair, which had been placed in the center of a circular area with no vegetation on it. While she was seated there, the old man introduced her to three young men he said were his assistants. Two were Indians and one was white.

It took the four of them less than an hour to construct a crate around the chair where Florinda was sitting. When they were finished, Florinda was encased snugly inside a crate, which had a lattice top to allow for ventilation. One of its sides was hinged in order to serve as a door.

The old man opened the door and helped Florinda to step out of it. He took her to the house and asked her to help him prepare her medicine, in order to have it handy for the time when the curer would return.

Florinda was fascinated with the way he worked. He made a potion out of plants with a pungent odor and prepared a bucket of a hot liquid. He suggested that for her comfort she should immerse her leg in the bucket, and if she felt like it, she should drink the concoction he had prepared before it lost its potency. Florinda obeyed him unquestioningly. The relief she felt was remarkable.

The old man then assigned her a room to herself and had the young men put the crate inside the room. He told her that it might be days before the curer would show up; in the meantime she had to follow meticulously all the instructions left for her. She agreed with him, and he produced a list of tasks. They included a great deal of walking in order to collect the medicinal plants needed for her potions, and her assistance in their actual preparation.

Florinda said that she spent twelve days there instead of eight, because her servants were late due to torrential rains. It was not until the tenth day that she discovered that the woman had never left and that the old man was actually the real curer.

Florinda laughed, describing her shock. The old man had tricked her into actively participating in her own cure. Fur-thermore, under the pretext that the curer demanded it, he put her inside the crate daily for at least six hours, in order to fulfill a specific task he had called the "recapitulation."

At that point in her account, Florinda scrutinized me and concluded that I had had enough and that it was time for me to leave.

On our next meeting, she explained that the old man was her benefactor, and that she was the first *stalker* that the women of her benefactor's party had found for the Nagual Juan Matus. But none of that was known to her then. Even though her benefactor made her shift levels of awareness and revealed this to her, it was to no avail. She had been raised to be beautiful and that had created a shield around her so impenetrable that she was impervious to change.

Her benefactor concluded that she needed time. He devised a plan to draw Celestino to Florinda's battleground. He made her see things about Celestino's personality that she herself knew to be true but had not had the courage to face on her own. Celestino was very possessive of everything he owned; his wealth and Florinda ranked high among his possessions. He had been forced to swallow his pride over his humiliation at the hands of the curer because the curer was cheap and Florinda was actually recuperating. He was biding his time, waiting for a moment when the cure would be complete in order to seek revenge.

Florinda said that her benefactor told her that the danger was that her complete recovery was going to be too quick and Celestino would decide, since he made all the decisions in the house, that there was no longer any need for Florinda to see the curer. Her benefactor then gave her a potion to apply on her other leg. The unguent was terribly pungent and produced an irritation on the skin that resembled the spreading of the disease. Her benefactor advised her to use the unguent every time she wanted to come back to see him, even though she did not need a treatment.

Florinda said that it took a year to be cured. In the course of that time, her benefactor acquainted her with the rule and drilled her like a soldier in the art of *stalking*. He made her apply the principles of *stalking* to the things she did daily; small things at first, leading up to the major issues of her life.

In the course of that year, her benefactor also introduced her to the Nagual Juan Matus, whom she described as very witty and thoughtful but still the most unruly and terrifying young man she had ever met. She said that it was the Nagual Juan Matus who helped her escape from Celestino. He and Silvio Manuel smuggled her out of the city through police and army roadblocks. Celestino had filed a legal complaint for desertion, and being an influential man, he had used his resources to try to stop her from leaving him.

Because of this her benefactor had to move to another part of Mexico and she had to remain in hiding in his house for years; this situation suited Florinda as she had to fulfill the task of recapitulating and for that she needed absolute quiet and solitude.

She explained that a recapitulation is the forte of *stalkers* as the *dreaming body* is the forte of *dreamers*. It consisted of recollecting one's life down to the most insignificant detail. Thus her benefactor had given her that crate as a tool and a symbol. It was a tool that would permit her to learn concentration, for she would have to sit in there for years, until all of her life had passed in front of her eyes. And it was a symbol of the narrow boundaries of our person. Her benefactor told her that whenever she had finished her recapitulation, she would break the crate to symbolize that she no longer abided by the limitations of her person.

She said that *stalkers* use crates or earth coffins in order to seal themselves in while they are reliving, more than merely recollecting, every moment of their lives. The reason why *stalkers* must recapitulate their lives in such a thorough manner is that the Eagle's gift to man includes its willingness to accept a surrogate instead of genuine awareness, if such a surrogate be a perfect replica. Florinda explained that since awareness is the Eagle's food, the Eagle can be satisfied with a perfect recapitulation in place of consciousness.

Florinda gave me then the fundamentals of recapitulating. She said that the first stage is a brief recounting of all the incidents in our lives that in an obvious manner stand out for examination.

The second stage is a more detailed recollection, which starts systematically at a point that could be the moment prior to the *stalker* sitting in the crate, and theoretically could extend to the moment of birth.

She assured me that a perfect recapitulation could change a warrior as much, if not more, than the total control of the *dreaming body*. In this respect, *dreaming* and *stalking* led to the same end, the entering into the third attention. It was important for a warrior, however, to know and practice both. She said that for women it took different configurations in the luminous body to master one or the other. Men, on the other hand, could do both with a degree of ease, yet they could never get to the level of proficiency that the women attained in each art.

Florinda explained that the key element in recapitulating was breathing. Breath for her was magical, because it was a life-giving function. She said that recollecting was easy if one could reduce the area of stimulation around the body. This was the reason for the crate; then breathing would foster deeper and deeper memories. Theoretically, *stalkers* have to remember every feeling that they have had in their lives, and this process begins with a breath. She warned me that the things she was teaching me were only preliminaries, that at a later time, in a different setting she would teach me the intricacies.

Florinda said that her benefactor directed her to write down a list of the events to be relived. He told her that the procedure starts with an initial breath. *Stalkers* begin with their chin on the right shoulder and slowly inhale as they move their head over a hundred and eighty degree arc. The breath terminates on the left shoulder. Once the inhalation ends, the head goes back to a relaxed position. They exhale looking straight ahead.

The *stalker* then takes the event at the top of the list and remains with it until all the feelings expended in it have been recounted. As *stalkers* remember the feelings they invested in whatever it is that they are remembering, they inhale slowly, moving their heads from the right shoulder to the left. The function of this breathing is to restore energy. Florinda claimed that the luminous body is constantly creating cobweblike filaments, which are projected out of the luminous mass, propelled by emotions of any sort. Therefore, every situation of interaction, or every situation where feelings are involved, is potentially draining to the luminous body. By breathing from right to left while remembering a feeling, *stalkers*, through the magic of breathing, pick up the filaments they left behind. The next immediate breath is from left to right and it is an exhalation. With it *stalkers* eject filaments left in them by other luminous bodies involved in the event being recollected.

She stated that these were the mandatory preliminaries of *stalking*, which all the members of her party went through as an introduction to the more demanding exercises of the art. Unless stalkers have gone through the preliminaries in order to retrieve the filaments they have left in the world, and particularly in order to reject those that others have left in them, there is no possibility of handling *controlled folly*, because those foreign filaments are the basis of one's limitless capacity for self-importance. In order to practice *controlled folly*, since it is not a way to fool or chastise people or feel superior to them, one has to be capable of laughing at oneself. Florinda said that one of the results of a detailed recapitulation is genuine laughter upon coming face to face with the boring repetition of one's self-esteem, which is at the core of all human interaction.

Florinda emphasized that the rule defined *stalking* and *dreaming* as arts; therefore they are something that one performs. She said that the life-giving nature of breath is what also gives it its cleansing capacity. It is this capacity that makes a recapitulation into a practical matter.

In our next meeting Florinda summed up what she called her last-minute instructions. She asserted that since the joint assessment of the Nagual Juan Matus and his party of warriors had been that I did not need to deal with the world of everyday life, they had taught me *dreaming* instead of *stalking*. She explained that this assessment had been radically modified, and that they had found themselves in an awkward position; they did not have any more time to teach me *stalking*. She had to stay behind, on the periphery of the third attention, in order to fulfill her assignment at a later time, when I would be ready. On the other hand, if I were to leave the world with them, she was exonerated from that responsibility.

Florinda said that her benefactor considered the three basic techniques of *stalking*—the crate, the list of events to be recapitulated, and the *stalker*'s breath—to be about the most important tasks a warrior can fulfill. Her benefactor thought that a profound recapitulation is the most expedient means to lose the human form. Thus it is easier for *stalkers*, after recapitulating their lives, to make use of all the *not-doings* of the self, such as erasing personal history, losing self-importance, breaking routines and so forth.

Florinda said that her benefactor gave all of them the example of what he meant, first by acting out his premises, and then by giving them the warrior's rationales for his actions. In her own case, he, being a master of the art of *stalking*, acted out the ploy of her disease and cure which not only was congruous with the warrior's way, but was a masterful introduction to the seven basic principles of the art of *stalking*. He first drew Florinda to his own battleground where she was at his mercy; he forced her to discard what was not essential; he taught her to put her life on the line with a decision; he taught her how to relax; in order to help her regroup her resources, he made her enter into a new and different mood of optimism and self-confidence; he taught her to compress time; and finally he showed her that a *stalker* never pushes himself to the front.

Florinda was most impressed by the last principle. To her it summarized everything she wanted to tell me in her last-minute instructions.

"My benefactor was the chief," Florinda said. "And yet, looking at him, no one would've ever believed it. He always had one of his female warriors as a front, while he freely mingled with the patients, pretending to be one of them, or he posed as an old fool who was constantly sweeping dry leaves with a handmade broom."

Florinda explained that in order to apply the seventh principle of the art of *stalking,* one has to apply the other six. Thus her benefactor was always looking on from behind the scenes. Thanks to that he was capable of avoiding or parrying conflicts. If there was strife, it was never directed toward him, but towards his front, the female warrior.

"I hope that you have realized by now," she went on, "that only a master *stalker* can be a master of *controlled folly. Controlled folly* doesn't mean to con people. It means, as my benefactor explained it, that warriors apply the seven basic principles of the art of *stalking* to whatever they do, from the most trivial acts to life and death situations.

"Applying these principles brings about three results. The first is that *stalkers* learn never to take themselves seriously; they learn to laugh at themselves. If they're not afraid of being a fool, they can fool anyone. The second is that *stalkers* learn to have endless patience. *Stalkers* are never in a hurry; they never fret. And the third is that *stalkers* learn to have an endless capacity to improvise."

Florinda stood up. We had been sitting, as usual, in her living room. I immediately assumed that our conversation was over. She said that there was one more topic to present to me before we said goodbye. She took me to another patio inside her house. I had never been in that part of her house before. She called someone softly and a woman stepped out from a room. I did not recognize her at first. The woman called my name and then I realized that she was doña Soledad. Her change was stupendous. She was younger and more powerful.

Florinda said that Soledad had been inside a recapitulating crate for five years, that the Eagle had accepted her recapitulation in place of her awareness and had let her go free. Doña Soledad assented with a movement of her head. Florinda abruptly ended the meeting and told me that it was time for me to leave because I had no more energy.

I went to Florinda's house many more times afterward. I saw her every time but only for a few moments. She told me that she had decided not to instruct me anymore because it was to my advantage that I deal only with doña Soledad.

Doña Soledad and I met several times, but whatever took place during our meetings is something quite incomprehensible to me. Every time we were together she would make me sit at the door of her room facing the east. She would sit to my right, touching me; then we would make the wall of fog stop rotating and both of us would be left facing the south, into her room.

I had already learned with la Gorda to stop the rotation of the wall; it seemed that doña Soledad was helping me to realize another aspect of that perceptual capacity. I had correctly detected with la Gorda that only a portion of us stopped the wall. It was as if suddenly I had become divided in two. A portion of my total self was looking straight ahead and *saw* an immobile wall to my right; while another larger portion of my total self had turned ninety degrees to the right and was staring at the wall.

Every time doña Soledad and I stopped the wall we remained staring at it; we never entered into the area between the parallel lines as the Nagual woman, la Gorda and I had done scores of times. Doña Soledad would make me gaze every time into the fog as if the fog were a reflective glass. I would experience then the most extravagant disassociation. It was as if I were racing at breakneck speed. I would see bits of a landscape forming in the fog, and suddenly I was in another physical reality; it was a mountainous area, rugged and inhospitable. Doña Soledad was always there in the company of a lovely woman who laughed uproariously at me.

My incapacity to remember what we did beyond that point was even more acute than my incapacity to remember what the Nagual woman and la Gorda and I did in the area between the parallel lines. It seemed that doña Soledad and I entered into another area of awareness that was unknown to me. I was already in what I thought was my keenest state of consciousness, and yet there was something even keener. The aspect of the second attention that doña Soledad was obviously showing me was more complex and more inaccessible than anything I had witnessed so far. All I could recollect was a sense of having moved a great deal, a physical sensation comparable to having walked for miles, or to having hiked on rugged mountain trails. I also had a clear bodily certainty, although I could not fathom why, that doña Soledad, the woman, and I exchanged words, thoughts, feelings; but I could not pinpoint them.

After every meeting with doña Soledad, Florinda would immediately make me leave. Doña Soledad gave minimal verbal feedback. It appeared to me that being in a state of such heightened awareness affected her so profoundly she could hardly talk. There was something that we were seeing in that rugged landscape besides the lovely woman, or something we were doing together that left us breathless. She could not remember anything, although she tried.

I asked Florinda to clarify the nature of my journeys with doña Soledad. She said that a part of her last-minute instruction was to make me enter into the second attention as stalkers do, and that doña Soledad was more capable than she herself was to usher me into the *stalker*'s dimension.

On the meeting that was to be our last, Florinda, as she had done at the beginning of our instruction, was waiting for me in the hall. She took my arm and led me to the living room. We sat down. She warned me not to try as yet to make sense of my journeys with doña Soledad. She explained that *stalkers* are inherently different than *dreamers* in the way they use the world around them, and that what doña Soledad was doing was trying to help me to turn my head.

When don Juan had described the concept of turning a warrior's head to face a new direction, I had understood it as a metaphor that depicted a change in attitude. Florinda said that that description was true, but it was no metaphor. It was true that *stalkers* turn their heads; however, they do not turn them to face a new direction, but to face time in a different way. *Stalkers* face the oncoming time. Normally we face time as it recedes from us. Only *stalkers* can change that and face time as it advances on them.

Florinda explained that turning the head did not mean that one sees into the future, but that one sees time as something concrete, yet incomprehensible. It was superfluous, therefore, for me to try to think out whatever doña Soledad and I were doing. All of it would make sense when I could perceive the totality of myself and would then have the energy necessary to unravel that mystery.

Florinda told me, in the spirit of someone giving a bonus, that doña Soledad was a supreme *stalker*; she called her the greatest of them all. She said that doña Soledad could cross the parallel lines anytime. Furthermore, none of the warriors of don Juan Matus' party had been able to do what she had done. Doña Soledad, through her impeccable *stalking* techniques, had found her parallel being.

Florinda explained that whatever I had experienced with the Nagual Juan Matus, or Silvio Manuel, or Genaro, or Zuleica were only minute portions of the second attention; whatever doña Soledad was helping me witness was still another minute, but different portion.

Doña Soledad had not only made me face the oncoming time, but she had taken me to her parallel being. Florinda defined the parallel being as the counterbalance that all living creatures have by the fact that they are luminous beings filled with inexplicable energy. A parallel being of any person is another person of the same sex who is intimately and inextricably joined to the first one. They coexist in the world at the same time. The two parallel beings are like the two ends of the same pole.

It is nearly impossible for warriors to find their parallel being, because there are too many distracting factors in the life of a warrior, other priorities. But whoever is capable of accomplishing this feat would find, in his parallel being, just as doña Soledad had, an endless source of youth and energy.

Florinda stood up abruptly and took me to doña Soledad's room. Perhaps because I knew that it was going to be our last meeting, I was taken by a strange anxiety. Doña Soledad smiled at me when I told her what Florinda had just told me. She said, with what I thought to be a true warrior's humbleness, that she was not teaching me anything, that all she had aspired to do was to show me her parallel being, because that would be where she would retreat when the Nagual Juan Matus and his warriors left the world. However, something else had happened which was beyond her understanding. Florinda had explained to her that we had boosted each other's energy and that had made us face the oncoming time, not in small doses as Florinda would have liked us to, but in incomprehensible gobbles as my unruly nature wanted it.

The result of our last meeting was even more baffling. Doña Soledad, her parallel being and I remained for what I felt was an extraordinarily long time together. I saw every feature of the parallel being's face. I felt she was trying to tell me who she was. She also seemed to be cognizant that this was our last meeting. There was such an overpowering sense of frailty in her eyes. Then a windlike force blew us away into something that held no meaning for me.

Florinda suddenly helped me to stand up. She took me by the arm and led me to the door. Doña Soledad walked with us. Florinda said that I would have a hard time remembering all that had transpired because I was indulging in my rationality, a condition that could only worsen because they were about to leave and I would have no one to help me to shift levels of awareness. She added that someday doña Soledad and I would meet again in the world of everyday life.

It was then that I turned to doña Soledad and begged her to drive me out of my indulging; I told her that if she failed she should kill me. I did not want to live in the meagerness of my rationality.

"It's wrong to say that," Florinda said. "We're warriors, and warriors have only one thing in mind—their freedom. To die and be eaten by the Eagle is no challenge. On the other hand, to sneak around the Eagle and be free is the ultimate audacity."

15

The Plumed Serpent

Having accomplished every one of the goals which the rule specified, don Juan and his party of warriors were ready for their final task, to leave the world of everyday life. And all that was left for la Gorda, for the other apprentices and for me, was to witness it. There was only one unresolved problem: What to do with the apprentices? Don Juan said that properly they should leave with him by becoming incorporated into his own group; however, they were not ready. The reactions they had while attempting to cross the bridge had demonstrated to him what their weaknesses were.

Don Juan expressed the feeling that his benefactor's choice to wait years before gathering a warrior's party for him had been a wise choice and had produced positive results, while his own decision to set me up quickly with the Nagual woman and my own group had nearly been fatal to us.

I understood that he was voicing this not as an expression of regret but as an affirmation of the warrior's freedom to choose and accept his choice. He said, furthermore, that he had seriously considered following his benefactor's example, and that if he had done so, he would have found out soon enough that I was not a Nagual like him and no one else besides me would have been engaged beyond that point. As it was, Lydia, Rosa, Benigno, Nestor and Pablito were seriously handicapped; la Gorda and Josefina needed time to perfect themselves; only Soledad and Eligio were safe, for they were perhaps even more proficient than the warriors in his own group. Don Juan added that it was up to the nine of them to take their unfavorable or favorable circumstances and, without regret or despair or patting themselves on the back, turn their curse or blessing into a living challenge.

Don Juan pointed out that not everything about us had been a failure—the small part that we had played amidst his warriors had been a complete triumph in as much as the rule fit every one of my party except me. I fully agreed with him. To begin with, the Nagual woman was everything the rule had prescribed. She had poise, control; she was a being at war and yet thoroughly at ease. Without any overt preparation, she handled and led all of don Juan's gifted warriors even though they were more than twice her age. These men and women asserted that she was a carbon copy of the other Nagual woman they had known. She reflected perfectly each one of the female warriors, consequently she could also reflect the five women don Juan had found for my party, for they were the replicas of the older ones. Lydia was like Hermelinda, Josefina was like Zuleica, Rosa and la Gorda were like Nelida and Soledad was like Delia.

The men were also replicas of don Juan's warriors; Nestor was a copy of Vicente, Pablito of Genaro, Benigno of Silvio Manuel and Eligio was like Juan Tuma. The rule was indeed the voice of an overpowering force that had molded these people into a homogeneous whole. It was only by a strange twist of fate that they had been left stranded, without the leader that would find for them the passageway into the other awareness.

Don Juan said that all the members of my party had to enter into that other awareness by themselves, and that he did not know what their chances were, because that was up to each one of them individually. He had helped everyone impeccably; thus his spirit was free from worry and concern and his mind was free from idle speculations. All that was left for him to do was to show us pragmatically what it meant to cross over the parallel lines in one's totality.

Don Juan told me that at best I could only help one of the apprentices, and that he had picked la Gorda because of her prowess and because I was already familiar with her. He said that I had no more energy for the others, due to the fact that I had other duties to perform, other paths of action, which were congruous with my true task. Don Juan explained to me that every one of his own warriors knew what that task was but had not revealed it to me, because I needed to prove that I was worthy of it. The fact that they were at the end of their trail, and the fact that I had faithfully followed my instructions made it imperative that this revelation take place, although only in a partial form.

When the time came for don Juan to leave, he let me know while I was in a state of normal awareness. I missed the significance of what he was saying. Don Juan tried to the very end to induce me to join my two states of awareness. Everything would have been so simple if I had been capable of that merger. Since I was not, and was only rationally touched by his revelation, he made me shift levels of awareness in order to allow me to assess the event in more encompassing terms.

He warned me repeatedly that to be in the left side awareness is an advantage only in the sense that our grasp of things is accelerated. It is a disadvantage because it allows us to focus with inconceivable lucidity only on one thing at a time; this renders us dependent and vulnerable. We cannot be on our own while being in the left side awareness and have to be cushioned by warriors who have gained the totality of themselves and know how to handle themselves in that state.

La Gorda said that one day the Nagual Juan Matus and Genaro rounded up all the apprentices at her house. The Nagual made them shift into the left side awareness, and told them that his time on earth had come to an end.

She did not believe him at first. She thought that he was trying to startle them into acting like warriors. But then she realized that there was a glow in his eyes that she had never seen before.

Having made them shift levels of awareness, he talked with every one of them individually and made them go through a summation, so as to refreshen all the concepts and procedures he had acquainted them with. He did the same with me. My appointment took place the day before I saw him for the last time. In my case he conducted that summation in both states of awareness. In fact, he made me shift back and forth various times as if making sure that I would be completely saturated in both.

I had been unable to recollect at first what had taken place after this summation. One day la Gorda finally succeeded in breaking the barriers of my memory. She told me that she was inside my mind as if she were reading me. Her assessment was that what kept my memory locked up was that I was afraid to remember my pain. What had happened at Silvio Manuel's house the night before they left was inextricably enmeshed with my fear. She said that she had the clearest sensation that I was afraid, but she did not know the reason why. Nor could she remember what exactly had taken place in that house, specifically in the room where we sat down.

As la Gorda spoke I felt as if I were plummeting into an abyss. I realized that something in me was trying to make a connection between two separate events that I had witnessed in my two states of awareness. On my left side I had the locked-up memories of don Juan and his party of warriors on their last day on earth, on my right side I had the memory of having jumped that day into an abyss. In trying to join my two sides I experienced a total sense of physical descent. My knees gave way and I fell to the floor.

When I described my experience and my interpretation of it, la Gorda said that what was coming to my right side awareness was doubtlessly the memory that had surfaced in her as

I talked. She had just remembered that we had made one more attempt to cross the parallel lines with the Nagual Juan Matus and his party. She said that the two of us together with the rest of the apprentices had tried once more to cross the bridge.

I could not bring that memory into focus. There seemed to be a constricting force that prevented me from organizing my thoughts and feelings about it. La Gorda said that Silvio Manuel had told the Nagual Juan Matus to prepare me and all the apprentices for their crossing. He did not want to leave me in the world, because he thought that I did not stand a chance of fulfilling my task. The Nagual disagreed with him but carried out the preparations regardless of how he felt.

La Gorda told me that she remembered I had driven to her house to take her as well as the other apprentices to Silvio Manuel's house. They remained there while I went back to the Nagual Juan Matus and Genaro in order to prepare for the crossing.

I did not remember it at all. She insisted that I should use her as a guide, since we were so intimately joined; she assured me that I could read her mind and find something there that would awaken my full recollection.

My mind was in a state of great turmoil. A feeling of anxiety prevented me from even focusing on what la Gorda was saying. She kept on talking, describing what she remembered of our second attempt to cross that bridge. She said that Silvio Manuel had harangued them. He told them that they had had sufficient training to try once again to cross; what they needed to enter fully into the other self was to abandon the *intent* of their first attention. Once they were in the awareness of the other self the power of the Nagual Juan Matus and his party would pick them up and lift them off into the third attention with great facility—something they could not do if the apprentices were in their normal awareness.

At one instant, I was not listening to la Gorda any more. The sound of her voice was indeed a vehicle for me. Suddenly the memory of the entire event surfaced in my mind. I reeled under the impact of remembering. La Gorda stopped talking, and as I described my memory she also recollected everything. We had put together the last pieces of the separate memories of our two states of awareness.

I remembered that don Juan and don Genaro prepared me for the crossing while I was in a state of normal consciousness. I rationally thought that they were preparing me for a jump into an abyss.

La Gorda remembered that to prepare them for the crossing Silvio Manuel had hoisted them to the beams of the roof strapped in leather harnesses. There was one in every room of his house. The apprentices were kept suspended in them nearly all day.

La Gorda commented that to have a harness in one's room is an ideal thing. The Genaros, without really knowing what they were doing, had hit upon the quasi-memory of the harnesses they had been suspended from and had created their game. It was a game that combined the curative and cleansing qualities of being kept away from the ground, with the possibility of exercising the concentration that one needs for shifting from the right to the left side consciousness. Their game was indeed a device that helped them remember.

La Gorda said that after she and all the apprentices had remained suspended all day, Silvio Manuel had brought them down at dusk. All of them went with him to the bridge and waited there with the rest of the party until the Nagual Juan Matus and Genaro showed up with me. The Nagual Juan Matus explained to all of them that it had taken longer than he had anticipated to prepare me.

I remembered that don Juan and his warriors crossed over the bridge before we did. Doña Soledad and Eligio automatically went with them. The Nagual woman went over last. From the other side of the bridge Silvio Manuel signaled us to start walking. Without saying a word, all of us began at once. Midway across the bridge, Lydia, Rosa and Pablito seemed incapable of taking one more step. Benigno and Nestor walked almost to the end and then stopped. Only la Gorda, Josefina and I arrived to where don Juan and the others were standing.

What happened next was very much like what had happened the first time we attempted to go through. Silvio Manuel and Eligio held open something I believed was an actual slit. I had enough energy to focus my attention on it. It was not an opening on the hill that stood at the end of the bridge, nor was it an opening in the wall of fog, although I could distinguish a foglike vapor around the slit. It was a dark mysterious opening that stood by itself apart from everything else; it was as big as a man, but narrow. Don Genaro made a joke and called it "the cosmic vagina," a remark that brought roaring laughter from his peers. La Gorda and Josefina held on to me and we stepped in.

I felt instantly that I was being crushed. The same incalculable force that had nearly made me explode the first time had gripped me again. I could feel la Gorda and Josefina merging with me. I seemed to be wider than they were and the force flattened me against the two of them together.

The next thing I knew I was lying on the ground with la Gorda and Josefina on top of me. Silvio Manuel helped us stand up. He told me that it would be impossible for us to join them in their journey at that time, but that perhaps later, when we had tuned ourselves to perfection, the Eagle would let us go through.

As we walked back to his house, Silvio Manuel told me almost in a whisper that their path and my path had diverged from each other that night. He said that our paths would never meet again, and that I was alone. He exhorted me to be frugal and utilize every bit of my energy without wasting any of it. He assured me that if I could gain the totality of myself without excessive drainage I would have the energy to fulfill my task. If I drained myself excessively before I lost my human form, I was done for.

I asked him if there was a way to avoid drainage. He shook

his head. He replied that there was a way, but not for me. Whether I succeeded or not was not a matter of my volition. He then revealed my task. But he did not tell me how to carry it out. He said that someday the Eagle would put someone in my path to tell me how to do it. And not until I had succeeded would I be free.

When we got to the house, all of us congregated in the large room. Don Juan sat in the center of the room facing the southeast. The eight female warriors surrounded him. They sat in pairs on the cardinal points, also facing the southeast. Then the three male warriors made a triangle outside the circle with Silvio Manuel at the vertex that pointed to the southeast. The two female couriers sat flanking him, and the two male couriers sat in front of him almost against the wall.

The Nagual woman made the male apprentices sit against the east wall; she made the women sit against the west wall. She then led me to a place directly behind don Juan. We sat there together.

We remained seated for what I thought was only an instant, yet I felt a surge of unusual energy in my body. I believed that we had sat down and then immediately stood up. When I asked the Nagual woman why we got up so quickly, she replied that we had been sitting there for several hours, and that someday, before I entered into the third attention, all of it would come back to me.

La Gorda stated that not only did she have the sensation that we sat in that room only for an instant, but that she was never told that it had been otherwise. What the Nagual Juan Matus told her afterward was that she had the obligation to help the other apprentices, especially Josefina, and that one day I would return to give her the final push she needed to cross totally into the other self. She was tied to me and to Josefina. In our *dreaming together* under Zuleica's supervision we had exchanged enormities of our luminosity. That was why we were able to withstand together the pressure of the other self upon entering it in the flesh. He also told her that it was the power of the warriors of his party which had made the crossing so easy this time, and that when she would have to cross on her own, she had to be prepared to do it in *dreaming*.

After we had stood up Florinda came over to where I was. She took me by the arm and walked around the room with me, while don Juan and his warriors talked to the apprentices.

She said that I should not allow the events of that night at the bridge to confuse me. I should not believe, as the Nagual Juan Matus had believed at one time, that there is an actual physical passageway into the other self. The slit that I had seen was simply a construct of their *intent*, which had been trapped by a combination of the Nagual Juan Matus' obsession with passageways and Silvio Manuel's bizarre sense of humor; the mixture of both had produced the cosmic vagina. As far as she was concerned, the passage from one self to the other had no physicality. The cosmic vagina was a physical expression of the two men's power to move the "wheel of time."

Florinda explained that when she or her peers talked about time, they were not referring to something which is measured by the movement of a clock. Time is the essence of attention; the Eagle's emanations are made out of time; and properly, when one enters into any aspect of the other self, one is becoming acquainted with time.

Florinda assured me that that very night, while we sat in formation, they had had their last chance to help me and the apprentices to face the wheel of time. She said that the wheel of time is like a state of heightened awareness which is part of the other self, as the left side awareness is part of the self of everyday life, and that it could physically be described as a tunnel of infinite length and width; a tunnel with reflective furrows. Every furrow is infinite, and there are infinite numbers of them. Living creatures are compulsorily made, by the force of life, to gaze into one furrow. To gaze into it means to be trapped by it, to live that furrow.

She asserted that what warriors call *will* belongs to the wheel of time. It is something like the runner of a vine, or an intangible tentacle which all of us possess. She said that a warrior's final aim is to learn to focus it on the wheel of time in order to make it turn. Warriors who have succeeded in turning the wheel of time can gaze into any furrow and draw from it whatever they desire, such as the cosmic vagina. To be trapped compulsorily in one furrow of time entails seeing the images of that furrow only as they recede. To be free from the spellbinding force of those grooves means that one can look in either direction, as images recede or as they approach.

Florinda stopped talking and embraced me. She whispered in my ear that she would be back to finish her instruction someday, when I had gained the totality of myself.

Don Juan called everyone to come to where I was. They surrounded me. Don Juan spoke to me first. He said that I could not go with them on their journey because it was impossible that I could withdraw from my task. Under those circumstances the only thing they could do for me would be to wish me well. He added that warriors have no life of their own. From the moment they understand the nature of awareness, they cease to be persons and the human condition is no longer part of their view. I had my duty as a warrior and nothing else was important, for I was going to be left behind to fulfill a most obscure task. Since I had already relinquished my life there was nothing else for them to say to me, except that I should do my best. And there was nothing for me to say to them, except that I had understood and had accepted my fate.

Vicente came to my side next. He spoke very softly. He said that the challenge of a warrior is to arrive at a very subtle balance of positive and negative forces. This challenge does not mean that a warrior should strive to have everything under control, but that a warrior should strive to meet any conceivable situation, the expected and the unexpected, with equal efficiency. To be perfect under perfect circumstances was to be a paper warrior. My challenge was to be left behind. Theirs was to strike onward into the unknowable. Both challenges were consuming. For warriors, the excitation of staying put is equal to the excitation of the journey. Both are equal, because both entail the fulfilling of a sacred trust.

Silvio Manuel came to my side next; he was concerned with practicalities. He gave me a formula, an incantation for times when my task would be greater than my strength; it was the incantation that came to my mind the first time I remembered the Nagual woman.

I am already given to the power that rules my fate.
And I cling to nothing, so I will have nothing to defend.
I have no thoughts, so I will see.
I fear nothing, so I will remember myself.
Detached and at ease,
I will dart past the Eagle to be free.

Ya me dí al poder que a mi destino rige.
No me agarro ya de nada, para así no tener nada que defender.
No tengo pensamientos, para así poder *ver*.
No temo ya a nada, para así poder acordarme de mí.   ·
Sereno y desprendido,
me dejará el águila pasar a la libertad.

He told me that he was going to reveal to me a practical maneuver of the second attention, and right then he turned into a luminous egg. He reverted back to his normal appearance and repeated this transformation three or four more times. I understood perfectly well what he was doing. He did not need to explain it to me and yet I could not put into words what I knew.

Silvio Manuel smiled, cognizant of my problem. He said that it took an enormity of strength to let go of the *intent* of everyday life. The secret that he had just revealed was how to expedite letting go of that *intent*. In order to do what he had done, one must place one's attention on the luminous shell.

He turned one more time into a luminous egg and then it became obvious to me what I had known all along. Silvio Manuel's eyes turned for an instant to focus on the point of the second attention. His head was straight, as if he had been looking ahead of him, only his eyes were askew. He said that a warrior must evoke *intent*. The glance is the secret. The eyes beckon *intent*.

I became euphoric at that point. I was at long last capable of thinking about something I knew without really knowing. The reason why *seeing* seems to be visual is because we need the eyes to focus on *intent*. Don Juan and his party of warriors knew how to use their eyes to catch another aspect of *intent* and called this act *seeing*. What Silvio Manuel had shown me was the true function of the eyes, the catchers of *intent*.

I then used my eyes deliberately to beckon *intent*. I focused them on the point of the second attention. All of a sudden don Juan, his warriors, doña Soledad, and Eligio were luminous eggs, but not la Gorda, the three little sisters, and the Genaros. I kept on moving my eyes back and forth between the blobs of light and the people, until I heard a crack in the base of my neck, and everybody in the room was a luminous egg. I felt for an instant that I could not tell them apart, but then my eyes seemed to adjust and I held two aspects of *intent*, two images at once. I could see their physical bodies and also their luminosities. The two scenes were not superimposed on each other but separate, and yet I could not figure out how. I definitely had two channels of vision, and *seeing* had everything to do with my eyes and yet was independent of them. I could still *see* the luminous eggs, but not their physical bodies when I closed my eyes.

I had at one moment the clearest sensation that I knew how to shift my attention to my luminosity. I also knew that to revert to the physical level all I had to do was to focus my eyes on my body.

Don Genaro came to my side next and told me that the
Nagual Juan Matus, as a parting gift, had given me duty,
Vicente had given me challenge, Silvio Manuel had given me
magic, and he was going to give me humor. He looked me up
and down and commented that I was the sorriest looking Nagual he had ever seen. He examined the apprentices and concluded that there was nothing else for us to do, except to be
optimistic and to look on the positive side of things. He told
us a joke about a country girl who was seduced and jilted by
a city slicker. When she was told on the day of her wedding
that the groom had left town, she pulled herself together with
the sobering thought that not everything had been lost. She
had lost her virginity, but she had not yet killed her piglet for
the wedding feast.

Don Genaro told us that the only thing that would help us
to get out of our situation, which was the situation of the jilted
bride, was to hold onto our piglets, whatever they might be,
and laugh ourselves silly. Only through laughter could we
change our condition.

He coaxed us with gestures of his head and hands to give
him a hearty ha ha. The sight of the apprentices trying to
laugh was as ridiculous as my own attempt. Suddenly I was
laughing with don Juan and his warriors.

Don Genaro, who had always made jokes about my being
a poet, asked me to read a poem out loud. He said that he
wanted to summarize his sentiments and his recommendations
with the poem that celebrates life, death and laughter. He was
referring to a fraction of José Gorostiza's poem, "Death Without End."

The Nagual woman handed me the book and I read the
part that don Juan and don Genaro had always liked.

> *Oh, what blind joy*
> *What hunger to use up*
> *the air that we breathe,*
> *the mouth, the eye, the hand.*

What biting itch
to spend absolutely all of ourselves
in one single burst of laughter.
Oh, this impudent, insulting death
that assassinates us from afar.
over the pleasure that we take in dying
for a cup of tea . . .
for a faint caress.

The setting for the poem was overpowering. I felt a shiver. Emilito and the courier Juan Tuma came to my side. They did not say a word. Their eyes were shining like black marbles. All their feelings seemed to be focused in their eyes. The courier Juan Tuma said very softly that once he had ushered me into the mysteries of Mescalito at his house, and that that had been a forerunner of another occasion in the wheel of time when he would usher me into the ultimate mystery.

Emilito said, as if his voice were an echo of the courier Juan Tuma's, that both of them were confident that I was going to fulfill my task. They would be waiting, for I would join them someday. The courier Juan Tuma added that the Eagle had put me with the Nagual Juan Matus' party as my rescue unit. They embraced me again and whispered in unison that I should trust myself.

After the couriers, the female warriors came to me. Each one hugged me and whispered a wish in my ear, a wish of plenitude and fulfillment.

The Nagual woman came to me last. She sat down and held me in her lap as if I were a child. She exuded affection and purity. I was breathless. We stood up and walked around the room. We talked about and pondered our fate. Forces impossible to fathom had guided us to that culminating moment. The awe that I felt was immeasurable. And so was my sadness.

She then revealed a portion of the rule that applies to the three-pronged Nagual. She was in a state of ultimate agitation and yet she was calm. Her intellect was peerless and yet she was not trying to reason anything out. Her last day on earth overwhelmed her. She filled me with her mood. It was as if up to that moment I had not quite realized the finality of our situation. Being on my left side entailed that the primacy of the immediate took precedence, which made it practically impossible for me to foresee beyond that moment. However, the impact of her mood engaged a great deal of my right side awareness and its capacity to prejudge feelings that are to come. I realized that I would never again see her. That was unbearable!

Don Juan had told me that on the left side there are no tears, that a warrior can no longer weep, and that the only expression of anguish is a shiver that comes from the very depths of the universe. It is as if one of the Eagle's emanations is anguish. The warrior's shiver is infinite. As the Nagual woman talked to me and held me, I felt that shiver.

She put her arms around my neck and pressed her head against mine. I thought she was wringing me like a piece of cloth. I felt something coming out of my body, or out of hers into mine. My anguish was so intense and it flooded me so fast that I went berserk. I fell to the floor with the Nagual woman still embracing me. I thought, as if in a dream, that I must have gashed her forehead in our fall. Her face and mine were covered with blood. Blood had pooled in her eyes.

Don Juan and don Genaro very swiftly lifted me up. They held me. I was having uncontainable spasms, like seizures. The female warriors surrounded the Nagual woman; then they stood in a row in the middle of the room. The men joined them. In one moment there was an undeniable chain of energy going between them. The row moved and paraded in front of me. Each one of them came for a moment and stood in front of me, but without breaking the row. It was as if they were moving on a conveyor that transported them and made each of them stop in front of me. The male couriers went by first, then the female couriers, then the male warriors, then the *dreamers*, the *stalkers*, and finally the Nagual woman. They went by me and remained in full view for a second or two, long enough to say goodbye, and then they disappeared into the blackness of the mysterious slit that had appeared in the room.

Don Juan pressed my back and relieved some of my unbearable anguish. He said that he understood my pain, and that the affinity of the Nagual man and the Nagual woman is not something that can be formulated. It exists as a result of the emanations of the Eagle; once the two people are put together and are separated there is no way to fill the emptiness, because it is not social emptiness, but a movement of those emanations.

Don Juan told me then that he was going to make me shift to my extreme right. He said that it was a merciful although temporary maneuver; it would allow me to forget for the time being, but it would not soothe me when I remembered.

Don Juan also told me that the act of remembering is thoroughly incomprehensible. In actuality it is the act of remembering oneself, which does not stop at recollecting the interaction warriors perform in their left side awareness, but goes on to recollect every memory that the luminous body has stored from the moment of birth.

The systematic interaction warriors go through in states of heightened consciousness is only a device to entice the other self to reveal itself in terms of memories. This act of remembering, although it seems to be only associated with warriors, is something that is within the realm of every human being; every one of us can go directly to the memories of our luminosity with unfathomable results.

Don Juan said then that that day they would leave at dusk and that the only thing they still had to do for me was to create an opening, an interruption in the continuum of my time. They were going to make me jump into an abyss as a means of interrupting the Eagle's emanation that accounts for my feeling that I am whole and continuous. The jump was going to be done while I was in a state of normal awareness, and the idea was that my second attention would take over; rather than dying at the bottom of the abyss I would enter fully into the other self. Don Juan said that I would eventually come out of the other self once my energy was exhausted; but I would not come out on the same mountaintop from where I was going to jump. He predicted that I would emerge at my favorite spot, wherever it might be. This would be the interruption in the continuum of my time.

He then pushed me completely out of my left side awareness. And I forgot my anguish, my purpose, my task.

At dusk that afternoon, Pablito, Nestor and I did jump off a precipice. The Nagual's blow had been so accurate and so merciful that nothing of the momentous event of their farewell transcended beyond the limits of the other momentous event of jumping to certain death and not dying. Awe-inspiring as that event was, it was pale in comparison to what was taking place in another realm.

Don Juan made me jump at the precise moment when he and all of his warriors had kindled their awareness. I had a dreamlike vision of a row of people looking at me. Afterwards I rationalized it as just one of a long series of visions or hallucinations I had had upon jumping. This was the meager interpretation of my right side awareness, overwhelmed by the awesomeness of the total event.

On my left side, however, I realized that I had entered into the other self. And this entrance had had nothing to do with my rationality. The warriors of don Juan's party had caught me for an eternal instant, before they vanished into the total light, before the Eagle let them go through. I knew that they were in a range of the Eagle's emanations which was beyond my reach. They were waiting for don Juan and don Genaro. I saw don Juan taking the lead. And then there was only a line of exquisite lights in the sky. Something like a wind seemed to make the cluster of lights contract and wriggle. There was a massive glow on one end of the line of lights where don Juan was. I thought of the plumed serpent of the Toltec legend. And then the lights were gone.